THE
TRUMAN COURT

THE
TRUMAN COURT

LAW AND THE LIMITS OF LOYALTY

Rawn James, Jr.

UNIVERSITY OF MISSOURI PRESS

Columbia

Copyright © 2021 by
The Curators of the University of Missouri
University of Missouri Press, Columbia, Missouri 65211
Printed and bound in the United States of America
All rights reserved. First printing, 2021.

Library of Congress Catalog-in-Publication Data

Names: James, Rawn, author.
Title: The Truman court : law and the limits of loyalty / by Rawn James, Jr.
Description: Columbia, Missouri : University of Missouri Press, 2021. |
    Includes index.
Identifiers: LCCN 2020048216 (print) | LCCN 2020048217 (ebook) | ISBN
    9780826222299 (hardcover) | ISBN 9780826274564 (ebook)
Subjects: LCSH: United States. Supreme Court--History. | Political
    questions and judicial power--United States--History. | Judges--United
    States--History. | Truman, Harry S., 1884-1972. | Warren, Earl,
    1891-1974. | United States--Politics and government--20th century.
Classification: LCC KF8742 .J36 2021 (print) | LCC KF8742 (ebook) | DDC
    347.73/2609046--dc23
LC record available at https://lccn.loc.gov/2020048216
LC ebook record available at https://lccn.loc.gov/2020048217

∞™ This paper meets the requirements of the
American National Standard for Permanence of Paper
for Printed Library Materials, Z39.48, 1984.

Typefaces: Spinoza and Franklin

For my sons, August and Charleston

CONTENTS

PROLOGUE

PRESIDENTS DO NOT NOMINATE LAWYERS to the Supreme Court of the United States hoping that, if confirmed by the Senate, these justices will draft eloquent opinions for the ages. No president has ever complained that a justice he named to the Court failed to become a profound purveyor of legal theory.

Rather, when presidents make lifetime appointments to any of the federal appellate courts, they do so with a politician's imperative: they want votes—not electoral votes but judicial votes. They hope that the judges they appoint will continue to share a worldview with the president who nominated them. This is especially true in the case of nominations to the Supreme Court. As Justice William O. Douglas, who served on the Court for thirty-four years after being nominated by President Franklin D. Roosevelt, acknowledged, "Most Presidents name Justices who, they think, will vote the way they would vote."[1]

Quite often, of course, this does not happen. A justice's perspective may change over time amid both the freedom and burden of a lifetime appointment. Becoming a justice imposes on a person the imperative of determining who he or she wants to be on the Court and in history. With their votes and written opinions, all justices draft the first versions of their own history. This is perhaps why few of them can restrain themselves to presenting workmanlike opinions—short, easily understood, and efficiently written. Institutional humility has been preached more than practiced by justices for at least a century.

Fate forced Franklin Roosevelt to wait four and a half years before nominating his first justice. In less time than that, his successor, Harry S. Truman, nominated three associate justices and the chief justice. At the dual dawns of the Cold War and the Civil Rights era, Chief Justice Fred Vinson and Justices Harold Burton, Tom Clark, and Sherman Minton formed a formidable bloc on the Court. They were often joined by Stanley Reed to comprise a controlling Court majority.

Truman's first nomination to the Supreme Court was a substantive show of bipartisanship. His second garnered widespread praise from across the political spectrum. His third nomination raised concerns that he was interested in naming only his personal friends to the nation's highest court. And his last seemed to confirm these misgivings, despite the nominee's legitimate qualifications. Two of the men Truman nominated had served in his administration; the other two had worked closely with him when he was a senator.

With the possible exception of the chief justice, Truman's nominees generated little expectation that they would become pillars of the Court. It seemed to some as though Truman considered Supreme Court seats to be but lofty patronage positions to which he was free to nominate his friends. As legal historian Del Dickson notes, "Perhaps unfairly, all four of Harry Truman's Supreme Court appointees are remembered—to the extent that they are remembered at all—as a mediocre group of political insiders and presidential cronies."[2] One assessment written in 1950 concluded, "Truman has not only tilted the Court steeply to the right but he has loaded it with mediocrity."[3] Justice Douglas, who served with all four Truman nominees, believed that "under Truman the Court sank to its lowest professional level until the [Chief Justice Warren] Burger Court arrived." This was because "Truman seemed to like picking mediocre men."[4]

Admittedly, the men Truman nominated to the Court are more forgotten than disparaged but either assessment misses the point: as doctrinally inconsequential as Burton, Clark, Minton, and Vinson might be individually, their collective performance on the Supreme Court—their unity and consistent ability to persuade at least one justice to join their ranks to form a majority—deserves examination and respect. They voted to uphold both questionable and admirable Truman administration policies. They supported the president so reliably that at least one observer at the time referred to them as "the four Trumanites."[5] They often supported the president who had nominated them, not from a sense of loyalty, although the sentiment unfortunately sometimes seems to have reared its head, but rather because they agreed with his administration on critical questions of constitutional law.

This allowed Truman to revolutionize the relationship between the president and the Supreme Court. Presidents before Truman tended to engage the Court defensively, only when necessary, when challenged to defend their actions or bills they had signed into law. Roosevelt grew so frustrated with the Court's consistent pattern of striking down New Deal laws that in 1937 he presented a "judicial reorganization plan" to add justices to the Court so that New Deal legislation might survive judicial review. Swiftly derided as a scheme to "pack the Court," Roosevelt's proposal died in Congress. Just a few years later, Truman was successfully engaging the Court to *advance*—not merely to defend—his administration's agenda.

Unlike presidents who came before him, but like nearly every president who has succeeded him, Truman engaged the Supreme Court almost as actively as he engaged Congress. He did this by consistently employing the Department of Justice as an executive agency intent on implementing administration policy through court victories. Truman used the judiciary to advance his political agenda when the Constitution, the Congress, and his conscience allowed no other path. Every president since has followed his lead. The way in which Harry S. Truman revolutionized the relationship between the president and the Supreme Court is the least-explored major facet of his legacy, but its effects have reverberated in nearly every presidential election and Supreme Court nomination since.

THE
TRUMAN COURT

CHAPTER ONE

"We Must Have Steel."

NIGHTFALL'S FULL MOONRISE FAILED TO pierce the gloom that descended on America's steel-mill towns as the sun set on April 8, 1952. Night fell especially dark in McKeesport, Pennsylvania, because the mill's mammoth, fiery Bessemer converter had been shut down. In nearby Clairton and Duquesne, an uneasy quiet prevailed, the massive gear-locked wheels of their mills having ground to a halt. Steamers fell still along the Monongahela River, their skippers unsure whether the coal in their holds from upriver mines would be needed in downriver mills.[1]

Tonight would be cold, with temperatures expected to drop into the low thirties, so steelworkers dressed tightly against the weather to wait together for midnight. In Duquesne they gathered around an old oil drum that someone had fired up to provide warmth. In other mill towns they warmed themselves near pot-belly stoves. Those who could afford to joined a number of those who could not in taverns and bars.

Six hundred fifty thousand steelworkers were set to strike the minute after midnight. Their strike would halt 95 percent of America's steel production. It was, as described by one union spokesman, a strike "which no one wanted—few could afford."[2] But the way the men and their elected union leaders saw it, they had little choice.[3]

President Harry S. Truman was scheduled to address the nation by radio and television at 10:30 p.m. about the impending strike. Steelworkers worried that he would harshly criticize them and their union.[4] So many industries, livelihoods, and families had already been hurt by the looming steel crisis and the steelworkers were not even on strike yet. They feared a backlash brewing. The federal government banned the shipment of any remaining steel to civilian industries to preserve the steel for national defense purposes, and executives in America's automotive industry, the largest consumer of steel, announced that they did not know how long they could keep their plants operating.[5]

More than ten thousand coal miners had been sent home in recent days as steel companies cooled their mills' blast furnaces, open hearths, and coke ovens.[6] Shops and restaurants in mining and mill towns had been quiet for weeks because households were foregoing all but the most basic necessities. As the strike deadline edged closer, steelworkers' hours were cut. Men earned less money while preparing to earn none.

Managers reduced steelworkers' hours because it was no small endeavor to shut down a steel mill without damaging its expensive equipment and furnaces. Prudent mills allowed themselves ninety-six hours to shut down.[7] Union leaders had agreed to provide at least that many hours' notice before going on strike and so on April 4 they confirmed to management and government officials that their strike would commence at 12:01 a.m. on April 9.[8] The mills swiftly furloughed or laid off tens of thousands of workers.

In response, thousands more steelworkers walked off the job. These so-called wildcat strikes broke out days before the midnight deadline at mills in Texas, Michigan, and Pennsylvania. At the Crucible Steel Company mill in Midland, Pennsylvania, picketing workers refused to let workers onto the premises unless they were engaged in shutdown operations.[9] At least one steelworker prepared to strike with a picket sign referring to Benjamin Fairless, president of U.S. Steel: "HE CAN'T BE FAIR—HIS NAME IS FAIRLESS."[10]

Anxiety, fear, and fury percolated amid the steelworkers in the moments before the president spoke. Their plight was bleak, and they did not expect this unpopular president to improve it.[11] "I'd give a thousand dollars right now," sneered one barstool-seated worker, "to see that man drop dead."[12] At 10:30 p.m. Eastern Standard Time, the president began to speak:

> My fellow Americans, tonight our country faces a grave danger. We are faced by the possibility that at midnight tonight the steel industry will be shut down. This must not happen. Steel is our key industry.
>
> It is vital to our defense effort. It is vital to peace. . . . If steel production stops, we will have to stop making the shells and bombs that are going directly to our soldiers at the front in Korea.[13]

By March 1951 half of all Americans considered Truman's decision to enter the war a mistake and most favored pulling American troops from Korea. After the Chinese Communists entered the conflict in November 1950, the war had become increasingly unpopular in America. The Truman administration engaged in truce negotiations but the war continued as the Communists repeatedly abandoned the talks. In large part because of the Korean War and the inflation it afflicted on the economy, Truman's approval rating fell to a dismal 23 percent.[14]

So tonight, Truman explained that the nation's steel production was essential not just for the unpopular war in Korea but for more admired military programs as well: "If steel production stops, we will have to cut down and delay the atomic energy program. If steel production stops, it won't be long before we have to stop making engines for the Air Force planes." He connected the war in Korea—a war into which he had led the country without seeking or receiving a congressional declaration of war— to the worldwide struggle against communism. "I have to think about our soldiers in Korea," he continued, "facing the Chinese Communists, and about our soldiers and our allies in Europe, confronted by the military power massed behind the Iron Curtain."[15]

Truman's primary problem was not that the war in Korea had become so unpopular in the two years since he first committed American troops and activated the draft; his problem was that *he* had become spectacularly unpopular by the spring of 1952. His political capital was virtually nonexistent. Even with his own Democratic Party in control of Congress, legislators all but ignored the president's Fair Deal initiatives. Just days earlier, on March 29, 1952, he had announced that he would not seek reelection.

In this hobbled state, Truman told the nation, "I am directing the Secretary of Commerce to take control of the steel mills and to keep them operating." He felt compelled to do so because, "with American troops facing the enemy on the field of battle, I would not be living up to my oath of office if I failed to do whatever is required to provide them with the weapons and the ammunition they need for their survival."[16]

Had Truman ended his speech there, the legal and political response to his decision to temporarily seize the steel industry might have been different.[17] After all, it was not unprecedented for the federal government to seize private companies. During World War I, when more than 1 million workers launched over four thousand strikes across the nation, President Woodrow Wilson seized numerous corporations. Wilson sometimes claimed that he was empowered to do so by specific statutes, while at other times he asserted that the Constitution justified his actions. Six months before the Japanese attack on Pearl Harbor, President Franklin Roosevelt ordered federal troops to take control of the North American Aviation plant in Inglewood, California, where labor unrest endangered the company's ability to deliver $200 million worth of orders to the American and British militaries. After America entered World War II, Roosevelt seized more than forty companies under the 1943 War Labor Disputes Act.[18]

President Truman's speech to announce and explain his reasons for seizing the steel mills by signing Executive Order 10340 could have been a short one. But it wasn't. The president and several members of his staff had begun drafting it at six that evening and worked on it until shortly before Truman began reading it live to the nation four and a half hours later.[19] After announcing his administration's seizure of the industry's mills, Truman had a good deal more to say, most of it about the steel companies' executives, whom he blamed for the entire ordeal. "Let me tell you how this situation came about," he said, and proceeded to describe how, when steelworkers met with management to negotiate their new contract, "the companies never really bargained. The companies all took the same position." They refused to consider raising workers' wages and improving working conditions "in spite of the fact that the steel industry was making very high profits." Lest a single listener misunderstand his position, the president declared,

> The plain fact of the matter is that the steel companies are recklessly forcing a shutdown of the steel mills. They are trying to get special, preferred treatment not available to any other industry. And they are apparently willing to stop steel production to get it.
>
> As president of the United States, it is my plain duty to keep this from happening. And that is the reason for the measures I have taken tonight.

Truman closed by asking the executives and union leaders to reconcile their differences and settle their dispute. It was clear which party he believed was at fault. Nonetheless, he asked both sides to resolve the matter equitably. To the nation he proclaimed with no apparent metaphorical intent, "We must have steel."[20]

* * *

At the end of Truman's speech, cheers erupted in homes, union halls, and taverns across America's steel-mill towns. Not only had the president supported their cause with his words but he was employing the full power of his presidency to keep them on the job. Millions who depended on the steelworkers' labor could not believe this extraordinary turn of events. "This is a Godsend to a lot of poor steelworkers and their families," said one local union vice president. "This is one of the greatest moments in history for them."[21]

Workers who supported Truman's actions entertained no pretense that his speech was even-handed. An electrician for the Jones & Laughlin Steel Corporation declared at a packed bar in Homestead, Pennsylvania, that Truman could win a third term as president. "He's lived up to what he ran for," the worker explained. "That was the cause of labor." A nearby millwright agreed that Truman's was "the best speech any man ever made for labor." Their wives were ecstatic that the massive strike had been avoided.[22] One worker's mother in McKeesport telephoned the local union hall to hear for herself. "Is it really over?" she asked. "Thank God—I've been praying that it would never start."[23]

Truman's harsh rhetoric against the steel companies struck some pro-business listeners as unseemly and even unpresidential. Republican senator Harry P. Cain of Washington told reporters that Truman's only goal in delivering that speech was to "cause dissension, turmoil and class conflict—this he did superbly."[24] Campaigning for the Republican presidential nomination, Ohio's Senator Robert Taft told overflowing arena crowds that Truman's decision to seize the steel mills presented "a valid case for impeachment."[25] Taft warned audiences that Truman so grossly misunderstood the limits of presidential power that "he might just as well go a step further and draft the steelworkers into the Army without the consent of Congress."[26]

Republicans were not alone in criticizing Truman's explanation of what caused the labor dispute. The *Washington Post* editorial board wrote, "With only a few changes, President Truman's speech on the steel seizure could have been written in the office of the CIO United Steel Workers."[27] Pulitzer Prize–winning *New York Times* reporter Arthur Krock rued "the thoroughly biased account [Truman] gave to the American people." Krock contended that the president's decision to seize the steel mills was "a striking example of bad government."[28] Other journalists agreed that, as one wrote, "President Truman virtually froze the government's position" in favor of the steelworkers.[29] In a second editorial, the *Washington Post* board argued, "Nothing either in the President's speech or in his executive order can be cited as justification for the seizure." Instead, his "seizure of the steel industry will probably go down in history as one of the most high-handed acts committed by an American president."[30]

* * *

Less than an hour after the president's radio and television address, attorneys for the Republic Steel Corporation and the Youngstown Sheet & Tube Company arrived at the Washington, DC, home of federal district judge Walter M. Bastian and rang the doorbell. When the judge answered the door, they handed him a motion seeking a temporary restraining order and an injunction to prevent the president's executive order from taking effect. Refusing to issue any orders without allowing the government equal opportunity to defend its position, Judge Bastian scheduled oral arguments for 11:30 the following morning.[31]

Administration officials and Department of Justice lawyers expected the steel companies to appeal their cases as far as the law permitted but they were not worried. Even if the companies appealed all the way up to the Supreme Court of the United States, and even if the requisite four justices voted to hear the case, the administration was confident that the Court would rule in its favor. Even legal commentators who were troubled by Truman's seizure of the steel industry conceded that the Supreme Court, comprised as it was, would validate the president's actions.

This was because by 1952 a five-justice majority of the Court viewed the nation, its government, and the threats seeking to endanger both in much the same way that Harry S. Truman did. He had nominated four of these men to the Court, including the chief justice of the United States. Truman had never been surprised by the Court he composed.

CHAPTER TWO

Justice Harold Burton

BY AUGUST 1945, HARRY TRUMAN was president and Justice Owen Roberts had resigned. Truman unexpectedly had the opportunity to nominate a justice to the Court. Selecting Roberts's replacement was neither the most difficult nor significant decision Truman had faced as president. In less than four months Truman had made more monumental decisions than some presidents make in an entire four-year term. Not for nothing did he title the first volume of his presidential memoirs *1945: Year of Decisions*.

Selecting a Supreme Court nominee was the new president's first significant, truly independent act as president. Unlike matters of domestic policy or the path toward victory in World War II, Truman could neither consult nor rely on plans already in effect when Franklin Roosevelt died. The *Washington Post* editorialized that selecting Justice Roberts's proposed replacement would "be a real test for President Truman." Whomever Truman nominated would likely say more about the new president than it would about the nominee himself: "Indeed, the type of appointment he makes will tell us a great deal about the quality of justice and the attitude toward the law of the land that the Truman Administration seeks to establish."[1]

African Americans saw opportunity in Roberts's departure. Andrew Ransom, a prominent attorney and professor at Howard Law School in Washington, DC, declared, "We suffer no injury by [Roberts's] resignation no matter who replaces him."[2] Roberts had been the lone dissenter in one of the few landmark civil rights cases ever decided by a non-unanimous Supreme Court. In *Smith v. Allwright*, he alone dissented from the Court's holding that a person's race may not prohibit him or her from voting in primary elections.[3] The *Chicago Defender* assessed the prevailing view in African American communities: "It is generally conceded that whoever replaces Justice Roberts as a member of the Supreme Court can scarcely afford to be any more conservative than he."[4]

By this time, many Americans had disabused themselves of the notion that the Court was an apolitical institution. Any belief that judges and justices decided cases irrespective of their own political predilections fell out of favor during the final years of Roosevelt's presidency. It simply seemed unrealistic in light of all the evidence to the contrary. Republican-appointed justices construed the Constitution in ways that favored the Republican Party's political agenda, and justices appointed by Democrats tended to do the same for the Democratic Party. Roberts's retirement left only one Republican appointee on the Court.

Rather than cling to seemingly outdated notions of judicial impartiality, Americans at the end of World War II wanted Truman to establish political balance on the Court. Soon after Roberts stepped down, a national Gallup poll indicated that 56 percent of Americans believed that the president "should appoint about the same number of Democrats and Republicans" to the Supreme Court. Just 9 percent believed that he should appoint only members of his own party. More tellingly, only 19 percent of those surveyed believed that the president should select Supreme Court nominees without regard to the nominees' political affiliation. By a margin of nearly three to one, Americans in 1945 believed that the president's first consideration in selecting a Supreme Court nominee should be the nominee's political party affiliation.[5] Owen Roberts's retirement left only one Republican appointee on the Court. Democratic senator Carl Hatch of New Mexico, who was a friend and supporter of the president, told reporters that it "would be wise" for Truman to nominate a Republican to fill the vacancy.[6]

* * *

Before they became justices, Roosevelt's nominees possessed scant judicial experience. Only Wiley Rutledge and Hugo Black had been judges: Rutledge had served for two years on the Court of Appeals for the District of Columbia, which, because it reviewed many federal regulations and practices, was (and remains) widely regarded as the second most important federal court in the nation. Black's judicial experience consisted of eighteen months' service as a police judge in Birmingham, Alabama.[7]

Their lack of judicial experience made it difficult to predict how Roosevelt's eight nominees would rule on questions of constitutional law. As Pulitzer Prize–winning historian David Garrow has noted, "Generally speaking, nominees who have evolved in unanticipated ways did not have federal court backgrounds. It's a response to the pressures of Washington, with the Supreme Court presenting legal questions they did not have to confront before."[8] Roosevelt's nominees confronted many legal questions for the first time after joining the Court. Despite having been appointed by the same president, their opinions scattered like buckshot.

It was ironic, considering the ordeal he endured to nominate them, that the justices Franklin Roosevelt named to the Supreme Court so openly disliked each other. In fact, "dislike" fails to convey the enmity they felt for each other. Justices Felix Frankfurter and Robert Jackson joined on one side against Justices Hugo Black, William O. Douglas, and Frank Murphy. Their feuds bore legitimate ideological foundations but turned regrettably personal.

Columnist C. P. Ives observed at the close of the Court's 1944–45 term: "One of the fascinating things about the new Supreme Court has been its tendency not merely to split but to splinter. Though Mr. Roosevelt named eight of the nine sitting justices, the state of disagreement on the court has worsened rather than improved." More than a few of the dissents filed during the term read like the justices were "thumbing each other's ideological eyeballs out" as they wrote "with vehemence."[9] Until Jackson made an intemperate eruption after the death of Chief Justice Harlan Fiske Stone and proved otherwise, the chief justice shouldered much of the blame for this decline in decorum.

* * *

For his part, Owen Roberts had grown weary of life on the Court. It was not so much that his judicial philosophy had changed as it was that the membership and ideological makeup of the Court had changed around him. During his most prominent years, Roberts had enjoyed being the all-important "swing vote" on the Court. Roberts seemed to exist, as one *New York Times* editorial put it, "in the exact center of the Court."[10] He created majorities by joining either the four conservative justices or the four moderate ones on any given case. Because his colleagues sought his deciding vote for their decisions, he held considerable influence over majority opinions without bearing the burden of having to write them.

After Roberts announced his retirement, Chief Justice Stone drafted the letter that a retiring justice traditionally received from his Court brethren. Knowing all too well how divided the Court was, Stone's letter to Roberts struck a comparatively neutral tone, uncharacteristic of previous letters

given to retiring justices. Stone handed off the letter to the senior associate justice, Hugo Black, requesting that he sign it and pass it to the next
justice.

Justice Black treated his colleague's retirement letter as if it were a
judicial opinion concerning a close question of constitutional law. He informed the chief justice that he objected to two phrases in the letter: one
expressing regret at Roberts's retirement and the other telling him, "You
have made fidelity to principle your guide to decisions." Black would sign
the letter only if Stone deleted those sentences, something that the chief
justice reluctantly agreed to do.[11]

By then, however, the other justices had learned of the wording. Felix
Frankfurter and Robert Jackson refused to sign the letter unless the sentence regarding Roberts's "fidelity to principle" was retained. Frankfurter
insisted that Stone's original draft paid deserving tribute to Roberts.
Frankfurter wrote in a memorandum to his brethren, "I *know* that that
was Justice Brandeis's view of Roberts, whose character he held in the
highest esteem."[12] William O. Douglas, however, agreed with Black that
the sentence should be deleted. Justices Frank Murphy, Stanley Reed, and
Wiley Rutledge expressed their willingness to sign either version.

In the end, no letter was sent. Because the justices could not agree on
wording, Owen Roberts did not receive even a card to commemorate his
retirement from the Supreme Court of the United States. He quietly returned to his native Pennsylvania, happy to leave the rancor behind him.[13]

* * *

Part of what Ohio senator Harold Hitz Burton liked best about serving in
the United States Senate was that he was able to return home frequently
and easily. By birth Burton was a New Englander, a faithful Unitarian
who, after attending Bowdoin College in Maine, graduated in 1912 from
Harvard Law School a few weeks before marrying Selma Florence Smith
one week shy of his twenty-fifth birthday. After his wedding he moved
with his bride to her home state of Ohio, where he joined her uncle's law
practice in Cleveland.

When the United States entered World War I, Burton joined the Army.
Burton, like Truman, served as an infantry officer leading men in combat
in France. He rose to the rank of captain and was awarded a Purple Heart
and Belgium's Croix de Guerre. After the Allies' victory, Burton returned
home to Cleveland, where he resumed practicing law, becoming a partner

in his own firm of Cull, Burton & Laughlin in 1925. He also taught corporate law at Western Reserve University.[14]

The lifelong Republican then entered politics and his rise was swift. In 1927 he won election to the East Cleveland Board of Education; the following year he was elected to the Ohio House of Representatives, in which he served until October 1929, when he went to work for the city of Cleveland, becoming the city's acting mayor in 1931. Four years later Burton was elected mayor of his adopted home city.

Cleveland in 1935 was deeply distressed. Its unemployment rate hovered near 25 percent while crime ran unbridled in the streets and alleys. Gangsters had so corrupted the police force that they operated with near impunity.

Mayor Burton believed that crime and unemployment were connected and attacked both on several fronts. He crossed party lines to support Roosevelt's Works Progress Administration because he wanted Clevelanders back at work. He acted aggressively to eliminate corruption in the police department and modernized the force by putting officers in automobiles for the first time. He hired Eliot Ness to be Cleveland's public safety director. Burton's reputation for clean living and honest governing earned him a reputation as the "Boy Scout Mayor."[15]

But the Boy Scout Mayor was as politically ambitious as he was personally reserved. In the spring of 1940, he sought to build on his success as the only three-term Republican mayor of mostly Democratic Cleveland when he decided to run for the U.S. Senate seat being vacated by retiring Democrat Vic Donahey.[16] Burton defeated former Democratic congressman James McSweeney on the same day that Roosevelt won Ohio's twenty-six electoral votes for the third time.[17] It rained all day in Cleveland but turnout remained strong on the mayor's home turf.[18] Voters statewide rewarded Burton's commitment to pragmatic problem-solving.[19] Ohio's voters continued their streak of being on the winning side of every presidential election since 1896.[20]

* * *

After taking the senator's oath of office on January 3, 1941, Harold Burton went to work in the same bipartisan manner that had succeeded in Cleveland. Democrats so respected his expertise in city affairs that they took the unique step of appointing him chairman of the Senate District Committee, which in the era before Washingtonians won the right to home rule in the 1970s controlled the city affairs of Washington, DC. Democratic senators conceded that the former mayor "was the best informed man available."[21] Senators of both parties praised him for having made significant improvements to Cleveland's infrastructure while reducing the city's public debt by $16 million.[22]

To be sure, chairing the Senate District Committee was not a coveted assignment. No one ran for the Senate hoping to become the *de facto* mayor of the District of Columbia. But Burton worked hard at the job. He was decades ahead of his time in supporting Washingtonians' struggle for home rule. Just a month after taking office he told a crowd of more than five hundred Washingtonians, "One of the greatest blessings of self-government should be its closeness to the people governed."[23]

Like any senator, though, Burton was more interested in national and international affairs than he was in DC's municipal management issues. His most significant legislative initiative was a bipartisan measure that illustrated his strong belief in internationalism framed by American leadership. With Senators Carl Hatch of New Mexico, Joseph Ball of Minnesota, and Lister Hill of Alabama, Burton in 1943 sponsored what became known as the B2H2 resolution, which established a sort of blueprint for international cooperation after World War II.

Senator Truman offered his unequivocal support for Burton's ambitious resolution, calling himself "100 percent" in favor of the bill. Truman declared that the United States "could not possibly avoid the assumption of world leadership after this war ended," and therefore "it was well to get Congress's view on the record now."[24] Ultimately the Senate passed an alternative bill offered by Texas senator Tom Connally but Burton appreciated Truman's strong support for his bill and the men became friends.

Burton and his wife enjoyed federal Washington's social scene, with Selma Burton becoming the guest of honor at a fashionable party at the Washington Club just a few months after her husband took office.[25] Happily married with four children—two married, one in college, and the youngest finishing preperatory school in New Hampshire—the Burtons took pleasure in the life that their position and finances afforded them in the nation's capital.[26]

Nonetheless, Ohio was their home and Burton was able to return more frequently and easily than most senators. Particularly during the summer months in the age before air-conditioning, the Baltimore & Ohio Railroad presented a welcome escape from Washington's stifling humidity. Just stepping into Union Station, with its polished floors and vaulted ceilings, promised relief from the heat and a respite from politics.

* * *

One September morning in 1945, White House officials stopped Senator Burton just before he boarded the train. The president wanted to meet with him. Burton suspected that his former colleague might be summoning him to discuss the sudden Supreme Court vacancy. An astute political riser since his days on the East Cleveland Board of Education, Burton knew Senate Democrats were publicly lobbying the White House to nominate Burton, in part because his confirmation would allow Ohio's Democratic governor to appoint his successor.[27] Journalists reported that Truman had decided to nominate a Republican to replace Roberts.[28] Privately, Truman continued to hold Burton in high esteem, considering him to be "the most conscientious and hard-working committee member I ever did know."[29] A chauffered car carried Senator Burton the seventeen or so blocks from Union Station to the White House.

"Harold," Truman said to Burton in the Oval Office, "I've made up my mind to appoint you to the Supreme Court."
"Harry, I would not ask for it."
"I know that. I would not appoint you if you did. But I will appoint you and you will take it."[30]

Burton protested that he had not practiced law in a decade.
"I have canvassed the whole field and I believed you are the best. . . . I started with you and I considered all the others, Parker, Phillips, Patterson and you know all the rest and I came back to you."[31] The president concluded, "I want someone who will do a thoroughly judicial job and not legislate. You are fitted for the court; you have a judicial temperament."[32] As a justice, he expected Burton to "find the law," because a group of unelected judges had no business "making law up there."[33]

* * *

In the White House on September 18, 1945, journalists crowded near the president for a short but news-making press conference. In three minutes

Truman announced, among other things, that he had accepted Secretary of War Henry L. Stimson's resignation, that he was reorganizing the Department of Labor, and that he had nominated Ohio Republican senator Harold H. Burton to the Supreme Court of the United States.

"Is there anything else, Mr. President?" a reporter asked to everyone's laughter.[34]

Truman quickly answered a few questions. Legendary *Atlanta Daily World* reporter Harry S. McAlpin, who had become the first African American reporter admitted to the White House press corps during Franklin Roosevelt's administration, wrote that Truman was "hurling headline stories at a rate of one per minute."[35] Six minutes after it began the briefing ended and correspondents dashed to the telephones.[36]

* * *

Public and political reaction to Burton's nomination was overwhelmingly positive. Burton was popular among his fellow senators.[37] Ohio's Republican senator Robert Taft was one of the president's most strident critics, but he praised Truman for nominating his fellow Ohioan, declaring that the president could not have selected "a better lawyer, a more impartial judge or a man of higher ideals."[38] Democratic senator Carl Hatch, who earlier had urged Truman to nominate a different senator, called Burton "an admirable choice from every standpoint except that of the senate. We will miss him very much as a senator."[39] Columnist Merlo Pusey praised Burton as "a middle-of-the-roader" whose "strong leanings toward progressive policies" was tempered by "a deep and conservative respect for our democratic institutions."[40] Burton was widely regarded as "a 'liberal Republican' of marked independence."[41] Editors of the *Baltimore Afro-American* wrote that, as mayor of Cleveland, Burton "proved able and distinguished himself," and noted that he had supported civil rights legislation in Congress.[42]

Burton's lack of deep legal experience troubled some skeptics. *Baltimore Sun* editors wrote that he was "not a judge. He is not a legal scholar. . . . Senator Burton has not even practiced law as his major business for more than a decade. His knowledge of American jurisprudence in general, his awareness of the subtle but urgent philosophical questions which now impinge on the Supreme Court of the United States are probably no greater than those of any other tolerably well-informed layman."[43]

That Burton and Truman were friends did not escape notice. News accounts reported that Burton was, as one reporter wrote, a "personal friend of the President and a prominent member of the Senatorial war investigating body [that] began its work as the Truman Committee."[44] Reporter Wesley McCune, who later worked in the Truman administration, recalled that, between Senators Truman and Burton, "it was love at first sight. Truman often told friends praiseworthy things about Burton's fair mindedness, teamwork and conscientious approach to the investigating power."[45]

But observers did not attribute Burton's nomination to his friendship with the president. Their relationship was viewed as incidental to an otherwise outstanding, bipartisan selection for the high court. The *Washington Post*'s editors dismissed the prospect of cronyism by declaring it "quite natural that [Truman] should have turned to Senator Burton, who had worked closely with him on the Truman Committee in investigation of the war agencies."[46]

Political ramifications of Burton's nomination were likewise dismissed. The fact that Ohio's Democratic governor would appoint Senator Burton's successor and presumably replace the nominee's Republican vote in the Senate with a Democratic one was regarded as a largely inconsequential coincidence. As harsh a critic as *New York Times* columnist Arthur Krock rejected as "absurd as well as petty" any suggestion that gaining an additional Democratic senator's vote played a large role in Truman's decision.[47]

Aside from the nominee himself, the one who reaped the greatest reward from the selection was President Truman. Editors of the *Washington Post* wrote that it was "of great significance that a Democratic president has had the courage to appoint a Republican justice." All remembered that Truman's four-term predecessor had never done so. Truman was commended for "recogniz[ing] the necessity of avoiding the reflection of only one party's philosophy on the bench."[48] Krock believed that Truman was running "a disorganized and confused Government when organization and clarity are greatly needed" but nonetheless praised Burton's nomination as proof of the president's independent thinking.[49] Nevada senator Pat McCarran, who chaired the Senate Judiciary Committee, effused that "the American government is to be congratulated on the president's action in naming [Burton.]"[50]

Ohio's suddenly celebrated son arrived back in Washington just before noon on Wednesday, September 19, after a quick trip home on the B&O Railroad. Burton said that he was "deeply appreciative of the confidence which the nomination expressed in me" but explained that he could "make no further statement until it has been sent to the Senate and confirmed."[51] He would not have to wait long.

Senators voted on his nomination less than twenty-four hours after it was announced.[52] The judiciary committee did not hold hearings. Senator Alben Barkley of Kentucky admitted that he had been told in the past it was bad practice to confirm any nominee without holding committee hearings but he was glad to do so in Burton's case. Senator Taft recalled his days with Burton at Harvard Law School. "There is no man I know of," Taft avowed, "who has higher ideals of government."[53] Before adjourning at 5:40 pm on September 19, 1945, the Senate voted unanimously to confirm Burton to the Supreme Court of the United States.[54] He would be the only Republican to take a seat on the Court from 1933 to 1953.

* * *

Of the contemporary observers examining Truman's decision to nominate Burton, *New York Times* Washington reporter Lewis Wood realized the point better than most when he wrote, "In many aspects, he resembles President Truman, for like the President, Mr. Burton is an early riser, works long hours and is fond of detail. . . . Like the President also, the nominee was a soldier in the first World War. He enlisted with the Ninety-first Division. . . . A first lieutenant and then a captain, he received the Order of the Purple Heart and won the Croix de guerre of Belgium."[55]

Burton's political beliefs closely aligned with Truman's and Truman knew this. Unlike Truman's future Supreme Court nominees—who were also his friends—the selection of Burton was not predicated upon a shared understanding of the judiciary's proper role in the federal system. Instead, what the president and his first nominee to the Court held in common was an understanding of how the federal government should affect the lives of everyday Americans: it should protect them from subversive threats, sometimes even at the expense of their individual liberties; it should seek to eradicate racial segregation; it should promulgate policy from its two elective branches; and it should project strength abroad through interventionist policies. "We must set an example for the world in our courts and elsewhere of what true justice for all and constitutional freedom for all really mean," Burton professed days before taking the bench. "I believe that international stability is a domestic necessity for America. . . . I believe in the American people and in our Constitution as the foundations of freedom and peace on earth."[56]

* * *

Eight minutes before noon on October 1, 1945, Court Marshal Thomas E. Waggaman called to those assembled, "ALL RISE!" A moment later, after entering through a side door, Harry Truman became the first sitting president ever to step into the red-carpeted courtroom.[57] He was accompanied by White House special counsel Samuel Rosenman and press secretary Charles Ross. By all accounts, the president appeared to be "in a jovial mood."[58] His entrance was not announced, and the startled crowd murmured with excitement.[59] Truman took a reserved seat at counsels' table in front of the justices, and from his wooden chair happily turned from side to side greeting thrilled court-watchers. Chief Justice Harlan Fiske Stone had officially administered the oath of office to former Senator Burton earlier that day in a private ceremony.

When the clock struck noon the traditional cry of "Oyez! Oyez!" rang out and all, including the president, rose as the robed justices emerged from behind the plush red velvet curtains hanging behind the bench.[60] Moments later, Burton stepped before Clerk of the Court Charles Elmore Cropley, who had worked in the building since 1912, first as a page boy, and whose death at age fifty-six nearly seven years hence would bring the chief justice to open the Court's term by reading a warm eulogy from the bench.[61] Cropley ceremoniously administered the oath to Burton as he had for every justice present. Marshal Waggaman then escorted Burton to the Court's most junior seat, endmost on the left side of the chief justice.

A Court official whispered into the president's ear. It was the justices' turn to show deference and they, along with the spectators, rose when Truman did. He left the courtroom through the same side door in which he had entered, and after the door closed behind him everyone again took their seats.[62]

A few days later, Burton wrote a note of gratitude to the president:

Dear Harry,

It was thoughtful and generous of you to come to the session of the Court on October 1st which included my introduction into the office to which you appointed me. . . . I only hope that I can justify the trust reposed in me.[63]

CHAPTER THREE

Attorney General Tom Clark

HARRY TRUMAN HAD KNOWN TOM Clark since Clark was the Department of Justice official charged by the Roosevelt administration with helping the Truman Committee investigate the defense industry. When Truman became president, he quickly sent Clark's name to the Senate for confirmation as the nation's attorney general, announcing the nomination during a White House press conference on May 23, 1945.

Clark, then forty-five years old and still working as a politically appointed attorney at DOJ, admitted to being surprised by the nomination, telling reporters moments after Truman's announcement, "I don't know just what to say. Naturally, I am grateful to the president for the appointment. I will serve to the best of my ability."[1] A holdover from the Roosevelt administration, Clark had been preparing to return to home and private practice in his native Texas. He and Truman had worked well together on the Truman Committee investigations, but unlike others whom Truman had befriended as a senator, Clark neither sought nor expected a job in the presidential administration. That the bowtie-wearing Clark was popular with Texas's formidable congressional delegation no doubt weighed in Truman's calculus.

Truman nominated Clark while his approval ratings were historically high. With the nation at war and still reeling from Franklin Roosevelt's death, Americans wanted to believe in their new president. They wanted to trust his judgment. Senators confirmed his nominees with little debate. Cries of cronyism and concerns about the quality of those nominees were still some time away.

While White Americans' reaction to Clark's nomination was largely positive, many African Americans expressed uneasiness. They had good reason to be wary. Clark was from Dallas. The senators and congressmen who recommended him had built careers on the Lone Star State's segregationist politics. It was well known that Roosevelt had put Clark in the Department of Justice at the behest of Senator Tom Connally, whom African American reporters described as a "rabid racist."[2] The day after Truman's press conference, the National Negro Council announced its opposition to Clark's nomination on the grounds that he, as a senior Justice Department official, had not worked to implement or even spoken in favor of the Supreme Court's landmark 1944 decision *Smith v. Allwright*, which held that Texas's Whites-only Democratic Party primary in Texas violated the Fifteenth Amendment.[3] Clark's deliberate silence on the case was remarkable because it originated in his home state.

After being nominated for attorney general, Clark broke his silence on *Allwright*. He granted an interview to the *Chicago Defender* to address African Americans' concerns about his nomination and to announce that the Justice Department under his leadership would enforce the *Allwright* decision nationwide. "Negro citizens can depend on me absolutely," he promised, "to enforce the provisions of the Constitution for the protection of all American citizens."[4] He denied reports that during the investigation of a Mississippi lynching victim, he had referred to African Americans by racial slurs, insisting, "The language attributed to me . . . is both unfortunate and inaccurate."[5]

An African American elevator attendant who had worked for years at DOJ defended Clark to reporters. She told them that, unlike most White men, Clark always removed his hat when he entered her elevator. In segregated Washington, DC, such small courtesies mattered. Louis Mehlinger, an African American lawyer at DOJ, recalled how he had spent years trying to join the Federal Bar Association but was denied on account of the association's racist admission policies. After Clark was elected president of the association, he ended the Whites-only admission policy and Mehlinger was able to join.[6]

* * *

Tom Clark's grandfather was a Confederate soldier killed on the battlefield at Allatoona Pass in the autumn of 1864. That soldier's second son, Clark's father, was born in Mississippi, educated at Ole Miss, and moved to Dallas in 1885 to open his law practice. He married fellow Mississippian Jeannie Falls and the couple had ten children. Tom, their seventh, was born in 1899, by which time several of his siblings had died. Both of Clark's parents were strident segregationists, even for their time. His mother "never forgave" Abraham Lincoln for signing the Emancipation Proclamation, a document his father declared was issued "in utter disregard and in violation of the Constitution."[7]

The Dallas of Tom Clark's childhood was segregated in every way. "whites only" and "colored only" signs designated which restrooms, water fountains, swimming pools, and transportation options residents could use. Legal and illegal violence against African Americans maintained the system. New, young White residents streamed into the city while most African Americans were either aging former slaves or those freedmen's children.

After graduating from high school, Clark enrolled in the Virginia Military Institute, where he excelled in VMI's rigorous academic and physical environment. By the end of his first year, however, his family's financial situation had worsened on account of his father's drinking problem. Clark withdrew from VMI and returned home to Texas, where he worked his way through the University of Texas and its law school.

By his own admission, Clark "did not do too well in law school."[8] He was more interested in socializing than studying and regularly skipped class. He kept a demanding social schedule, remaining active in Delta Tau Delta, the fraternity that he had pledged in college, and joining both Pi Sigma Alpha, an honorary political science fraternity, and Apha Phi Epsilon, a literary and public speaking fraternity. He became chairman of the student publications board, which published the yearbook and several university newspapers. In what little time remained, Clark courted Mary Ramsey, a strawberry blonde who lived in the sorority house across the street from his fraternity house. The tall, lanky man paying his own way through school was, according to the Pi Beta Phi sorority housemother, "a big man on campus."[9]

Clark so neglected his studies that as graduation day grew near, it became unclear whether he would graduate from law school. The dean summoned the young man to his office to explain the gravity of the situation. It would be particularly unfortunate for a student who had overcome so many financial obstacles to find himself academically ineligible to graduate. Clark took the dean's warning to heart. He scored so highly on his final examinations that professors agreed to excuse his habitual absences and permit him to graduate with his class in the fall of 1922. In three years he had earned both his bachelor's degree and bachelor of laws degree

(an L.L.B, the precursor to today's juris doctorate degree.) He returned
to Dallas to practice law with his father and brother Bill, and he married
Mary Ramsey two years later.

* * *

It might be said that Tom Clark went to Washington in his brother's
place. Bill Clark's friend Percy Rice had successfully managed Senator
Tom Connally's 1934 campaign. Impressed with Bill Clark's legal work,
Connally asked if he would to come to Washington to work as an assistant attorney general. Bill declined but said his brother Tom might be
interested. After some back and forth with the Roosevelt administration,
Connally secured a position in the Department of Justice for thirty-seven--
year-old Tom Clark, who moved his young family to Washington for what
he presumed would be a few years' stay.

When he reported to the main Justice building on Pennsylvania Avenue,
Clark learned that he had not been hired to serve as an assistant attorney
general. He had been hired as an assistant *to* the attorney general—a job
with much less authority, responsibility, and prestige. Connally had just
announced his opposition to Roosevelt's so-called Court-packing plan.
Roosevelt refused to place several men whom Connally had recommended
for administration jobs; Clark was lucky to have received a position at all.

* * *

Japan attacked the U.S. Naval Base at Pearl Harbor on December 7, 1941. A
few weeks later Roosevelt signed Executive Order 9066, which authorized
the War Department to move "any and all persons" to areas specifically
designated by the secretary of war as suitable for their residence.[10] While
the president's order avoided any mention of race or ethnicity, nearly all
the American citizens and residents the government forcibly relocated
were of Japanese ancestry.

Seventy percent of the Japanese Americans relocated to internment
camps were American citizens. They received little notice before being
ordered to leave their homes with whatever few possessions they could
carry to the camps, which were surrounded by barbed-wire fences and
patrolled by armed guards. In 1943 and 1944 the Supreme Court affirmed
the government's power to impose curfews on Japanese Americans and to
imprison any of them who refused to obey orders to leave their homes.[11]

Administration officials asigned Clark to work with the U.S. Army to
move Americans of Japanese descent to internment camps. He inspected

locations to assess their suitability to become camps, meeting with local officials at remote sites in Colorado, Utah, Idaho, Oregon, and other western states. Clark tapped career DOJ attorneys to assist political appointees in prosecuting those who resisted the Army's relocation orders. He worked in the western states until May 1942, when he returned to Washington.

In later years Clark deeply regretted having helped establish the internment camps. "I got back to Washington as soon as I could," he recalled. "I didn't care for [the internment program] and I should not have participated in it." The assignment haunted him for decades. "I have made a lot of mistakes in my life," he rued thirty years later. "One is my part in the evacuation of the Japanese from California."[12] But during the war Clark objected neither to the internment program nor his role in implementing it.

The Roosevelt White House was pleased with his work. When he arrived back in Washington, the administration offered him a commission as a senior Army officer but Clark respectfully declined. He wanted to return to the Justice Department and get back to doing lawyer's work.

Attorney General Francis Biddle promoted Clark to chief of DOJ's newly created war frauds section. Clark was disappointed, having hoped for a more established, higher-ranking position. Serving as director of the war frauds section, however, proved to be a serendipitous assigment that changed Clark's life and career, this at a time when Senator Harry Truman was gaining national recognition as chair of a special Senate committee to investigate the national defense industry.

Clark, as chief of the new war frauds section, became Truman's primary contact in the Department of Justice. The men worked well together and became friends. A few years later Truman became president of the United States, fired the attorney general who had repeatedly denied Clark the most senior positions in DOJ, and asked Clark to become attorney general in his place.

* * *

A proud family man who washed the dinner dishes at home, Tom Clark differed from many of his contemporaries in that he would have left Washington had his wife, Mary, and their two children, William Ramsey and Margaret, wanted to do so. Their family life was not wholly subordinate to his career. Luckily for him, they were enjoying their lives in the District of Columbia. Mary Clark especially relished federal Washington's social scene. The *Washington Post* described her as "enjoying a school girl thrill at Mr. Clark's new job."[13]

Mary was just about to leave for a lunch with friends at the Mayflower Hotel when her husband, calling from a pay phone, excitedly told her that the president would announce his appointment as attorney general later that afternoon.[14] A few weeks later the Clarks were the guests of honor at an annual Father's Day "mint julep party and reception" at friends' well-appointed home on Chesapeake Street NW, and just a few days after that they were feted again at a cocktail party at the Statler Hotel.[15]

Rank-and-file Justice lawyers welcomed Clark's nomination. He had worked alongside career attorneys both in Washington and in western states for years. One attorney declared that "there never was an appointment of an Attorney General that was more popular in the Department. This man has come up from the ranks of lawyers here. He has been in the field. He knows their problems. When he hears a lawyer in the Criminal Division has won a tough case, he writes him a congratulatory note. In long hand."[16]

Some Roosevelt appointees in the Justice Department doubted Clark was up to the job. Outgoing Attorney General Francis Biddle did little to conceal his disappointment at being replaced and privately suggested that Clark was an unwise choice. At a June staff meeting, Clark asked political appointees to continue working in their positions after he became attorney general. He expected to rely on their experience and advice. Several surprised him by declining his offer, with three assistant attorneys general submitting their resignations before he was sworn in.[17]

Although disappointed, Clark paid little mind to their departures. He had been in Washington long enough to know many attorneys who would happily replace the Roosevelt appointees. Roosevelt had been president for more than twelve years; it would take some time for the Roosevelt era to end. Clark, who was nominated just weeks into Truman's presidency, was at the vanguard of a new legal era.

In front of 1,500 people gathered in the great hall of the Department of Justice, Tom Clark was sworn in as attorney general of the United States on July 1, 1945. "I shall be the people's lawyer," he declared in a speech before the Maryland Bar Association just hours later. "The people's lawyer to see that the innocent are protected, the guilty punished, monopolies, trusts and restraints in interstate business prevented, the public purse guarded, civil liberties preserved and Constitutional guarantees held inviolate—that is my goal."[18]

CHAPTER FOUR

The Court Truman Inherited and a Justice Abroad

HAVING SERVED AS ATTORNEY GENERAL, an associate justice on the Supreme Court, and chief justice of the United States, Harlan Fiske Stone was one of the most respected jurists of his time. To this day he is the only justice in American history to have served both as the most junior member of the Court and as chief justice. A Republican nominated him to the Court and a Democrat named him chief justice.

During his sixteen-year tenure as an associate justice, Stone established himself as an independent voice on the Court. He advocated for judicial restraint irrespective of politics. The lifelong Republican consistently voted to uphold New Deal laws Republicans opposed. His time as an associate justice was successful.

His shorter, four-year tenure as chief justice was less so. He was surrounded by seven Roosevelt nominees on the Court but was unable to lead them to unity, or often even to clearly stated explanations of the law. Concurring opinions muddled majority decisions and dissenting opinions abounded. Even though much of this was beyond Chief Justice Stone's control, discord came to characterize the Court under his leadership.

* * *

Harlan Fiske Stone was born in hardscrabble rural New Hampshire in October 1872, and despite being born on winter's edge, he grew big for his age. He played football, excelled in school, and was quite popular. Friends called him "Doc." At Amherst College his classmates foresaw that "Doc Stone will take warning and proceed to be the most famous man in [the class of] '94."[1]

In the class behind Stone's was a Vermont shopkeeper's taciturn son who, having been born on the Fourth of July in 1872, was a few months older than "Doc." Stone and Calvin Coolidge became friends. Their paths diverged after graduation but would converge again. Stone became a professor at Columbia University School of Law, where he earned his colleagues' respect and his students' admiration. Among his students was a financially strapped westerner named Bill Douglas who one day would join him on the Supreme Court. Stone became dean of the law school, serving for thirteen years before returning to private practice in 1923.

That same year, Coolidge became president of the United States. He asked Stone to be his attorney general.[2] The Senate easily confirmed him, and Stone left his lucrative private practice to join Coolidge's cabinet.

Stone's predecessor, Harry M. Daugherty, had been forced to resign during congressional investigations of the rampant corruption at the Department of Justice. Stone sought to eradicate the graft.[3] He stopped the Bureau of Investigations—predecessor to the Federal Bureau of Investigation—from spying on American citizens solely because they belonged to political fringe groups. At a press conference Stone explained, "The Bureau of Investigations is not concerned with political or other opinions of individuals. It is concerned only with their conduct and then only with such conduct as is forbidden by the laws of the United States." He gave voice to a tenet that later would guide his civil liberties jurisprudence on the Court: "When a police system passes beyond these limits, it is dangerous to the proper administration of justice and to human liberty, which it should be our first concern to cherish."[4]

In 1924 Stone appointed J. Edgar Hoover to lead the FBI. It was the most significant decision he made as attorney general, perhaps in his entire career. Hoover would lead the FBI for the next fifty years, running roughshod over the Department of Justice's professed ideals and professional standards. The FBI director routinely ordered agents to investigate American citizens based not on evidence of criminal activity but on the basis of their political beliefs.

In time, Stone grew defensive about having appointed Hoover. In a letter to Harvard Law School professor Felix Frankfurter, with whom Stone would later serve on the Court, he confided that he shared the professor's concerns about Hoover but, "I suppose, in his case . . . one must take the fat with the lean."[5] The extent of Hoover's transgressions would not become fully known until the 1970s, when Congress at last investigated his decades-long term as director of the FBI.

* * *

Stone had been attorney general for less than a year when Coolidge nominated him to fill the Supreme Court vacancy created in 1925 by Joseph McKenna's resignation.[6] Stone's nomination surprised senators for two reasons: first, he had been attorney general for just nine months, and second, he did not hail from a western state, as did the Californian McKenna.[7] Geographical representation on the Court mattered politically in the era before common air travel. None of the remaining eight sitting justices were from the West Coast. For his part, Stone had recommended to the president that he nominate New Yorker Benjamin Cardozo. But Coolidge instead nominated his fellow New Englander.

Senators' concerns about Stone's nomination helped create one of the most dramatic rituals in federal government. He became the first Supreme Court nominee to testify before the Senate Judiciary Committee.[8] It came to be because Stone, while in private practice, had represented Wall Street banks in all sorts of legal matters. The Coolidge administration in which he served as attorney general was so ardently pro-business that lawmakers worried that if Stone were confirmed to the Court, he would become a lifetime vote for Wall Street. To alleviate these concerns, Stone offered to testify under oath before the Senate Judiciary Committee. After the first-ever Senate confirmation hearing, Stone was confirmed by a vote of seventy-one to six.[9]

In 1925 Chief Justice William Howard Taft and the so-called Four Horsemen—Justices Pierce Butler, James McReynolds, George Sutherland, and Willis Van Devanter—comprised a reliable right-wing majority on the Court. Because Stone had been "kicked upstairs" from the arch-conservative Coolidge administration, many expected him to become a sixth majority vote. But he quickly surprised his fellow justices and Court commentators by consistently voting to uphold Congress's power to regulate markets and protect workers' rights. Despite having been named to the Court by Coolidge, Stone later voted to uphold New Deal legislation enacted by Roosevelt and the Democratic-led Congress. He came to deplore the reactionary conservatism of the Four Horsemen and often joined dissents written by Oliver Wendell Holmes and Louis Brandeis but rarely dissented alone. As years passed and Roosevelt's nominees joined the Court, Stone wrote more majority opinions.[10]

* * *

To show that he had put the Court-packing controversy behind him, on June 12, 1941, Roosevelt nominated Harlan Fiske Stone, a Republican nominee to the Court, to be chief justice of the United States. It had been thirty-one years since a president had nominated a member of the opposition party for that position.[11] Stone's nomination was particulary suprising because he had opposed Roosevelt's Court-reform proposal. When reporters asked Stone for his reaction, he struck a humbled note, replying, "The responsibility is so great, that it doesn't create any sense of elation."[12]

Many had expected Roosevelt to nominate Attorney General Robert Jackson as chief justice.[13] Instead, Roosevelt nominated Jackson to replace retiring justice James McReynolds. Jackson sought to quell rumors that he was miffed at not receiving the chief justice nomination: "I am glad to go on a bench over which Harlan Stone presides. His experience, his record and his character make his choice so obviously fitting that it should meet with universal approval."[14] Jackson also knew that he was forty-nine and Stone was sixty-eight years old. The Associated Press reported that Stone was "healthy and spry for his 68 years," but all knew that he could retire at age seventy and receive his full salary for the remainder of his days.[15] The Senate confirmed Stone by voice vote on June 27, 1941. He would serve as the nation's chief justice until his death nearly five years later.

Jackson had been Roosevelt's first choice for chief justice. But the ever-wily Felix Frankfurter persuaded Roosevelt to nominate Stone for the center seat by arguing that a Republican nomination would advance national unity. Ensuing years would reveal that Roosevelt sowed a problem when he assured Jackson that he would be named chief justice when Stone retired.[16] By then, Truman was president.

Former chief justice William Taft advocated a concept he called "mass[ing] the Court."[17] Taft so believed that the Court should speak with one voice that he would pressure a justice who dissented from a majority opinion to refrain from filing a written opinion. As a result, the dissent rate during Taft's tenure was an astonishingly low 9 percent.[18] Taft's successor, Chief Justice Charles Evan Hughes, continued, albeit with less success, Taft's emphasis on massing the Court.

Roosevelt's predecessor, Herbert Hoover, intended to elevate Stone from associate to chief justice in 1930 but Taft, who knew that he was dying, convinced Hoover not to nominate the former Columbia Law School dean. "Stone is not a leader," Taft told the president, "and would have a great deal of trouble in massing the court."[19] Hoover heeded Taft's advice and nominated Hughes instead. When Stone finally did become chief justice, Taft's advice proved prescient, for a reason inconceivable to Taft or Hughes: unlike them, Stone had no interest in "massing the Court."

* * *

It might have been naive to think that Stone could foster unity, or even cordiality, among the justices. This was because, as an associate justice, he had committed an egregious public breach of decorum that shook the Court. It was perhaps a far-fetched notion that the man who had so embarrassed the Court could effectively lead it just a few years later.

Back when he was an associate justice, Stone enjoyed early morning strolls around his tony neighborhood in northwest Washington. He was occasionally joined by Marquis Childs, an ambitious reporter for the *St. Louis Post-Dispatch*. Stone's mammoth frame would lumber up Massachusetts Avenue as if physically burdened by the troubles on his mind. The considerably younger Childs, who would die comfortably forty-four years after Stone's unexpected death, strolled alongside him, asking and listening.

Stone was worried about the Court. He had served with the Four Horsemen during the years when they habitually substituted their own judgment for that of the elected branches. With help from Chief Justice Hughes, the Horsemen had successfully stymied enactment of the New Deal on which Roosevelt had campaigned. The Court began to restrain itself only after Roosevelt proposed his so-called Court-packing plan.

Stone explained to Childs that the justices' political beliefs again threatened the Court. Roosevelt's first nominee, Justice Hugo Black of Alabama, failed to appreciate that he was no longer a senator. Stone did not deny Black's intellectual fitness or his unassailable work ethic. But Black seemed intent on continuing his congressional crusade on behalf of the poor and dispossessed, regardless of the legal precedents guiding the case at bar. During his first year on the Court, he filed more dissents than most of his colleagues. Black addressed issues that had not been argued on appeal in opinions roiling with what Stone viewed as political proselytizing. He was becoming, in Stone's eyes, a problem.[20]

Childs wrote a scathing article reporting that there was an unnamed "new man on the bench who has had no judicial experience and only a comparatively limited legal experience who is not a help to his colleagues in the first two or three years." After the article's publication, Childs prepared for severe professional fallout. Supreme Court justices—more than presidents, senators, or representatives—believed in the confidentiality of their private communications. But the next time Childs met Stone for an early morning walk, the big New Englander congratulated him on the piece, beaming that it was "just what is needed to educate the public."[21]

Childs could hardly hide his relief before Stone wondered why the writer should shy away from seeking the widest audience for his work. A scoop like this should not be limited to the *St. Louis Post-Dispatch*. Childs should consider conveying this important story nationwide.

Several months later, after more walks with Stone, Childs published an article in the May 1938 issue of *Harper's Magazine*. Entitled "The Supreme Court Today," it was as scandalous a story as had ever been published about the Court. Competing newspapers and magazines printed excerpts, with the *Washington Post* publishing its story beneath the headline "Black Embarrasses Colleagues in Supreme Court, Writer Says." Unlike Childs's earlier *Post-Dispatch* reporting, the *Harper's* article named Hugo Black as the source of his fellow justices' ire.

According to the article, Black caused his colleagues "acute discomfort and embarrassment" because of his "lack of legal knowledge and experience." Childs reported that Black's lack of knowledge of "the whole range of the law and the great body of Supreme Court decisions" forced his colleagues to pick up his slack and work "at considerable strain." The Alabaman's alleged deficiencies, Childs wrote, hampered his ability to do his job:

> It comes back to the matter of craftsmanship. A man with only a limited experience with the law, such as Justice Black, finds it extremely difficult to maintain the pace of the Court. So far the cases that have been assigned to him have been relatively simple. Nevertheless several opinions he has written have been rephrased by other members of the Court and they have been subsequently released with something less than satisfaction.[22]

Childs's critique of Black's performance continued in this vein with remarkable detail. He obviously had received information from at least one member of the Court. After grapevine gossip revealed that Childs occasionally accompanied Stone on his morning walks, it became clear who was the inside man.

A media maelstrom ensued. Reporters deluged Stone's office with telephone calls seeking comment. His secretary, Gertrude Jenkins, felt besieged. She dashed from the Court building to a nearby payphone. She called Childs and yelled into the receiver, "Reporters are hounding me. What shall I say?"

"Deny everything!"

"I always told the Judge he talked too much," Jenkins sighed as she hung up the phone. She denied everything but it was useless. Reporters knew that it was Stone who had trashed Black.

Justice Black's many supporters sought to turn the tables by calling every reporter in their card files to extol his considerable intelligence and judicial temperament. Meanwhile, Stone's office continued to deny what the federal city knew to be true.

The most calm person amid the unprecedented furor was Hugo Black himself, who seemed entirely unperturbed by the whole ordeal. As Stone dispatched emissaries to repeatedly deny that he was the source for Childs's reporting, Black declined every request for comment. When one of Stone's closest friends contacted Black to assure him that Stone had nothing to do with the *Harper's* article, the Alabaman replied, "I can assure you that I am not disturbed in the slightest by the matter to which you referred."[23] Such was the state of the Supreme Court Harry Truman inherited. And just weeks after becoming president, Truman exacerbated matters by placing further strain on the Court.

* * *

On May 2, 1945, Justice Robert Jackson accepted Truman's appointment to become the United States' chief counsel to prosecute the senior Nazi officials at the International Military Tribunal in Nuremberg, Germany. Jackson neither consulted nor informed Chief Justice Stone of his appointment before publicly announcing it.[24] Jackson announced a six months' leave of absence from the Court, but the Nuremberg trials would cause him to miss the entire term.[25]

Misgivings about Jackson's new assignment spread rapidly. Court rulings during the Great Depression had shown Americans from all walks of life how directly the Court's composition could affect their lives. Regular citizens were concerned about the possible effects of Jackson's absence.

Minnesota representative Joseph P. O'Hara, a Republican who, like Truman, had led soldiers in battle as an Army captain in World War I, introduced a bill to forbid justices from accepting extraneous assignments. The *Washington Post* noted that Jackson was not the first justice in recent years asked to perform extrajudicial duty: "Justice [Owen] Roberts was similarly drafted to direct the Pearl Harbor investigation. Under its present burden of work, the court can ill afford to lose the services of one of its members, even during the summer months customarily used by the justices to prepare for the next season's work."[26] Editors at the *Baltimore Sun* agreed that, although Jackson was an excellent selection, his position as a Supreme Court justice should have disqualified him: "In naming Justice Jackson as counsel for the United States in the cases against the top war criminals, President Truman has put the country's interests in excellent hands. One would have expected in advance that this assignment would go to somebody less busy than a Supreme Court justice."[27]

Jackson's fellow justices were not keen on his becoming the nation's chief war-crimes prosecutor. Why he had accepted such a demanding request confounded them. Douglas believed Jackson accepted the assignment because he planned to run for governor of New York, or perhaps even for president, and surmised that prosecuting former Nazis was politically advantageous "since the Jewish vote is important in many parts of our country."[28] Although Jackson's political ambitions were an open secret in federal Washington, his decision to serve in Nuremberg had more to do with seeking a respite from the increasingly bitter atmosphere on the Court than with courting any particular group of voters. Chief Justice Stone was particularly concerned about the number of four-to-four decisions that would have to be held over until Jackson's return. Stone himself had previously declined a request from President Roosevelt to assume responsibilities beyond his Supreme Court duties.[29]

Jackson's decision to accept Truman's Nuremberg assignment came at considerable cost to him and the Court. That he did not consult or even inform any of his fellow justices before accepting only added to their frustration. Douglas and other justices believed that Jackson should have resigned from the Court before accepting a post in the executive branch of government.[30]

Chief Justice Stone and Justices Black, Douglas, and Murphy not only disagreed with Jackson's leave of absence, they took issue with the legitimacy of the Nuremberg proceedings. Calling the unprecedented trials a "high-grade lynching party," Stone declared, "I don't care what he does to the Nazis, but I hate to see the pretense that he is running a court and proceeding according to common law. This is a little too sanctimonious a fraud to meet my old-fashioned ideas."[31]

Columnist Drew Pearson reported on Jackson's reaction to this disapproval in his widely read column "The Washington Merry-Go-Round." Reporting that Jackson was "all steamed up over his job as war criminals prosecutor," Pearson explained that Jackson believed in the work he was leaving to do. He was irritated at his fellow justices' unwillingness to wish him well in the endeavor. Pearson reported that Jackson was "ready to retire from the court if his black-robed colleagues don't like his taking time off to prosecute the Nazis."[32]

Jackson's threat to retire might have had more to do with his frustration with serving on the Court with Hugo Black than anything else. Before Truman asked him to serve in Nuremberg, Jackson was already considering resigning from the Court. He loathed the thought of serving another year with Black, whom he believed did not understand or accept that he no longer was a partisan senator but was now a justice.[33] Jackson thought the Alabaman made the conferences unbearable. At the wedding reception for Dean Acheson's daughter in 1943, Jackson pulled aside Frankfurter to ask, "Do you feel as depressed as I do after these Saturday conferences?" Frankfurter replied, "I certainly do," and both men attributed their malaise to the burden of being subjected to Black's weekly haranguing about "justice and right and decency and everything."[34]

By the time he left for Germany, Jackson had come to loathe Black. Distance would not quell his enmity. Before Jackson returned to the bench, he would spark a conflagration that would ensnare the president and mortify the Court.

But for now, in his public statement accepting the assignment, Jackson tacitly acknowledged the quandary posed by his leave of absence. "It is a labor I would not have sought," he admitted, "but I accept the assignment by the Commander in Chief with a sense of my inadequacy and with complete dedication I will see it through."[35] He began hiring staff members and disappointed civil rights supporters by appointing a segregationist attorney to choose which former Nazi officials the United States should recommend for prosecution.[36]

On May 22, 1945, Jackson departed for Europe with U.S. Army colonel John Amen. Their immediate destination was London, where they planned to begin what Jackson called an "examination of important witnesses, documents, reports, captured orders and other evidence that might be used in the trial of the major criminals before an international military tribunal."[37] During his time abroad Jackson and his fellow prosecutors reviewed more than 100,000 German documents, 25,000 photographs, and millions of feet of film.[38]

Once in Germany, he moved into a well-landscaped estate a few miles northwest of Nuremberg. A small staff tended to his needs, and U.S. Army staff sergeant Moritz Fuchs served as his bodyguard. The two men became close friends. Jackson so appreciated Fuchs's untiring vigilance that Jackson nominated him for the Army Commendation Medal. In May 1955, seven months after sixty-two-year-old Jackson died of a sudden heart attack, Sergeant Fuchs, who had served under General George Patton during World War II, was ordained a Catholic priest in Syracuse, New York. Jackson's widow, Irene, who had met her husband's bodyguard after the Nuremberg trials ended, traveled to Syracuse to attend Moritz Fuchs's ordination and first Mass.[39]

Attorney General Tom Clark came to Nuremberg on an Army plane in July 1946 to be present at the opening of the trials. He supported the trials but not Truman's selection of a Supreme Court justice to serve as chief prosecutor. Clark did not publicly comment on the matter until after he retired, however, when he said that Jackson "should never have been prosecutor on the Nuremberg Trials. That was a great mistake. Justices should not accept these outside appointments while they are sitting on the court."[40]

Jackson's performance as the United States' lead counsel in Nuremberg drew mixed reviews. Courtroom spectators watched Nazi general Hermann Goering confound and fluster Jackson over the course of two and a half days of cross-examination.[41] Goering seemed to gain the advantage with each question Jackson asked. Jackson lost his composure, flinging off his interpreters' headphones and shouting at the judges,

> I respectfully submit to the Tribunal that this witness is not being responsive. It is perfectly futile to spend our time if we cannot have responsive answers to our questions. This witness, it seems to me, is adopting and has adopted in the witness stand and in the dock an arrogant and contemptuous attitude toward the Tribunal which is giving him the trial which he never gave a living soul nor dead ones either.[42]

He appeared to have lost control of his witness and himself.

As the trials dragged on, Frankfurter sought to reassure Jackson that all was well back in Washington, but even this consolation came with qualification. In one letter, Frankfurter wrote, "Whatever I may think about a Justice of the Supreme Court taking on other jobs—and I am afraid I am impenitent on that subject—I never had any doubt about the profound importance of your enterprise and equally no doubt that you would discharge the task according to the finest professional standards both intellectually and ethically."[43]

CHAPTER FIVE

"The Very Nearly Indispensable Man"

FREDERICK MOORE VINSON LIKED TO tell people that he had been born in jail. His father, James Vinson, was the jailer in Louisa, Kentucky, a rural town on the banks of the Big Sandy River. The Vinsons' home, where Fred was born on January 22, 1890, was attached to the jail. James would bring his young son with him to the nearby Lawrence County Courthouse, and these visits sowed the seeds of Fred's interest in the law.[1]

Tragedy struck when James Vinson died. Fred was still a very young boy, and his mother, Virginia, struggled financially. To make ends meet, she took in boarders at their home. Fred took on whatever work he could find after school and during the summer months.

He graduated from Louisa High School and enrolled in Kentucky's Centre College, from which he graduated at the top of his class in 1909. He was also the best shortstop in the school's history. Vinson then worked to pay his way through Centre College School of Law, where he won the school's two most prestigious academic prizes before graduating in 1911 and returning to Louisa to practice law. Two years later he was elected city attorney. During World War I, he joined the Army and was at the Central Officer's Training School at Camp Pike, Arkansas, when the war ended. Vinson returned to Kentucky and, in 1923, won a special election for an open seat in the House of Representatives. Voters sent the jailer's son to Congress, where he became an effective advocate for Franklin Roosevelt's New Deal.[2]

Vinson chaired the tax subcommittee of the House Ways and Means Committee, and his mastery of federal tax law soon stood unmatched in Congress. The Kentuckian's only line in the sand was that he refused to increase taxes on tobacco. Minnesota congressman Harold Knutson, a Republican who opposed nearly every measure Vinson proposed, acknowledged on the House floor, "The gentleman from Kentucky is the greatest authority on taxation that has served in this House in the 21 years I have been a member of this body."[3]

Although it might have surprised those who came to know him after he left Congress, Fred Vinson was a powerful orator. His rich baritone filled the House chamber as easily as it did committee hearing rooms. After Vinson addressed the packed House one afternoon, one of his principal adversaries proclaimed on the floor, "In all the time I have served in this House I can recall no time when there has been a finer exhibition of the artistic accomplishments of a great advocate than you have just witnessed." Applause flooded the chamber. "There was the mark of a genius."[4]

In November 1937, Roosevelt nominated Vinson to be a judge on the United States Court of Appeals for the District of Columbia Circuit. Because its jurisdiction largely consisted of appeals from federal agencies, the U.S. Court of Customs and Patent Appeals and the U.S. Court of Claims, the DC Circuit Court of Appeals was widely viewed as second only to the Supreme Court in national importance. The Senate confirmed him less than a month later, and he resigned from Congress to take his seat on the bench.

Vinson proved to be an efficient and ideologically reliable judge. He sat on 439 cases and wrote 107 majority opinions. Of those, 25 were appealed to the Supreme Court. The Court granted *certiorari* review of just 4 of those 25, overturning his opinion in 3 of them. In the 439 cases he judged, Vinson dissented only 5 times. More tellingly, a full 85 percent of his majority decisions favored the government's position. Of his twelve majority opinions in criminal cases, only three rulings favored the defendant.[5]

This consistency revealed Vinson's two-pronged judicial philosophy, at least as it existed then. First, he tended to defer to the legislative and executive branches. He presumed that their actions were valid unless they clearly violated the Constitution. Second, Vinson was a strong believer in *stare decisis*, the legal doctrine that forms the basis for common law by mandating that courts follow the decisions of courts in previous cases involving similar facts. On the DC Circuit Court of Appeals, Vinson was loath to distinguish cases from those already decided by precedent. His deference to the executive and legislative branches combined with his adherence to *stare decisis* established his philosophy and practice of judicial restraint.

As if his duties on the DC Circuit Court of Appeals were not consuming enough, Vinson was appointed by Chief Justice Stone in March 1942 to serve as the chief judge of the newly formed Emergency Court of Appeals. Congress established this court in the Emergency Price Control Act to adjudicate complaints regarding price limits on commodities and rents set by the federal price administrator to keep inflation at bay. Vinson's selection and performance as chief judge of the Emergency Court of Appeals—while maintaining his duties on the DC Circuit Court of Appeals—solidified his reputation as one of Washington's most able and versatile public servants.

Due in large part to his success as chief judge of a newly created court, Roosevelt asked Vinson to relinquish his lifetime appointment to the federal bench and become the director of the Office of Economic Stabilization (OES), a powerful position crucial to the nation's continued economic recovery during World War II. On May 28, 1943, after less than five years on the federal bench, Vinson resigned and accepted Roosevelt's nomination to lead the OES. He had no regret about leaving the judiciary, explaining, "I had a feeling that I was not making much of a sacrifice in the war and it was up to me to do something more than sit on the bench and listen to lawyers' arguments."[6] Senators knew Vinson well by now and confirmed him by a voice vote without a word of debate.[7]

Director Vinson's primary duty was to use whatever means were legally available to the federal government to prevent inflation. New Deal programs and, more forcefully, jobs created by the war effort had pulled the nation from the depths of the Great Depression. But rising prices of household goods threatened the recovery. Vinson had to resist political pressure from both labor and industry management. He earned universal praise for his even-handed leadership of the OES, where he served for two years. His service as director there made Vinson famous. Americans across the country learned why political insiders referred to him as one of the "strong men" in federal service.[8]

In 1945 Roosevelt nominated Vinson to be the federal loan administrator, placing him at the helm of the $40 billion Reconstruction Finance Corporation. He had hardly settled in there when Roosevelt appointed him director of war mobilization and reconversion. Not long thereafter, at his vacation home in Georgia, Franklin Delano Roosevelt died.

* * *

During the first three months of his presidency, Harry S. Truman replaced
scores of Roosevelt's appointees, including cabinet officials. He had been
president for a little more than six weeks on May 23, 1945, when he accepted the resignations of the attorney general, the secretaries of labor
and agriculture, and the war food administrator. At a White House press
conference late that afternoon, a reporter asked, "Mr. President, were any
of the resignations requested by you?"

"They were not," Truman responded. "I have the resignation of every
member of the Government who *can* resign since I have been president!"
The reporters laughed with him. "I can accept them or not as I choose."[9]

Henry Morgenthau had been treasury secretary for eleven years by
the time Truman became president. Roosevelt and Morgenthau had been
neighbors in Dutchess County, New York, years ago, and Roosevelt had
deeply trusted Morgenthau. Truman had no such relationship with the
treasury secretary, who came to realize that, despite remaining in the
cabinet, he no longer was among the White House's closest advisors.
The Treasury Department was one of the most efficiently run agencies
in government, and after more than a decade at its helm, Morgenthau
undisputedly had helped make it so.[10] Nonetheless, he soon caught wind
of rumors that Truman planned to replace him with Fred Vinson.[11]

Morgenthau called Clinton P. Anderson, the secretary of agriculture,
to discuss his standing with the new president. "I think I'd better have
a showdown," Morgenthau confided. "I think I should ask the President
whether he definitely wanted me to remain with him during the rest of his
term."

Anderson counseled against it, telling him, "Truman is funny about
things like that."

But Morgenthau already had made up his mind. At his next White
House appointment, he asked Truman if he could expect to be treasury
secretary for the remainder of the president's term.

"I can't make a promise like that," Truman replied.

"Well, in that case I will have to resign."

The president handed him a sheet of paper: "Start writing."[12]

Morgenthau became the sixth Roosevelt cabinet official to depart during
Truman's short time in office.[13] No one begrudged the new president's right

to choose his advisors but Truman seemed intent on dismantling the previous administration after professing to anyone who would listen that he never wanted to be president. Once the Senate confirmed Morgenthau's successor, Truman's men would comprise a majority of the ten-position cabinet.[14] Roosevelt's appointees greeted the sudden shift in tide with gallows humor, asking each other privately, "When are they going to throw you a farewell cocktail party?"[15]

* * *

The day after Morgenthau resigned, the White House announced that Truman would name Fred Vinson to replace him. Federal Washingtonians praised the nomination, with Vinson being called "the very nearly indispensable man" in the nation's government.[16] This latest nomination solidified Vinson's place among the most respected men in public life. Even Morgenthau, while publicly refuting reports that Truman had demanded his resignation, offered nothing but praise for Vinson, saying, "If I could have picked a successor, I would have chosen Fred Vinson."[17]

The Senate Finance Committee voted to approve Vinson's nomination without holding hearings, and the full Senate unanimously confirmed his nomination later that same day.[18] Fifty-five-year-old Vinson was sworn in as secretary of the treasury in the Capitol's House Ways and Means Committee room on July 23, 1945.[19]

* * *

Treasury Secretary Vinson immensely enjoyed his job, relishing the freedom of having no one left in Washington to impress. On account of his reputation and fast friendship with Truman, he soon became the most influential member of Truman's cabinet. Professionally he was happier than he had been since his days serving in Congress years ago.

He was also terribly worried. The end of World War II presented enormous challenges to the nation's economy, which was unprepared to absorb the impending postwar boom in unemployment. More than 10 million men and women in uniform would be discharged from the armed forces and searching for civilian jobs. Another 10 million Americans in private industry worked in jobs directly related to the wartime defense effort. They too would be seeking new jobs.

To prevent the possible unemployment boom, Treasury Secretary Vinson proposed to Congress an employment stimulus plan consisting of $5 billion worth of individual and corporate tax cuts scheduled to take effect in 1946. Among its provisions, Vinson's plan mandated that, now that the war had ended, 12 million of the nation's lowest income earners would be relieved of their federal tax burden. The second prong of Vinson's proposal, dubbed the "full-employment program," mandated the federal government spend whatever became necessary to invigorate the economy sufficiently to reach full employment. Only with this balanced, aggressive approach, he contended, could the federal government protect the value of the dollar and prevent staggering levels of unemployment. He was the first treasury secretary to call for tax reductions since Andrew Mellon in 1929.[20] One reporter accurately described Vinson as a "moderate progressive . . . not a prisoner of the Wall Street bankers, or of the classical economists or of the Southern Old Guard."[21]

Vinson lobbied members of both parties to support his full-employment program. Democrats were divided on the plan, while Republicans wanted to increase the proposed tax reductions. Vinson urged his former colleagues not to cut taxes more than the plan called for because doing so would upset the fiscal balance on which the program relied.[22] Vinson spoke to reporters to explain that what the Republicans wanted to do was "not the way to cut taxes."[23]

Regrettably for Vinson's proposal, 1946 was an election year. Members of Congress were in a generous mood. Despite his urging them not to do so, they cut taxes by $1 billion more than Vinson had requested.[24] Lawmakers also rejected the extensive role Vinson envisioned the federal government would play in staving off staggering rates of postwar unemployment. Rather than commit to funding whatever proved necessary to reach full employment, Congress committed to providing only "such volume of Federal investment and expenditure that may be needed" for "creating and maintaining" the conditions favorable to reaching maximum employment.[25]

* * *

Vinson and Truman quickly formed a close friendship that touched the course of American events more than any other in its time. The two men thought alike, with each grounded in the pragmatic politics of the possible. This was how they had won elections in their rural border states. It was how they had risen to the heights of federal power, past and above men with better education, more money, and politically connected families. Each man saw in the other someone particularly American, whose high position confirmed to the other that he too belonged.

Beginning shortly after Vinson became his treasury secretary, Truman sought Vinson's advice not just on economic matters but on the vast array of decisions he confronted daily. Truman regularly consulted Vinson before making major decisions. He valued Vinson's vast experience, detailed knowledge of the federal bureaucracy, and proven good judgment.

CHAPTER SIX

Death of a Chief Justice

AS AN ASSOCIATE JUSTICE FOR nearly sixteen years, Harlan Fiske Stone had chafed under the rigid leadership styles of Chief Justices William Howard Taft and Charles Evans Hughes. When Stone was nominated to be chief justice, he nonetheless expressed admiration for his predecessor's undeniable managerial skills, saying, "I should be happy if the thoroughness and efficiency of the recent chief justice could be maintained."[1] But he wanted to change the way the Court decided cases.

Taft and Hughes vigorously advocated for public and official recognition of the Supreme Court as an equal branch of government. Taft successfully lobbied Congress to fund the construction of a Supreme Court building so justices would no longer have to meet in an unused conference room in the Capitol, as they had ever since the Court moved from Philadelphia to Washington in 1790. Likewise, Hughes deftly deflected Roosevelt's purported concern for the advanced age of the justices during the Court-packing controversy. Taft and Hughes conducted the Court's business with martial efficiency because any signs of inefficiency or sloth would have impeded their efforts to protect and strengthen the Court as a coequal branch of the federal government.

Stone took the helm under no such pressure. No Court-packing scheme threatened the judicial branch, and construction of the Supreme Court's majestic building was completed six years before he became chief justice. Stone therefore was able to focus his attention inward, encouraging debate in a freewheeling fashion anathema to his predecessors. As a former law school professor, he relished lengthy, probing discussions of the issues presented by each case. He conducted the Court's weekly conferences in the exact opposite manner as either Taft or Hughes. The pace of the Court's business slowed considerably. No one questioned the new chief's thoroughness, but efficiency quickly proved alien to his administration of the Court. He also ended the practice of discouraging dissenters from filing dissents. When he was an associate justice, Stone had so enjoyed dissenting that Taft privately called him a Bolshevik. As chief justice, Stone preferred that the Court speak with one voice but believed in the contemporary and historical value of dissenting opinions, which he believed could educate the public.

* * *

Cases that the Supreme Court elects to decide are argued in public. Briefs filed with the Court are made public. When the Court reaches its decisions, the legal justifications and explanations for those decisions are made public. But how members of the Court reach those decisions—how the majority forms, whether it is challenged, and how it survives—is kept entirely private. It always has been. This is the conference, and it is difficult to overstate its importance to Supreme Court jurisprudence.

One day a week during each term, Stone and the associate justices met for the conference. They wore business suits—robes were reserved for the courtroom—and gathered around a twelve-foot-long mahogany conference table in a private room. Their high-backed leather and mahogany chairs, like the table, had been handmade by the Court's team of carpenters. The red volute carpet beneath the heavy table was laid when the building opened in 1935 and remains there today.[2] Only justices were permitted into the room, and interruptions were as discouraged as they could be without being forbidden. Law clerks, stenographers, and custodial staff could not enter the room during the conference. If there was a need for water or any other such thing, the junior justice left the room to order it or retrieve it himself. Even during the months when the Court was not in session, the conference room remained closed to visitors.[3] Outside the conference room and the courtroom, the justices rarely saw each other. The conference was the primary venue for chief justices to exercise their limited power over the Court's decision-making.

The chief justice sat at one end of the table opposite the senior associate justice. The three most senior justices sat to the chief's right and the four junior justices to his left. On both sides they sat according to seniority. The most junior justice sat closest to the door so that he— and, beginning in 1981, she—could most easily answer any impertinent knocking, relay legal research requests to law clerks, or simply ask for lunch. During the conference, the chief justice often sought to resolve not only pending cases but also administrative matters better decided with all justices present.

When the Court prepared to discuss a case, the chief justice spoke first. He summarized the case and the issues presented and typically stated how he thought the case should be decided. When he finished, the senior associate justice spoke, followed by the remaining seven justices in order of seniority. The more senior justices usually spoke longer than the junior justices if for no other reason than that there were only so many perspectives on a given case. When discussion on a case ended, the justices voted in reverse order of seniority. If the chief justice was in the majority, he decided who would write the opinion of the Court; if he was in the minority, then the most senior justice in the majority assigned the opinion.

Chief Justices Taft and Hughes mastered the conference. Hughes continued Taft's practice of focusing on efficiency and collegiality. At the conference they forced justices to decide cases the same week they were argued. Taft and Hughes spent hours preparing for each conference, memorizing the facts of each case and honing the legal arguments supporting the results they sought. Seeking to construct consensus among their colleagues, they preferred presiding over debates rather than entering the fray. To a man their fellow justices recalled with gratitude how their conferences began exactly on time and ended at an appointed hour.

As chief justice, Stone discarded the unwritten rules and mores of the Taft and Hughes Courts. He was far more interested in spirited debate than he was in "massing the court." When summarizing cases, Stone spoke at considerable length. He often interrupted other justices when it was their turn to speak. Before long, the associate justices took to interrupting each other as well. The conference atmosphere swiftly deteriorated.

After allowing conferences to run for hours, Stone then allowed them to end without resolution. Cases were held over for continued discussion in the following weeks' conference. "We were always in conference," Justice William O. Douglas recalled. "He couldn't move the cases along."[4] Outsiders noticed the Court's new dilatory pace. The *New York Times* reported that, as several important cases "remain unsettled even after two or three months," Court watchers had begun to "surmise a lack of harmony within the closed conference room."[5]

Ideological differences mixed with personal feelings in the freewheeling conferences. Felix Frankfurter criticized Hugo Black as "the cheapest soapbox orator," who turned every conference into "a championship by Black of justice and right and decency and everything, and those who take the other view are always made out to be the oppressors of the people and the supporters of some exploiting interest." He charged Frank Murphy, whom Frankfurter regarded as little more than a misplaced career government bureaucrat, and William Douglas, whom he openly despised, as spending their time at conference "me-tooing Black" by chiming in as if on cue, "I agree with Justice Black." Frankfurter began referring to Black, Douglas, and Murphy as "the Axis."[6]

Had the justice's souring moods been confined to the conference, their acrimony might have remained private or merely the subject of Washington gossip. Unfortunately, the vitriol, stoked by the contentious and lengthy conferences, reared its head in the justices' dissents—which they were writing with increasing regularity. Under Chief Justice Stone, the Supreme Court produced dissenting opinions at a higher rate than at any previous time in American history.[7] The percentage of non-unanimous decisions rose during Stone's tenure from 36 to 56 percent.[8] In 1943, for the first time in history, most of the Court's rulings—a full 58 percent—were divided decisions.[9] A remarkable one-third of divided rulings during the 1944 term were five-to-four decisions.[10]

Justices discarded the restraint with which they had proceeded in their disagreements when Taft and (to a lesser degree) Hughes led the Court. This was due in large part to Stone's belief that dissenting opinions detracted neither from the dignity of the Court nor his reputation as chief justice. He thought that a justice who disagreed with the majority should not be discouraged from writing a well-reasoned dissent.

Journalists eagerly covered the divided Court, which, according to one correspondent, was featured on newspapers' "front pages more sensationally than any time since the historic battle over the Roosevelt-sponsored 'court-packing' bill several years ago." As the New York Times reported, "In recent years the justices have usually shrouded their sharpest remarks in the privacy of the locked conference chamber, keeping them locked away from the public. It is only lately that the wrangling has broken again into the open through caustically phrased dissents."[11]

That the justices disagreed with each other so vehemently also was strange because nearly all of them had been nominated by the same president. In a precursor to criticism that would later plague Truman's Court nominations, Roosevelt was accused of attempting to mold the Court into an ideological extension of his administration. Roosevelt nominated lawyers on whom he could rely to uphold the constitutionality of New Deal legislation. Most of them had helped draft, promote, or enforce New Deal programs. For example, Stone, as an associate justice, had voted to uphold New Deal laws before Roosevelt, in an apparently bipartisan gesture, elevated him to chief justice. The *Washington Post*'s editors struck a popular cord when they wrote, "In spite of Mr. Stone's elevation to the Chief Justiceship, the President had laid this high tribunal open to the charge of being a New Deal Court. For an agency of government that must be impartial and independent if it is to retain public confidence and function successfully, this preponderance of Administration men may be a formidable handicap."[12]

By the 1940s, however, the constitutionality of the New Deal was largely a settled question. Even before Roosevelt amassed eight nominees on the Supreme Court, the judiciary's post-1937 decisions acknowledged that the federal Constitution empowered Congress and the president to enact New Deal laws. The era of so-called substantive due process jurisprudence was over.

On the post–New Deal cases, the men Roosevelt nominated to the Court were fiercely divided. Their written opinions laid bare these divisions. One unnamed justice lamented in his chambers to White House press secretary Jonathan Daniels, "Hell, they said the Court lost prestige because we were all Rooseveltian rubber stamps. Now they are giving us the devil because we're divided."[13] Stone echoed this sentiment in a speech at a judicial conference in Asheville, North Carolina. He derided as unrealistic "thoughts that justices of the reorganized court would have one mind and hearts that beat as one." Despite the fact that the Court consisted almost entirely of Roosevelt nominees, the justices remained independent thinkers. "There [are] still those rugged individualists in our midst who like to express their opinions," he remarked good-naturedly, "and many dissenting votes are cast."[14]

* * *

On Easter Monday 1946, the justices took their places on the bench to announce the Court's decisions. Lawyers, journalists, messengers, and spectators filled the plush-curtained courtroom. It was the first time in three weeks the Court had convened.

In *Girouard v. the United States*, the Court held by a vote of five to three that an alien could not be denied U.S. citizenship on the grounds that, if naturalized, he would refuse to bear arms in the nation's defense. Written by Justice Douglas, *Girouard* effectively reversed precedent, including a case in which Stone had espoused a position precisely opposite to the one he currently professed.[15] Stone dissented in *Girouard*, arguing that Congress had made clear that his previous interpretation of the Naturalization Act of 1940—the interpretation the Court was now adopting—was incorrect. Rather than enjoy victory in his earlier dissent becoming the majority opinion, Stone deferred to what he viewed as Congress's expressed will. Justices Stanley Reed and Felix Frankfurter joined his dissent, which Stone read aloud in the courtroom. The chief justice concisely captured the ethos of judicial restraint in his closing line: "It is not the function of this Court to disregard the will of Congress in the exercise of its constitutional power."[16]

As the clock neared two in the afternoon, Justice Hugo Black announced three decisions and Reed followed by announcing a decision in another case. As Reed spoke, Stone became oddly preoccupied with the papers in his hand. A lock of hair fell over his forehead atop his thick, horn-rimmed eyeglasses, and uncharacteristically, he did not swipe it back into place. When Reed finished, all eyes returned to the chief justice to announce the next decision. Stone mumbled incoherently. He appeared suddenly disoriented. Then with visible effort he managed to say, "The case should be stayed . . . and investigation . . ."[17]

Black, the senior associate justice, rose from his seat, followed wordlessly by the remaining justices. Together they helped Stone to his feet and led him from the courtroom to his nearby chambers, where Capitol physician George W. Calver examined him.[18] An associate of Stone's personal physician arrived, and both doctors agreed that the seventy-three-year-old had suffered "a small attack of indigestion." Stone's wife drove him home, where he obeyed doctors' orders to rest. Several hours later he suffered a massive cerebral hemorrhage and died at quarter to seven that evening.[19]

* * *

The chief justice's dramatic departure from the bench and death just hours later stunned the nation. Questions abounded: Had Stone been taken to the hospital rather than to his home might he have lived? Had he suffered a heart attack on the bench? Clerk of the Court Elmore Cropley told reporters that the chief justice had worked quite hard over the three-week recess and had "probably overtaxed himself."[20] The usually loquacious Frankfurter told reporters that he "was too overwhelmed to say anything."[21] Former chief justice Hughes said that he was "inexpressibly shocked and grieved by the sudden death of Chief Justice Stone."[22]

David Brinkley reported to television viewers on NBC that Truman, who had been president for slightly longer than a year, had gone to bed aboard the U.S.S. *Princeton* in the Atlantic Ocean when an urgent message from the White House reached the vessel. Assistant press secretary Eben A. Ayers awakened the president to deliver the news.[23] Upon learning of Stone's death, Truman issued a statement that was immediately radioed to the homeland. "The death of Chief Justice Stone," the president said, "is a grievous loss to the country. He was a great jurist and a great American. I am terribly shocked."[24]

Former justice Owen J. Roberts, enjoying his retirement in Phoenixville, Pennsylvania, perhaps best summarized the personal side of the man with whom he had seldom agreed: "No matter what a person's status in life, Justice Stone was vitally interested in his welfare. He had heartfelt and very real and deep sympathy for them."[25]

* * *

Harlan Fiske Stone's service as chief justice was, in the final analysis, an undistinguished ending to a superb legal career. He was an effective attorney general who left his mark on the Department of Justice despite leading it for less than a year. True judicial modesty characterized his sixteen years as an associate justice. He habitually ignored his own political preferences when deciding cases, deferring instead to the elected branches of government.

As chief justice, he inherited a fractured Court. Frankfurter, despite having persuaded Roosevelt to nominate Stone as chief justice, bedeviled Stone the same as he bedeviled every other chief justice with whom he served. Justices Robert Jackson and Hugo Black stoked their internecine feud like a fire they feared would go out. Most importantly, the issues on which most justices agreed faded to the background as constitutional questions on which they disagreed rose to the forefront. Even had Stone wanted to mass the Court, any efforts in this arid landscape likely would have failed. The general consensus was that, as one contemporary writer

observed, Stone's work as a justice was "outstanding" but "he had been a
failure as a presider."[26] Even Stone's closest allies on the Court considered
his tenure as chief justice to be unsuccessful.[27]

* * *

Justice Robert Jackson famously remarked, "Washington adores a
funeral—especially if it ushers in a vacancy."[28] More than two thousand
mourners attended Harlan Fiske Stone's funeral, but the chief justice had
scarcely been laid to rest before speculation over his successor subsumed
the federal city. Journalists competing for sources and scoops claimed to
have identified the men Truman was most likely to nominate.

Truman had been president for just fifty-four weeks. During that time
he had negotiated terms of victory in Europe, authorized the nuclear
bombing of Japan, parried with business leaders over threatened strikes
in crucial industries, and begun the monumental task of easing America's
wartime economy into the peace while keeping both inflation and another
depression at bay. His first Court nomination had revealed little by way of
what judicial philosophy he sought in a potential justice. Harold Burton
was a qualified man whom Truman knew and trusted and who agreed with
Truman on most significant policy matters. Burton had not been on the
Court long enough to have decisively proved otherwise.

White House officials quietly put to rest rumors that the president
was considering Secretary of War Robert Patterson, a Republican, for the
chief justice nomination. Although he had nominated Republican senator
Harold Burton to replace retiring Republican appointee Justice Owen
Roberts, Truman's aides explained, Truman had been under no obligation
to do so. He certainly was not obligated to nominate another Republican
to replace a man whom Calvin Coolidge had nominated to the Court.[29]

Washington's soothsayers took this news as confirmation that Truman
planned to nominate one of the associate justices to be chief justice and
then nominate a new associate justice to the Court. The *Washington Post*
declared that it was "virtually certain" that the next "chief justice will be
drawn from among the eight associate justices."[30] One front-page headline
announced, "Chief Justice to Be Chosen from Court Membership."[31] The
New York Times reported, "There seemed no doubt that the head of the
court would be elevated from among the present members, and a new man
named to take his place as an associate."[32]

Once observers concluded that Truman would nominate an associate justice to replace Stone, they began debating which the president would tap. Some reports asserted that he was deciding between Stanley Reed and Robert Jackson, while others claimed that the nominee would be either William Douglas or Jackson. Still others claimed that Hugo Black or Jackson would be selected for the center seat.[33] At least one Washington journalist reported that Truman's advisors believed Jackson to be too politically astute and energetic to remain sequestered in the judicial branch: they wanted Jackson to be Truman's vice presidential running mate in the upcoming 1948 election.[34]

Because most everyone agreed that Truman was closely considering Robert Jackson for the nomination, Jackson quickly became the presumed nominee. "Stone's Post Likely to Go to Jackson" blared one *Baltimore Sun* headline.[35] Word leaked that Franklin Roosevelt had committed to nominating Jackson upon Stone's death or retirement.[36] More substantively, Jackson's jurisprudence closely resembled that of the former chief justice. And on a Court characterized by distant, often cold relationships, Jackson and Stone, both of whom had grown up on farms, had shared a warm friendship. Columnist Marquis Childs eloquently wrote that, both judicially and personally, Stone and Jackson "shared a realism that seemed to come out of the soil of an earlier America."[37] One could be forgiven for thinking that Truman, who as a young man tilled Missouri's soil on a plough's lone seat behind a mule, had already made his decision when he invited former Chief Justice Charles Evan Hughes to the White House to discuss the Supreme Court vacancy.

* * *

By limousine the retired chief justice traveled the one and a half miles from his home at 22nd and R Streets NW to the White House. He arrived promptly for his three o'clock meeting, looking spry for his eighty-four years.[38]

Truman spent thirty minutes with Hughes, who had been closely following recent events on the Court. The rancor and divisions among the justices was terribly unfortunate. Because the Court was so fractured, however, Hughes warned Truman against nominating an associate justice to be chief justice. He encouraged Truman to select a distinguished jurist who could unite the Court's warring factions.[39] Attorney General Tom

Clark, who attended the meeting, recalled, "We had to figure out just who would be the best peacemaker." Hughes told the president that "Vinson would be an ideal person" for the job.[40]

A throng of reporters peppered Hughes with questions as he left the White House. "No comment," he said to them with a smile. "Thank you." He stepped into the limousine waiting to ferry him back to his Dupont Circle home.[41]

Hughes's advice aligned with Truman's thinking. The Court needed a proven leader who could unite the Court. Of the eight associate justices, only Black and Burton had held elective office. The remaining six had excelled in academia, private practice, or as political appointees but they had never on their own behalf forged compromise with political opponents. In order to do so on the bench, Truman reasoned, they needed to be led by an impeccably credentialed man who had not only personally participated in such compromises but had forged them on the national stage. These requirements shortened Truman's list of potential nominees but it is unlikely that his list had ever been a long one. Jackson's credentials, impressive though they were, did not fit the bill.

Moreover, Robert Jackson was Roosevelt's man, not Truman's. Yes, Jackson had agreed to accept the arduous Nuremberg assignment at Truman's behest. But it was Roosevelt, not Truman, who had brought the high-school-educated New Yorker to Washington. Jackson had been Roosevelt's solicitor general, attorney general, and seventh nominee to the Court. The fact that Court observers so unanimously believed Jackson would be the president's choice for chief justice showed how little the Washington press corps understood Harry S. Truman fifty-four weeks into his presidency.

CHAPTER SEVEN

"The General Utility Man of Government"

ON JUNE 6, 1946, SEVERAL weeks after Chief Justice Stone's death, Fred Vinson attended a reception at the White House. He had been treasury secretary for almost a year. Truman asked him to step away with him for a moment so that they might talk privately. Once they were alone, Truman asked, "Fred, how would you like to be chief justice?"

Vinson later said that his own eyes "lit up" as he replied, "It would be quite an honor."

Truman slapped him on the back. "Well, maybe you will be." The president told him to say nothing about the matter to anyone, and the two friends rejoined the reception.[1]

Stone's death presented what Truman believed to be an opportunity to unite the fractured Supreme Court under a new leader. Vinson possessed both federal judicial experience and proven conciliatory skills. Truman advisor Clark Clifford said, "Once the president had heard about the problems on the Court, I rather doubt he seriously considered anyone else."[2] "I think that the reason President Harry Truman appointed Fred Vinson as chief justice," offered federal judge Mac Swinford of Kentucky, "was because they were so much alike. I think that Harry Truman was intellectually honest and I think Fred Vinson was intellectually honest. I think that was the cementing of their friendship and their mutual respect for each other."[3]

* * *

At his next news conference, Truman announced that he would nominate Vinson to be chief justice of the United States. The news surprised many, including several senators who expressed disappointment that Vinson would be leaving the Treasury Department.[4] Republicans had hoped that Truman would nominate a Republican because Stone's passing left just one member of their party, Truman nominee Harold Burton, on the bench.

Kentuckians were surprised because so many of them had believed that Vinson would run for the Senate seat soon to be vacated by A. B. "Happy" Chandler.[5] After the president's announcement, Vinson would only say, "I am profoundly grateful for President Truman's confidence."[6]

Later that evening, Congressman Lyndon Johnson and his wife, Lady Bird, hosted a dinner party at their home in northwest Washington. Speaker of the House Sam Rayburn and Justice William O. Douglas were among the guests who toasted Vinson's nomination. With bibulous enthusiasm, Johnson then suggested that he, Rayburn, and Douglas go to Vinson's apartment on Connecticut Avenue to personally congratulate him.

When they arrived, Vinson was not at home. His wife, Roberta, answered the door—in tears.

"Why're you crying?" Douglas asked.

"I never wanted my husband to be chief justice!" Roberta cried.

Johnson, Rayburn, and Douglas tried to console her, employing more than one scotch and soda in their cause. Mrs. Vinson explained that her husband, who had discussed with her every potential career change throughout his career, had not talked with her before accepting the nomination. She had learned the news from a radio report. That he had made his decision without so much as calling her was devastating. She spoke as if they had separated, sobbing, "I can never go back to Fred."

Vinson finally arrived home a short time later, stunned by the emotional scene in his living room. He explained to Roberta that he had tried numerous times to reach her, calling several homes or establishments where he thought she might be. Of course he wanted to talk with her, and he abhorred the fact that she had learned of his nomination from a news report. She accepted his explanation, and the couple and their unexpected guests celebrated his nomination with refreshed cocktails.[7]

* * *

Vinson had been a star shortstop at Centre College in Danville, Kentucky, before playing semiprofessional baseball on several teams. The future lawyer was almost as well known for arguing with umpires as he was for his talent.[8] He felt called to public service. Throughout his years in Washington he attended Washington Senators' games whenever his schedule allowed. He loved the game and knew it well.

In 1944 the American and National League baseball team owners asked him to leave federal service to become baseball commissioner. Team owners offered him a salary of $100,000—more than six times his government pay. Vinson declined their offer.[9] "After all," he reasoned, "we've only one life to live and when the country needs one's services, I believe that it is one's duty to serve."[10]

The chief justice's salary of $20,500 was but a fraction of the baseball commissioner's but it would be more than Vinson had ever earned. A lifetime appointment at that salary promised the Vinsons a level of security they had never known. As Douglas recalled, "Fred had very, very little of the worldly goods and practically no insurance."[11]

A primary reason why Vinson's nomination surprised so many federal Washingtonians was because they knew how much Truman relied on Vinson's advice and counsel. The president rarely made a major decision without consulting his treasury secretary. Truman described Vinson as "a straight shooter, who knows Congress and how they think."[12] Observers presumed that Truman would no longer confer with Vinson once he because chief justice. They were wrong.

Truman was not alone in holding Vinson in high esteem. Vinson was one of the most popular members of the Truman administration, enjoying respect and friendship from both Republicans and Democrats. He maintained numerous friendships on Capitol Hill with representatives and senators of both parties. Members of Congress were disappointed that Truman was asking Vinson to leave the Treasury Department, where his economic and tax expertise were being put to excellent use. Speaker of the House Rayburn, whose campaign for majority leader years earlier had been run by Vinson, enjoyed smoking breaks with him whenever the treasury secretary's duties brought him to Capitol Hill.[13] One of Vinson's former House colleagues recalled, "I never served with anyone more able than Fred Vinson and with a more impressive and striking personality than Fred Vinson."[14] Had he remained in the House of Representatives, there was little doubt that Vinson could have become majority leader.[15]

Supporters of Vinson's nomination did not claim that the former appellate judge was a brilliant legal mind. Instead, they described him as a man with the skills needed to soothe the strife afflicting the Court. Democratic senator Claude Pepper of Florida declared, "It seems that Mr. Vinson is the general utility man of the government. He has performed with distinction wherever he has served and no doubt will as Chief Justice." Moreover, because Justice Jackson had missed the entire term as he served in Nuremberg, the Court had held more than twenty-one cases for decision. Jackson's absence, combined with Stone's death, left the administrative functions of the Court in need of immediate attention. To this end, Colorado's Democratic senator Edwin Johnson noted, "Much of the important work of the chief justice is administrative and Fred Vinson has proved himself a very capable administrator and coordinator."[16]

As Democratic activist and future historian Arthur M. Schlesinger, Jr., wrote in *Fortune* magazine, "It will be hard for [Vinson] to cope intellectually with men like Black and Frankfurter: his mind does not move fast in the same way. . . . Vinson will have to influence the Court by a certain massive instinct for practicality."[17]

* * *

The day after Truman announced his nomination, Vinson was scheduled to deliver the commencement address at the University of Kentucky. Before an all-White audience at a public university that refused to admit African American applicants, Truman's nominee for chief justice delivered a stirring address extolling American freedom. "None of us wants to lose any of those personal liberties we won in 1776," he told the graduates. "We never want to be afraid to speak or listen, to read or write what we please. We never want to be afraid to worship as we see fit. . . . We do not want to be told where or how to live. We want to govern ourselves. . . . This is what we mean when we say freedom. . . . This is what we mean when we say we want security."[18]

The Senate confirmed Vinson's nomination by a voice vote with no debate.[19]

CHAPTER EIGHT

Open Warriors and Assassins

JUST DAYS AFTER THE DEATH of Harlan Fiske Stone, newspapers began reporting that Truman had decided to nominate Justice Robert Jackson for chief justice. This was untrue, as were the more devastating reports that followed: Truman had changed his mind and decided *not* to nominate Jackson after learning that if he did, Justices Hugo Black and William Douglas would resign. The *Washington Post* reported that the president had been preparing to announce Jackson's nomination for chief justice when "Black, the most brilliant member of the court's left wing, let it be known that the choice of Justice Jackson would be exceedingly distasteful to him." Justice Frank Murphy was reported "to have intimated that he would resign if Jackson became his chief."[1]

None of this was true. Truman had not received a warning from anyone on the Court. Even if he had, it is unlikely it would have affected his decision because if any justice resigned in protest, Truman would get to nominate the successor, his third Court nominee in a little more than a year.

Jackson had been away from the Court for an entire term now, the first justice ever do to so. After Chief Justice Stone's death, the Court consisted of just seven justices, and as the end of the term grew near, nineteen cases already had been scheduled for reargument.[2] Jackson's extended absence had shackled the Court's ability to function.

When Jackson learned in Nuremberg that Truman had nominated someone else for chief justice, he was apoplectic. He had read the news articles reporting that the president had planned to nominate him until other justices intervened. Now a crestfallen rage overwhelmed him. Arthur Schlesinger, Jr., wrote that Jackson "reacted as a G.I. would to rumors of his wife's infidelity."[3] He lost perspective, ensnaring Truman in what remains one of the most bizarre and unfortunate episodes in Supreme

Court history. Jackson knew that the other justices were irritated and a even bit angered by his absence, but he did not believe that this was why one or more of them had blocked his nomination for chief justice. Seeds of his undoing were sown, he believed, during the previous term, when the justices considered the *Jewell Ridge Coal* case.

* * *

In *Jewell Ridge Coal Corporation v. Local No. 6167, United Mine Workers of America*, corporate employers in 1945 asked the Court to decide whether the time miners spent traveling underground between the company's coal mines constituted compensable work under the Fair Labor Standards Act of 1938.[4] Justice Black joined the Court in deciding the case despite the fact that the attorney for the coal miners, Crampton Harris, had been Black's law-firm partner twenty years earlier. In conference, Jackson declared that Harris's involvement required Black to recuse himself. Black refused. Court precedent allowed him to sit on the case: earlier justices such as Pierce Butler and Owen Roberts had sat on several cases argued by their former law partners.[5] Conversely, Chief Justice Stone, when faced with a similar situation in an earlier case, had recused himself.[6] Jackson demanded that Black step down from the case. Again Black refused.

Jackson became visibly irate when Black provided the fifth vote to form a bare majority in favor of the coal miners. Murphy wrote for the Court and cited "'a realistic attitude' toward 'human beings'" as a commonsense basis for his majority opinion.[7] In a blistering dissent joined by Roberts, Frankfurter, and Stone, Jackson selectively quoted then-Senator Hugo Black to support the position now opposed by Justice Black.[8]

Jewell Ridge Coal Corporation petitioned for a new hearing, arguing that Black should have recused himself on account of his former fiduciary relationship with Crampton Harris. The Court denied the request. Jackson thought the Court should accompany its rehearing denial with an explanation. After some negotiation among the justices, he presented a draft stating, "There is no authority known to me under which a majority of this Court has power under any circumstances to exclude one of its duly commissioned justices from sitting or voting in any case."[9] After more negotiation, he revised the statement to read that "the Court was without power to pass on the question of qualifications," implying that if the Court had such power, it would have precluded Black from sitting on the *Jewell*

Ridge case.[10] Black refused to agree to any comment on his participation in the case, declaring that "any opinion which discussed the subject at all would mean a declaration of war."[11] In the end, the Court included no statement concerning Black's participation in the case. It denied Jewell Ridge's petition for a rehearing on June 18, 1945.

Jackson then took the extraordinary step of issuing a concurring opinion on a rehearing denial. In it he reiterated his assertion that the Court lacked authority to exclude one of its members from voting on a case. Valid as his point might have been, it appeared that he could not let it go. His focus on Black's participation in the case was especially curious because, if Black had recused himself, the miners nonetheless would have prevailed: the Court's vote would have been split four to four and therefore the lower court ruling in favor of the miners would have stood. Rarely unwilling to stir the pot of dissent on the Court, Frankfurter joined Jackson's concurrence.[12]

Jackson now believed that it was his concurring opinion that had inspired Black to dissuade President Truman from nominating him as chief justice. That Truman might not have nominated him regardless of the *Jewell Ridge* decision appeared not to have occurred to Jackson.

* * *

Almost immediately after Fred Vinson's nomination was announced, Jackson cabled a message from Germany to the White House to provide his perspective on the contentious deliberations in the *Jewell Ridge* case. Jackson's missive, purporting to be an explanation of his concurring opinion, was in fact a vituperative attack against Black for refusing to recuse himself. Jackson informed Truman that he planned to cable the message to select members of Congress.

Truman asked Jackson to withhold his statement until he returned home. Jackson disregarded the president's request and on June 10, 1946, sent his message to the chairmen of the House and Senate Judiciary Committees, as well as to the press in Nuremberg.[13] Then he held a press conference in Germany.[14]

"The President has nominated an upright, fearless and well-qualified man for Chief Justice of the United States," Jackson began. After noting that "Mr. Vinson's task is most difficult," Jackson wrote that, as much as certain problems had been discussed, the difficulty Vinson faced in uniting the Court was underestimated. This was because divisions ran deeper than the public knew. Widespread popular belief was that Vinson, once confirmed as chief justice, would "face a mere personal vendetta among justices which can be soothed by a tactful presiding officer. This," Jackson explained, "is utterly false. The controversy goes to the reputation of the Court for nonpartisan and unbiased decision." He described his disagreement with Hugo Black as a "feud" about which Congress had "a right to know the facts and issues involved." He described in detail the justices' private deliberations and accused Black of making "publicized threats to the President." After charging Black with threatening "war" against him, Jackson vowed, "If war is declared on me I propose to wage it with weapons of an open warrior, not those of a stealthy assassin." In ruling for the miners, Black had "reversed the position he had taken as a Senator." It was the second case in as many terms in which Black's former law partner had argued a case before the Court and won. "However innocent the coincidence of these two victories at successive terms by Justice Black's former law partner, I wanted that practice stopped." Jackson claimed that he was not at all seeking to impugn Black's "honor." Rather, he was posing a "question of judgment as to sound judicial policy." Black's practices risked "bring[ing] the Court into disrepute." Jackson closed by threatening against the practice being "ever repeated while I am on the bench."[15]

* * *

In the Court's history no one could recall "even a remote parallel" to Jackson's tirade.[16] Some members of Congress called on both Black and Jackson to resign.[17] As one columnist wrote, "The country has never seen a time when the Supreme Court was as low in public credit as it is in the wake of this row."[18] Illinois senator Scott Lucas, one of the congressmen insisting that both justices should step down, asserted, "There can't be any confidence in the Court as long as the feud goes on. For the good of themselves, for the good of the Court, and for the good of the country, both Justices should resign."[19] Reports persisted that Jackson or Black or both would quit, with some wondering whether Truman would seek to broker a peace between the justices.[20]

Reporters, followed by their readers and listeners, were flabbergasted. The Associated Press called it "an unprecedented attack on a colleague of the United States Supreme Court."[21] Jackson's private feud with Black was suddenly very public, and it immediately damaged the Court's reputation. No longer was concern about Court dysfunction limited to journalists and Court watchers. Regular Americans were now worried.

The *New York Times* editorial board gave voice to a popular plea when it called for Congress to delineate circumstances under which justices would be required to recuse themselves but Congress passed no such law.[22]

Truman called Black to offer his support, telling him, "Don't get into a pismire with Bob Jackson."[23] Truman's admonition was unnecessary. Black maintained a steely silence throughout the entire ordeal. When pressed by reporters, the sixty-year-old southerner replied, "I haven't made a statement of any kind since coming up here [to the Court]. I don't expect to make any now."[24] He refused to comment on any of Jackson's allegations because doing so would have violated his ideals of judicial propriety.[25]

Conversely, Jackson considered resigning from the Court, telling Frankfurter that he wondered "whether this is a good use of one's life." He expressed no regret for his actions: "I am certain that the position on the bench would have been intolerable if I had not taken this audacious and desperate step. I am not sure that it will be tolerable after it." Ironically, it was Jackson's odium for Black that kept him on the on the Court. "Black, as you and I know," Jackson continued, "has driven Roberts off the Bench and pursued him after his retirement. Now if he can have it understood that he has a veto over the promotion of any Associate, he would have things about where he wants them."[26]

Although styled as a defense of his own notions of judicial propriety, Jackson's statement was widely taken as an outburst borne in his frustration at having been passed over again for the chief justice nomination. He embarrassed himself, and his reputation never fully recovered. Any hope he had harbored of being elected to political office vanished along with his chances of ever being elevated to chief justice.

Years later Douglas suggested that Jackson personally never rebounded from the ordeal or his disappointment of being passed over for chief justice. "It did, I think, have a side effect on Bob Jackson's whole life," Douglas told an interviewer. "He became morose and bitter. He was not the happy, freewheeling, ebullient, friendly person that we had known as Solicitor General and later as Attorney General."[27]

Jackson's resentment affected his work on the Court. He became sullen, less persuasive in the conference, and antagonistic toward the chief justice. "I really think," Vinson remarked privately, "that Bob Jackson will make a personal target out of everyone who sits here as Chief Justice."[28]

Congress considered holding investigatory hearings on the Court. New Mexico senator Carl Hatch told reporters that Jackson's "charges are so grave that I cannot comment on them." He said that any congressional investigation should begin in the House of Representatives because only the House could initiate impeachment proceedings.[29] By the end of June, reports surfaced that Jackson himself was pushing for a congressional investigation. Renowned civil rights attorney Belford V. Lawson told reporters that if the reports were true, Jackson would have to resign from the bench: "It is inconceivable that he would expect to remain a member of that body while insisting on an investigation. This action would make his position untenable."[30] The reports turned out to be false, but the fact that reporters and lawyers viewed such a remarkable scenario as entirely plausible indicated how far in esteem the Court—and Jackson—had fallen.

* * *

On the same day that Truman announced Vinson's nomination for chief justice, Frankfurter, who was widely recognized as an authority on Supreme Court history during his decades as a professor at Harvard Law School, wrote to Justice Frank Murphy about the state of the Court. Frankfurter's assessment was dire:

1. Never before in the history of the Court were so many of its members influenced in decisions by considerations extraneous to the legal issues that supposedly controlled the decisions.
2. Never before have members of the Court so often acted contrary to their convictions on the governing legal issues in decisions.
3. Never before has so large a proportion of the opinions fallen short of requisite professional standards.[31]

Many Americans attributed the Court's recent flurry of dissenting opinions to the simple fact that the justices seemed not to like one another. The invective in some dissents and Jackson's furious epistle from Nuremberg supported this misperception.

But the justices' disagreements were mostly jurisprudential. They fundamentally disagreed not just on major issues of constitutional law but also on whether the judicial branch should play a role in even determining some of those issues. They disagreed on whether the protections established in the Bill of Rights applied to state governments. They disagreed on whether and when the federal government could restrict one's right to speak freely, and conversely, whether and when the federal government could compel one to say or do something, such as pledging allegiance to the flag of the United States.

Had the Court's turmoil been primarily the result of personality clashes and private feuds, the new chief justice would have been well-suited to quell the discord. Throughout federal Washington, Vinson was known for his patience, respect for differing opinions, and ability to conciliate disputes.[32] Unfortunately, the justices' disagreements were substantive and jurisprudential—as well as personal.

This was the state of the Supreme Court of the United States when Fred Vinson became chief justice. Brilliant though they might have been, the men Roosevelt named to the Court had shown an almost churlish disregard for the institution's stability and reputation.[33] The most powerful judges in the nation seemed to lack judicial temperament. As President Truman observed, the "Supreme Court has really made a mess of itself."[34]

CHAPTER NINE

"A Man to Trust"

WHEN CHARLES EVAN HUGHES BECAME chief justice of the United States on a cold February day in 1930, he took the oath of office in the Supreme Court's old offices in the Capitol building. There was no Bible and the clerk of court administered the oath. Eleven years later when Harlan Fiske Stone became chief justice, he took the oath of office at his vacation lodge in Estes Park, Colorado.[1] President Truman believed that such haphazard ceremonies were unbecoming the leader of the third coequal branch of government. Perhaps because he had taken the president's oath of office in the Cabinet Room of the White House upon Roosevelt's sudden death, when Chief Justice Stone did not even don a judicial robe but instead wore a suit like the other grave-faced men gathered for the solemn event, Truman was sensitive to the symbolism of such ceremonies.

Moreover, in light of the Court's recent difficulties, Truman believed that a man should not emerge from behind a closed door having just become the chief justice of the United States. Instead, the American people should be able to witness his swearing-in by radio, in person, and even on film. Only twelve of Truman's predecessors had nominated a chief justice. He relished the privilege and believed that Fred Vinson was "a man to trust."[2] The president would give the new chief justice the inauguration he himself had not had.

* * *

White House police officers counted 4,464 spectators filing through security gateways to the public viewing area on the south grounds of the White House. Gates opened at 10:30 a.m. but throngs had begun lining up hours before then. Many of the men wore short sleeves and women carried parasols for shade. Most carried cameras, and as soon as they gained admittance to the grounds, began snapping shots of each other and their children romping about the greenery. Ropes in front of the viewing area marked the seating space for members of Congress and administration officials. Justices Hugo Black, Wiley Rutledge, and Harold Burton interrupted their summer vacations away from Washington to attend. Justice Robert Jackson professed to be unable to escape his duties in Nuremberg but sent Vinson a congratulatory telegram. General Dwight D. Eisenhower attended, as did former Attorney General Homer Cummings.[3] From the White House's south portico Speaker of the House Sam Rayburn, first in line of succession for the presidency now that the man elected vice president was president, served as the master of ceremonies, proclaiming that it was "a deep, personal pleasure for me to participate in" Vinson's swearing-in ceremony.[4] Families gathered around their radios in homes across the nation.

In many ways, Vinson's ceremony was more grand than Roosevelt's fourth inauguration, which had also taken place on the south portico of the White House because Roosevelt did not think it proper to hold a splendid inauguration on the steps of the Capitol in the midst of World War II. Vinson's investiture bore the bearings of an historic event. Eighty-five members of the U.S. Navy Band wearing their summer whites played works by Tchaikovsky and Chopin as dignitaries and members of the public filed onto the White House grounds.[5]

A navy trumpeter let fly a flourish to quiet the crowd. Truman emerged from the White House. Tradition and expectation dictated that the band play "Hail to the Chief" at the president's entrance but Truman had issued orders that the song not be played. This was the chief justice's day.[6]

Speaker Rayburn introduced D. Lawrence Groner, chief judge of the U.S. Court of Appeals for the District of Columbia and one of Vinson's close friends. Judge Groner, in his black robe, invited the Vinson family to take their places before him. Fifty-six-year-old Fred Vinson placed his hand on a Bible that had been given to him and Roberta on their wedding day twenty-three years earlier in Louisa, Kentucky. Roberta now held the Bible, standing with their two sons, Fred and Jim, as well as the woman they admiringly introduced as "the oldest living Vinson," Fred's cousin Belle Vinson Hughes, who had traveled from Huntington, West Virginia. There were two oaths to be taken, the judicial oath and the constitutional oath. After the recitation of each one, Vinson declared in his heavy baritone, "I do, so help me God."[7] He kissed the Bible and stepped aside for Rayburn to introduce the president of the United States.

Truman delivered what the Associated Press called "a brief, informal speech."[8] He called the day "a most auspicious occasion," telling the crowd,

> Only thirteen presidents have had the honor and the privilege of appointing a chief justice of the United States. That duty fell upon me. It was one on which I labored long and faithfully.
>
> I finally decided to make the secretary of the Treasury the chief justice. . . . And the one regret that I had was losing Mr. Vinson from the cabinet of the president. The Supreme Court is at the top of the judicial branch. All of us have the utmost respect for the courts of the country, and we know that the respect will be enhanced when Mr. Vinson becomes chief justice of the United States actively on the bench.

"It is a pleasure for me to have you all here today to witness this ceremony," he told the crowd. "This is the thirteenth time that this ceremony has been performed. Mr. Vinson is the thirteenth chief justice and I think that is lucky for the United States and lucky for Mr. Vinson." After a quick pause, he added, "At least I hope it is."[9] Everyone laughed, and Truman and Vinson shook hands.

The chaplain of the Senate, Reverend Frederick Brown Harris, delivered a benediction, after which Lieutenant Charles Brendler led the U.S. Navy Band in a spirited recital of the national anthem.[10] The ceremony ended ten minutes after it began. Spectators began to exit through the gates. Truman and the Vinson family left the portico for the East Room. Here the new chief justice stood at the head of the receiving line, shaking hands with scores of invitees offering best wishes to the man charged with uniting the fractured Supreme Court.[11] With remarkable prescience, one account predicted, "His best chance of a high pedestal in history is to become known as the man who brought stability to the Supreme Court in a troubled time. There are as many reasons as there are associate justices why he will probably not achieve that place."[12]

* * *

At noon on Monday, October 7, 1946, the Supreme Court term opened with Chief Justice Vinson at the helm.[13] Court-watchers anticipated friction in the new term, which began four months after Justice Robert Jackson's unprecedented letter and press conference.[14] Jackson had returned from Germany just a week earlier.[15] Court-watchers anticipated "perhaps the tensest atmosphere surrounding the opening of a term in all the 157 years of the tribunal's life."[16]

Anyone hoping for a sign of discord was disappointed. Courtesy and calm reigned. Despite his apoplexy at not having been nominated for chief justice, Jackson had cabled Vinson from Nuremberg to congratulate him. The newly sworn-in chief justice replied by letter on June 26, beginning his note "Dear Bob" and acknowledging that Jackson's telegram "made me very happy. I want to thank you most sincerely for cabling me so promptly, and to tell you that I am looking forward to our association on the Court."[17]

There was much work to be done. Twenty-one cases had been held over from the previous term. The justices had to prepare for and hear rearguments for each of them. They also had to decide which of the five hundred pending petitions for *certiorari* to grant.[18]

On the bench during that first Monday session, Jackson sat three places to the left of the new chief justice, and Hugo Black, still the senior associate justice, sat directly to the chief's right. Roberta Vinson sat in the crowded courtroom next to First Lady Bess Truman. Justice Black opened the proceedings by formally announcing the nomination and confirmation of the chief justice and informing the crowded courtroom that the chief justice had already taken all the necessary oaths of office. Vinson then took control of the proceedings.[19] The Court's opening session lasted just twenty-one minutes. The justices appeared amiable and relaxed. "Tranquility Reigns as Vinson Opens Supreme Court Session" read the next day's *Washington Post* front-page headline.[20]

* * *

Vinson had reported to work in his chambers weeks before that first Monday in October. As one workday drew to a close, Douglas paid him a visit. Vinson greeted him as he greeted most everyone he met: "What do you know?" Although they did not yet know each other well, the two men, both raised by widowed mothers in rural poverty, talked so easily that Vinson lost track of time. He abruptly told Douglas that he had to get home—he and Roberta were expected at a formal dinner scheduled to begin in an hour.

Douglas watched Vinson press a button to signal for his secretary. When she stepped through the door, he said, "Send for the Court car."

Vinson and Douglas walked together down two flights of stairs to the garage, where they waited for some time. Eventually, a Ford pickup truck lurched from around the corner and stopped before them. "What's this?" Vinson asked.

"The Court car," Douglas replied—knowing there was no such thing. Vinson's secretary had convinced an acquaintence to give him a ride. Douglas opened the door and climbed in, followed by the incredulous chief justice.

When he was treasury secretary, Vinson had had thirty cars at his command. Becoming chief justice of the United States suddenly seemed like a demotion. Later, Vinson formally asked Congress to appropriate funds to furnish a car for the chief justice. As popular was he was with legislators, his request was denied.[21]

* * *

For his part, Jackson was still smarting over criticism of his performance at the Nuremberg trials. Consensus among lawyers was that the high-ranking Nazi military leader Hermann Goering had bested Jackson during his cross-examination. Goering was convicted and sentenced to death by hanging. But on October 15, 1946, the day before he was scheduled to be executed, Goering committed suicide in his cell by biting into a glass vial of cyanide. Debate persists to this day on when and how he obtained the poison, but in a note found in his cell he declared that he felt "no moral obligation to submit to my enemies' punishment. Therefore I have chosen to die like the great Hannibal."[22]

When reporters asked him if he had any comment on Goering's death, Jackson held forth at length, telling them, "If Goering had been made of the stuff that could walk to the gallows voicing some patriotic sentiment such as our Nathan Hale's regret that he had but one life to give to his country, he might have become a German martyr-hero. This was Goering's great ambition . . . dreaming himself a sort of Teutonic Napoleon." Jackson called the Nazi an "arrogant" witness who gave "speeches from the witness box and coached other defendants to do the same." Then he described Goering's suicide "as anti-climactic as a burlesque after a Wagnerian overture," the act of a man who "lacked the character" to face his punishment and whose suicide "killed the myth of Nazi bravery and stoicism and deep conviction."[23]

Privately Jackson expressed happiness that the Allies' military commanders had prohibited prosecuting attorneys from attending the hangings. He was dismayed when photographs of Goering's corpse and those of the men who had been hanged were released to the press. The complexity of the entire ordeal, and what he believed it might have cost him, weighed heavily on Robert Jackson.

CHAPTER TEN

Meatless On-Strike Midterm Elections

FRED VINSON'S GRAND WHITE HOUSE swearing-in ceremony provided Truman with a couple days of much-needed positive news coverage, with the 1946 midterm elections less than a month away. But soon after Vinson's investiture, the public and the press largely turned their attention away from the troubled Court and back to the president, whose popularity was plummeting.

Truman's approval rating had dropped from a stunning high of 87 percent down to 32 percent. His level of unpopularity was, however, not unprecedented: Roosevelt had polled at an approval rating of just 39 percent in June 1939.[1] The difference Democrats faced in 1946 was that this would be the first election in eight years in which the nation was neither fighting nor preparing for war. As the Supreme Court began its first term under Vinson, President Truman girded himself for the harshest political season of his career.

For sixteen years most registered independent voters had voted for Democratic candidates. In 1944 Roosevelt won 62 percent of the independent vote. A Gallup poll conducted two weeks before the 1946 midterm elections indicated that 59 percent of independents planned to vote for the Republican candidate in their congressional races. Many of them viewed Truman as the incompetent leader of a party that had been in power for too long. When asked which party they thought would do a better job of handling the most important issues of the day, 60 percent of all voters answered the Republican Party. There was, as George Gallup wrote, "a sharp change in the public's feeling about the sort of job Mr. Truman has been doing as President."[2]

To be sure, Democrats should have expected to lose congressional seats because a Democrat occupied the White House—and had done so for sixteen years. Since the Civil War, in every midterm election except one, the president's party—whether Democratic or Republican—had lost seats in the House of Representatives. The only exception was the Democratic landslide of 1934 that sent newcomers like Harry Truman to Washington.[3] So regular was the biannual midterm loss of seats that Democratic senator Carl Hatch of New Mexico went so far as to propose eliminating midterm elections and permitting House members to serve four-year terms.[4]

This year, however, promised to differ in an order of magnitude. The president's party was expected to lose so many congressional seats that control of both chambers was up for grabs for the first time in recent memory. Democratic fundraisers tried their best to prevent the impending onslaught by raising and spending unheard-of amounts of money to support their candidates. Party treasurer George Killion generously funded campaigns, spending a then-extraordinary sum of $1.5 million by mid-October. But the party's prospects remained dim.[5]

Truman was so unpopular that the Democratic Party dispatched Speaker of the House Sam Rayburn to stump for candidates in the president's home state of Missouri. In Columbia, Rayburn extolled Truman for doing a "magnificent and stupendous job." He sought to connect Truman's less than two-year-old presidency with Roosevelt's twelve years in office, saying, "I fear what might happen if old-time reactionary Republican leadership comes into power. Plain people will not give up their social and economic gains of the last four Administrations without a struggle."[6]

Republican candidates for local and state offices sought to capitalize on Truman's unpopularity by nationalizing their races. Even politicians who were not on the ballot sought to raise their profiles by attacking the president. New Jersey governor Walter E. Edge charged in a speech that Truman was "harassed and indecisive" with a cabinet "split with extreme and contrary views."[7] Democratic expectations sank so low that just drawing even with the Republicans seemed out of reach.[8]

* * *

The most immediate cause of Truman's unpopularity was the sudden scarcity of household goods. After surviving the deprivations of the Great Depression and years of wartime rationing, Americans expected to enjoy some measure of prosperity in peacetime. Instead, they encountered bare grocery shelves and shortages of basic goods. In Illinois, flour was in such short supply that bread lines reminiscent of the Depression snaked down city blocks. A group of women in Denver hijacked a bread delivery truck.[9]

Federally imposed price controls enacted during World War II were all that stood between the nation's economy and runaway inflation. Because the law required these controls to end on June 30, 1946, Truman asked Congress in January 1946 to send him by the first of April a bill extending the price controls. Congress, which was still controlled by Democrats, did not pass such a bill until the end of June, and the one they ended up passing was too weak to prevent inflation. Truman vetoed it. Price controls ended as scheduled at midnight on June 30.

Over the next two weeks, prices rose more than they had in the previous three years.[10] The price of everything from automobiles to coffee beans rose drastically. American households from coast to coast were buffeted by the sudden price increases for which they blamed the Truman administration.[11] Congress then passed a revised price control bill that differed little from the bill Truman had just vetoed, and he reluctantly signed it. Price controls were reinstated just weeks after being lifted.

With price caps reimposed on meat products, ranchers and stockmen refused to send their cattle to packinghouses. Steaks and ground beef vanished from store shelves. Families' frustrations reached the boiling point because their nation, widely recognized for the first time in its history as the most powerful in the world, was now forced to deal with a manmade meat shortage.

Republican congressional candidates wasted no time in capitalizing on voters' vexation. Their campaign workers drove sound trucks down city streets, speakers blaring to frustrated grocery shoppers lining the sidewalks: "Ladies, if you want meat, vote Republican!"[12] "The Truman slogan," one Republican quipped, "ought to be 'Let 'em eat horsemeat.'"[13] Republican attacks gained traction among beef-deprived homemakers, who picked up on the suggestion and took to calling the president "Horsemeat Harry."[14]

With just three weeks remaining before the midterm elections, Democratic candidates acknowledged, "Meatless voters are opposition voters." They beseeched the White House to "do something, anything, to get meat on the table."[15] Speaker Rayburn, dismayed by the whole affair, exclaimed, "This is going to be a damned beefsteak election!"[16]

Delicatessens and butcher shops closed. Their apron-clad workers sometimes picketed out front as if on strike, their signs reading "we want meat!" or "forced to close." Grocery stores and restaurants hung signs in their windows reading "no meat." As political pressure mounted, Secretary of Agriculture Clinton B. Anderson told reporters that the president was "now considering a decision" to end the national meat shortage.[17] As most Americans hoped Truman would ease the price restrictions on meat, the White House announced the president would address the nation.

Among the options Truman and his advisors were considering was ordering the federal government to seize the nation's cattle. Ranchers did not dispute that they possessed more than enough livestock to end the meat shortage. If the federal government took ownership of the cattle, it could order the ranchers to bring the animals to slaughter. Truman rejected this option because the logistics of executing it promised to be unwieldy. Whether such a move was constitutional seemed not to worry him.

Senator Robert Taft later fumed to reporters, "He considered seizing all the cattle in the United States—confiscation of all the property of the farmers in cattle—and dismissed it, not because it was arbitrary and un-American, but because this country was so big that he could not do it, at least before the election."[18] It was extraordinary that Truman had closely considered seizing all the nation's cattle to alleviate a politically created meat shortage. His decision five and a half years later to seize the nation's steel mills, therefore, may not have been a difficult question for him.

On October 14, 1946, Truman spoke to his largest radio audience since the end of World War II. He angrily blamed the national meat shortage on "a few men in the Congress who, in the service of selfish interests, have been determined for some time to wreck price controls no matter what the cost might be to our people." This "reckless group of selfish men" bore "the real blame" because it was they "who, in the hope of gaining political advantage, have encouraged sellers to gamble on the destruction of price control."[19] As much as he detested doing so, Truman announced that he was ending meat price caps.

Meat prices soared. Chicken quickly reached a dollar per pound in some markets while beef prices varied widely even within the same city. Reporters advised that "housewives" go to the market "armed with a full purse if she's interested in such staples as butter."[20] NAACP executive director Walter E. White called the on-again-off-again meat control fiasco "a spectacle of ineptitude for the so-called greatest nation on earth."[21]

* * *

In the wake of the president's meat speech, the Democratic Party's national chairman asked Truman to make himself scarce during campaign season. There was no place where the party could expect him to help his fellow Democrats. Republicans could scarcely believe their good fortune. As *Time* magazine's congressional correspondent wrote in an internal memorandum, "Harry Truman could not carry Missouri now."[22]

Truman complied with his party's request. He eschewed the campaign trail and avoided discussing the upcoming elections. When a reporter asked at a late October press conference whether he would like to make a bet on any of the congressional races, he replied that wagers were illegal in his home state of Missouri. Another reporter observed that time was "running short" and asked if he would be making any campaign speeches. Truman answered that he had no plans to do so.

The journalist followed up: "Why are you not going to speak on behalf of the Democrats?"

Visibly irritated, Truman retorted that he had not said he would make no speeches, only that he presently had no plans to do so.[23] But in the end he did not give a speech for any of his party's candidates. They likewise avoided mentioning him, with some even playing old recordings of the late Franklin Roosevelt's speeches to rally their crowds at campaign events. Democratic West Virginia senator Harley Kilgore, a friend of Truman's, explained that any candidate who so much as mentioned Truman's name would hear boos and catcalls from the crowd. "Here was a man who was actually doing an excellent job," Kilgore recalled, "but the most you could do was to defend him in a humorous fashion by using the old Western saloon refrain: 'Don't shoot our piano player. He's doing the best he can.'"[24]

Truman spent the days before the midterm election with his family in Independence, Missouri, where he refused reporters' repeated requests for comment. Wearing a natty tan suit and carrying an American Legion cane a friend had given him years ago, the president strolled about town with his Secret Service detail and a gaggle of journalists in tow. Here in Independence, adults jumped out of their cars to shake his hand and children asked for his autograph.[25] He visited his barber for a haircut and his tailor for a topcoat and appeared entirely unconcerned about the expected Republican rout. On Election Day Truman, Bess, and their daughter, Margaret, voted at the town's Memorial Hall before boarding the president's armored train car for the trip back to Washington.[26]

* * *

After the votes were counted, the extent of Americans' discontent with Truman and the Democratic Party could hardly have been clearer. Republicans won the 1946 midterm elections by historic margins, gaining control of both chambers of Congress and a majority of governorships for the first time in seventeen years. Republicans gained 55 seats in the House of Representatives and 12 in the Senate, seizing control of the House by a margin of 246 to 188 and the Senate by a margin of 45 to 41. GOP candidates won in nearly every region of the country, resulting, according to a *New York Times* editorial, "in gains so generally distributed as to leave no doubt that there has been a swing of sentiment on a nationwide scale against the Democratic Administration."[27] Candidates in Democratic strongholds such as Chicago, New York City, and Detroit lost to Republicans who successfully nationalized their campaigns.

African American voters, many of whom had left the South in the Great Migrations, comprised a swing voting bloc in several races. Republicans competed for votes they had often conceded during the Roosevelt years. They reminded voters that the Democratic Party was home to the nation's most virulent racists. Democratic senator Theodore Bilbo of Mississippi had admitted on NBC's television program *Meet the Press* three months before the elections that he was a member of the Ku Klux Klan.[28] Senator John Holmes Overton of Louisiana publicly declared less than two weeks before the election, "We don't want the Negroes in the party. They don't belong in the Democratic Party."[29] In Taylor County, Georgia, a Black man who voted in the Democratic primary was found dead the next day.[30]

The influential editors of the *Baltimore Afro-American* were exasperated not only with racism in the Democratic Party but with what appeared to be rampant incompetence. "We have had enough, actually, more than enough!" they wrote. The intolerable state of affairs led them to urge their readers: "Everywhere that Republican candidates for office are the equal of or better than the Democratic candidates, they should be supported so that we can have, without a doubt, a Republican House and Republican Senate." It was not unusual for the *Afro-American* to endorse Republican candidates, but it was bold for the editors to confront Truman's often repeated, self-told tale that he was the man who never wanted to be president: "If Mr. Truman did not want the presidency at the death of Mr. Roosevelt, there is no reason why we should elect him to office in 1948."[31]

A Republican defeated Truman's handpicked candidate in Missouri's fifth congressional district. The president's mother, brother, and sister lived in the district and cast their ballots for Truman's man, Enos T. Axtell.[32] As unaffected by political vagaries as the president often feigned to be, Margaret Truman described the Republican landslide in that race as "mortifying" for her father.[33]

* * *

Tradition dictated that a large delegation of public officials greet the president's train when it pulled into Washington's Union Station. But as Truman stepped off the train from Independence after the 1946 midterm elections, Undersecretary of State Dean Acheson was the only official on the platform to greet him. About this time Truman wrote, "Never was so lonesome in my life."[34]

Reporters asked for his thoughts on the Republicans' winning both houses of Congress, but smiling, with a book tucked under his arm, Truman again declined to comment. Administration officials also refused to discuss the elections for several days.[35] Nearly a week after the election, Truman said, "I accept their verdict in the spirit in which all good citizens accept the result of any fair election." His approval rating had plummeted to less than 20 percent.[36]

Democratic senator J. William Fulbright of Arkansas publicly suggested that Truman become the first president to resign from office. A former Rhodes scholar who studied at Oxford University, Fulbright compared Truman to a prime minister who had lost a vote of confidence in Parliament. He contended that Truman should appoint a Republican secretary of state who, under the rules of succession then in effect, would become president upon Truman's resignation because there was no sitting vice president. "It would probably be the wisest thing for the president to do," Fulbright reasoned, saying that the great majority of voters "have registered their belief that domestic progress and international tranquility can be better won by the Republican Party. That we [Democrats] do not share this belief is beside the point—the people have spoken."[37] Fulbright publicly urged Truman to appoint Republican senator Arthur H. Vandenberg of Michigan to become secretary of state and the next president of the United States, noting Vandenberg's foreign policy experience.[38]

Editors of the *Atlanta Constitution* and the *Chicago Sun* joined Fulbright's call for Truman's resignation, with *Sun* publisher and editor Marshall Field declaring that it would be a "patriotic" move.[39] The *New York Times* declared that the president should remain in office, adding that they doubted he would resign: "A quitter he has never been."[40] The White House declined to comment on Fulbright's suggestion, but Truman thereafter referred to the Arkansas Democrat as "Senator Halfbright."[41]

CHAPTER ELEVEN

Labor's Troubled Waters

NINETEEN FORTY-SIX WAS THE YEAR of strikes. In January, more than 900,000 American workers were on strike in industries ranging from manufacturing to electrical companies. Newspaper readers in Cleveland went without their daily papers when the printing pressmen went on strike for higher wages.[1] One hundred city employees in Stockton, California, declared a strike after being denied overtime pay for week-end work.[2] The Connecticut state police were called to keep the peace at a machinists' picket line in Stamford; a week later, the city ground to a halt when employees of businesses throughout downtown walked out in a demonstration of solidarity, forming a crowd of ten thousand in the town hall square.[3] Telephone operators in Washington, DC, staged a one-hour "sit-down strike" that disrupted long-distance calls to and from the nation's capital, with Washington Telephone Traffic Union president Mary Gannon speaking out "against [the] sweatshop practices" of the Chesapeake & Potomac Telephone Company.[4] In Chicago, the Mid-West Truck Operators Association's two thousand members continued their strike into its seventh week.[5]

All this happened during the first week of January 1946. By year's end, 116 million eight-hour workdays had been lost due to strikes.[6] The year produced the largest strike in American history in the steel strike, the longest major automobile strike (General Motors), and two crippling maritime strikes. Labor turmoil seriously damaged the nation's transition from a wartime to a peacetime economy.[7]

When replacement workers arrived at the Western Electrical Company in Kearny, New Jersey, on January 5, 1946, several of the twelve thousand striking workers attacked them, leaving fedoras and newspapers littered across the sidewalk.[8] In February and March, 700,000 steel workers,

263,000 packinghouse workers, 200,000 electrical workers, and 50,000 telecommunication workers joined those already on strike.[9]

Violence at the picket lines contributed to the sense of bedlam. Riot police in Detroit prevented a thousand striking General Motors workers from setting upon white-collar employees seeking to enter GM's corporate office building. The helmet-clad officers deterred violence but the office workers were so intimidated by the strikers that most of them fled.[10] Chicago police battled picketers at the stockyards.[11] It seemed that a workers' revolt gripped the nation.

* * *

The Republican landslide of 1946 politically freed Truman from having to maintain the federal government's Roosevelt-era relationship with labor unions. Truman remained pro-labor, but unions' postwar tactics affected his opinion of them.

Truman's most potent weapon to prevent labor strife from crippling the nation's economy was the War Labor Disputes Act. Section 3 of the act authorized the president to take possession of a facility necessary for the war effort if the president decided that a strike would interrupt or damage the nation's defense efforts. The act granted this authority to the president until six months after the cessation of hostilities, and Truman did not declare an end to World War II hostilities until December 31, 1946.[12]

In 1945 and 1946, Truman seized control of companies pursuant to the War Labor Disputes Act numerous times. He issued executive orders instructing the federal government to take possession of the Illinois Central Railroad on August 23, 1945; numerous oil-refining and pipeline properties on October 4, 1945; the Capital Transit Company on November 21, 1945; the Great Lakes Towing Company on November 29, 1945; several meatpacking companies on January 24, 1946; the railroads on May 17, 1946; the bituminous coal mines on May 21, 1946; and the Monongahela Connecting Railroad on June 14, 1946.[13] Seizing temporary control of private businesses to ward off the devastating effects of a strike became almost routine for Truman early in his presidency—so much so that one might understand why he came to believe that the power to do so emanated from the presidency itself rather than from a specific act of Congress.

Truman's seizure of the coal mines in May 1946 was the most consequential of these postwar seizures. That one proved the Truman administration not only would stand up to the nation's most powerful unions but was willing and able to punish them. And when labor leaders protested that the president had exceeded his constitutional authority, they pleaded their case before a Supreme Court that was increasingly given to seeing things Harry Truman's way.

* * *

After his presidency, Truman acknowledged, "Labor unrest is inevitable in a free economy; it is part of the struggle for adjustment to shifting economic conditions." Personally and politically, Truman had long supported labor, determined to protect those he often called "the little guy." While claiming to view labor disputes as "inevitable," Truman tended to treat them as national emergencies, regularly inserting himself, like Roosevelt had before him, into industrial labor disputes. He believed that it was his "responsibility as Chief Executive to see that the public was not injured by private fights between labor and management or among the unions themselves."[14]

Unlike Roosevelt, however, Truman in 1946 had no Great Depression or World War II around which to rally workers and management. America's economy had thrived during the war but struggled to stabilize during reconversion to the new peace. Union leaders prepared their members for the difficulties they knew reconversion would bring. Teamsters Union president Daniel J. Tobin struck a conciliatory tone: "I'm asking labor in all its division to give [Truman] an honest chance to make good. . . . Remember we are going into a period of perhaps serious readjustment and unemployment. All of us may have to make sacrifices. Labor will, I'm sure, understand that President Truman has a difficult task before him."[15]

America's reconversion to a peacetime economy proved even more traumatic than Tobin predicted. Companies across the nation laid off workers. Most of those who were not laid off saw their work hours reduced. During the war, most employees had been working at least forty-eight hours per week and getting paid time and a half for every hour over forty, amounting to the equivalent of fifty-two hours of work at straight pay. When companies reduced the hours of millions of workers to forty hours per week without raising their wages, those workers' take-home pay fell dramatically.[16]

Union leaders during the war—largely because their members were working so many hours—had agreed to forgo wage and benefit increases. This allowed companies to submit to the federal government's stringent price controls, which in turn held down the cost of living. With the war now won, workers sought the raises they had forsaken during the conflict. Wages, therefore, were the root cause of 1946's cataclysmic labor disputes. Despite the price controls, corporate profits had swelled during the war. Workers began to demand what they viewed as their overdue fair share of those profits. And with the expiration of the War Labor Disputes Act, they regained their right to strike.

*　*　*

Not for nothing was John L. Lewis, president of the United Mine Workers of America (UMW), widely considered one of the most powerful men in America. Coal was the life-blood of the nation's economy: it powered 62 percent of the nation's electrical power, 55 percent of all industrial energy, and 95 percent of locomotives on railways from coast to coast.[17] Lewis was a miner and the son of miners. He had led the UMW for thirty years and his credibility among its rank-and-file members was unassailable. They would honor any strike he called. On April 1, 1946, on Lewis's orders, 400,000 miners in 21 states went on strike.

Unlike workers in other industries, coal miners were not striking primarily for wage increases. Their prime goal was to create a welfare fund to provide medical care for aged and injured miners. To finance the program, Lewis sought a ten-cent royalty payment on each ton of coal mined. As UMW president, he would exercise complete control over the welfare fund.

Coal company executives balked at the idea. They thought Lewis was trying to shake down their companies. Yes, mining was inherently dangerous work, but this was why miners earned better pay and benefits than laborers in other industries. And for years Lewis had refused to negotiate more strict safety provisions into miners' contracts.

Truman sympathized with disabled miners and their families, but he was bothered by Lewis's insistence on having sole control of the fund. He believed that the strike was "a new grab for more power on the part of the miners' boss."[18]

Truman hosted Lewis and coal company representative Charles O'Neill at the White House no fewer than six times, but his attempts to mediate were unsuccessful. By mid-May, nearly every aspect of American life was affected by the strike. Cities limited the availability of electricity, trains ran on reduced schedules, and factories reduced workers' hours because there was less coal to power their plants. The nation's economy—already fragile during its reconversion to peacetime production—was buckling under the pressure. It could not withstand a long-term coal strike.

On May 22, 1946, Truman signed an executive order instructing the federal government to seize the coal companies pursuant to the War Powers Act. Federal officials seized the mines the next day. Interior Secretary Julius A. Krug ordered coal executives to maintain the mines in working condition during the seizure while government officials negotiated with union leaders.

A week later, the Truman administration reached an agreement with the UMW. The government granted nearly all of the union's demands. Coal executives were livid. But under the War Powers Act, they were effectively powerless to change the agreement. At four in the afternoon on May 29, Krug and Lewis signed the contract at the White House. Truman sat next to Krug, emphasizing his imprimatur on the deal that became known as the Krug-Lewis Agreement.[19]

Coal miners returned to work, and the government prepared to return ownership of the mines to the coal companies. Nearly ninety tons of coal had been left in the mines during the strike. It was time to get back to work.

Surprisingly, the one-sided deal was met with bipartisan praise. Truman happily remarked that his labor policies had succeeded in getting leftist Democratic senator "Claude Pepper, [conservative Republican senator Robert] Taft, the communist *Daily Worker* and the *Wall Street Journal* all in accord."[20] But the strike had proved costly to all involved, exacting $160 million in miners' wages and at least $14 million in company profits.[21]

Just a few months later, however, on October 22, before the government had fully returned ownership of the mines to the companies, Lewis threatened to call another strike on November 1, four days before Election Day, if Krug did not agree to renegotiate the contract. Lewis threatened to void the UMW's contract with the federal government. As columnist Walter Lippmann explained, Lewis "has taught the miners not to work without a contract. When he wants them to strike, he does not tell them to strike. He tells them there is no contract, and they stop working."[22]

Days after threatening to strike, Lewis publicly lambasted Truman in a bitter screed delivered at the UMW convention. He declared that the president of the United States was "a man totally unfitted for the position. His principles are elastic and he is careless with the truth. He has no special knowledge of any subject and he is a malignant, scheming sort of individual who is dangerous not only to the United Mine Workers, but dangerous to the United States of America."[23] Lewis plainly intended to challenge the federal government while embarrassing the president in the process.

Interior Secretary Krug refused to reopen negotiations so soon after signing the current contract, particularly since the union had gotten nearly everything it wanted. But Krug did agree to discuss specific points in the contract. He was willing to permit "an outstanding jurist" to settle the difference in how the government and the union interpreted two contract provisions concerning vacation pay and royalties on produced coal.[24] Lewis responded that Krug's refusal to renegotiate the entire contract would constitute a "breach of the contract and will void the Krug-Lewis agreement."[25] Of course, if the agreement was voided, then there would be no contract and the miners would stop working, following their rule that "when no contract exists, no work is done."[26]

* * *

While Lewis was making his demands, Truman was enjoying a working vacation—on his physician's advice—at the navy base on Key West he visited so often that it became known as the Little White House.[27] He fumed at Lewis's latest strike threat, summoning several of his closest advisors to the Little White House to decide how to respond. When they arrived, the president told his men, "This time I mean to slap that so-and-so down for good. Now you fellows tell me the best way to do it."[28]

Two days before Lewis's deadline, the Department of Justice filed a motion in federal court seeking a temporary injunction that would prevent Lewis from canceling the UMW's contract. Attached as exhibits to the motion were affidavits from high-ranking government officials, including Interior Secretary Krug, Secretary of War Robert Patterson, and Secretary of the Navy James Forrestal.[29] Arguing that a work stoppage would "adversely affect great public interests and seriously endanger the public welfare and safety," the administration urged the court to issue a restraining order against Lewis and the UMW.[30]

Federal district judge T. Alan Goldsborough received the case. Goldsborough had represented Maryland's first congressional district as a Democrat from 1921 until 1939, when Roosevelt nominated him to the federal bench. After reviewing the affidavits describing how deeply the impending strike would damage the economy, Goldsborough issued a temporary restraining order without hearing oral arguments. The order enjoined Lewis from voiding the Krug-Lewis Agreement and ordered the UMW to remain on the job. Goldsborough signed the order at 12:50 p.m. Two U.S. marshals rushed to Lewis's office on 15th and I Streets NW in Washington, DC, to serve the restraining order on him personally.[31]

Truman administration officials seemed eager to present their disagreement with the union as a contest between Lewis and the president. Reporters relayed details of how Truman was directing every aspect of the government's response to Lewis's strike threat. The White House made public Truman's orders to "fight it out" with the labor leader.[32] "Every step that is being taken," press secretary Charles G. Ross told reporters, "is being taken in accordance with his instructions."[33] Another administration official explained Truman's thinking: "It is not that the president is spoiling for a fight with Lewis. It is as simple as this: Somewhere, sometime, the Administration must find out who is more powerful—Lewis or the government. This looks like the best time. The president is not going to knuckle down to Lewis."[34]

CHAPTER TWELVE

The Chief Takes Charge

EVEN AFTER THE DISTRICT COURT issued a temporary restraining order, John Lewis refused to retract his strike threat. On November 20, 1946, coal miners walked off the job. Nearly every coal mine in the nation shut down. Lewis had openly defied a federal court order.

The fact that miners walked out did not mean they were happy about it. Some refused to hide their displeasure with having to endure another strike so soon after their fifty-nine-day strike just a few months ago. "A lot of us are getting tired of having to go out on strike every time Lewis decides to make a splash," groused one miner.[1] Adding to their anxiety was the fact that Christmas was less than a month away. As one Pennsylvania miner put it, "Christmas is a tough time to be on strike."[2]

Not only was Christmas season a difficult time for miners to strike; winter was a hard time for most Americans to endure the effects of a coal strike. Local governments reimposed wartime restrictions on electricity consumption, and the federal government restricted nonessential railroad travel. National sentiment quickly coalesced against the strike. Editors at the *Washington Post* captured the popular view when they wrote that, by defying a federal court's order, Lewis had "directly challenged the power of the Government to save the Nation from disaster."[3]

The 400,000 striking miners knew that popular opinion had turned against them: "We turn on the radio or pick up the paper and find out everybody in the country is against us. There is no sense to it."[4] Winter's cold contributed to some miners' second thoughts. John Rastoka remained a strong Lewis supporter but the strike worried him: "I sit at home by the radio with my wife and hear about Denver being out of coal and think that maybe there's a baby or somebody cold because they can't get coal, and I'm a coal miner. Sometimes it makes you wish we hadn't gone out until April."[5]

But whether a miner agreed or disagreed with Lewis's decision was irrelevant; he would walk out when his union walked out. "A man who scabs against his brothers might as well be dead. He can never live down his disgrace," one veteran miner explained, before adding ominously, "His wife and children must pay for his crime. I have worked in the mines for 30 years. I never saw a man turn against the union without regretting it for the rest of his days."[6]

* * *

Back in Washington, Judge Goldsborough held Lewis and the union in contempt of court. Four days later, attorneys for Lewis and the union filed briefs contesting not just the contempt citation but the restraining order itself. They argued that the order was invalid because the court lacked jurisdiction to issue it.

The union's argument was forceful in its simplicity: in 1932 Congress passed the Norris-LaGuardia Act to prevent courts from issuing restraining orders or injunctions against unions that were on strike or planning to strike. The act expressly eliminated federal courts' jurisdiction to issue such orders in labor-management disputes. When the federal government seized the mines, it became the miners' employer. Therefore, the current standoff between Lewis and the Truman administration was an employer-employee dispute over which the federal courts had no jurisdiction. Judge Goldsborough's temporary restraining order therefore did not legally bind Lewis or the union.

Attorney General Tom Clark's team of Department of Justice lawyers, led by Assistant Attorney General John F. Sonnett, countered that Congress did not intend for the Norris-LaGuardia Act to apply to disputes between the government and unions. Their reply brief contended that the case turned not on the rights of labor but rather on the safety and security of the nation.

Goldsborough deliberated for three days before ruling for the government. He ordered Lewis and the union to stand trial on the contempt charges beginning the following Monday. The judge intended to try both defendants on charges of both civil and criminal contempt charges, for which the penalties ranged from a small fine to a considerable fine and imprisonment.

"If they try to put Lewis in jail or fine our union," one miner warned, "you'll see the AFL and CIO stopping work everywhere. It'll be [chaos] all over the country."[7] Perhaps heeding such warnings and preferring not to make Lewis a martyr, counsel for the government requested that the criminal proceedings against Lewis be dropped. Sending Lewis to jail would not end the coal strike.[8]

The trial opened on December 2 and concluded at noon the next day. Ruling that Lewis and the UMW were in contempt of court, Goldsborough levied punishing fines: he ordered Lewis to pay $10,000 and the union to pay $3.5 million. It was the harshest financial penalty ever imposed in a labor contempt-of-court case. The union's attorney immediately pleaded that the fines amounted to "cruel and unusual punishment," but the judge refused to reconsider the fines.[9]

Lewis left the federal courthouse smoking a cigar beneath a dark fedora. He did not order the miners back to work and gave no indication that he would. He instead seemed intent on defying the expressed will of the entire federal government.

Lewis's power over the American economy was clear to any American alive at the time. Seventy thousand steel workers, fifty thousand railroad workers, and forty thousand automobile industry workers had been furloughed, laid off, or otherwise idled because of the coal strike.[10] Even the student writers of the *Harvard Crimson*, who were unlikely to work on the railroads or in factories, worried over Truman's decision to stage a showdown with Lewis: "'Who is stronger—the government or Mr. Lewis?' . . . There is no question as to its outcome—John L. can beat anything, weight for age, at any distance."[11] The students expressed publicly what many in Washington feared privately.

* * *

Attorneys for both sides sought leave to appeal directly to the Supreme Court. And they took the extraordinary step of asking to meet with the chief justice to discuss their petitions. Vinson agreed to meet with them.

Shortly after that meeting, Lewis stunned the nation by ordering the miners to return to their jobs immediately, where they would work under the same pay and conditions that were in effect when the strike began.[12] In a brief statement, Lewis said that the Supreme Court "during its period of deliberation [would be] free from public pressure superinduced by the hysteria of an economic crisis."[13] That Lewis's about-face came so swiftly after his attorneys and government counsel met with the chief justice was a fact lost on no one.

Regardless of the circumstances under which it arose, no one doubted that the 400,000 striking miners would heed Lewis's order to return to work. "The boss has said it, and that's all," quipped the UMW district president in Charleston, West Virginia.[14] Miners did not automatically follow Lewis's lead on political matters—they disregarded his calls to vote against Roosevelt in 1940 and 1944—but on contract matters, his word was law.[15] They returned to work.

The U.S. Postal Service lifted weight and size limitations on parcel shipments and railroad companies prepared to return to full service. Mayors ended "brownout" electricity rationing in cities across the nation. Homeowners and storekeepers were allowed to turn on their Christmas lights for the first time in weeks.[16]

Lewis's decision to end the strike was a major victory for the Truman administration. Although Truman's rhetoric continued to reflect New Deal thinking, his actions and two Supreme Court nominees indicated that he was forging a more conservative Democratic path than Roosevelt had. Coal miners noticed. Bill Baker, a former local union president in Russellton, Pennsylvania, told one reporter, "Truman is not our kind of Democrat. If [the Truman administration] can get away with things like this, it's time for us to get our own labor party and put our own ticket into the field."[17]

Lewis's decision to stand down marked the point of Truman's newfound independence. Truman's close advisor Clark Clifford recalled some years later, "I think you can put your finger on winning this showdown with Lewis as the moment when Truman finally and irrevocably stepped out from the shadow of FDR to become president in his own right. . . . I can tell you, there was a big difference in the Old Man from then on."[18]

* * *

Two days later, on December 9, the Supreme Court announced that it would hear the case, agreeing to the parties' request to bypass the court of appeal. The justices set oral arguments for January 14, 1947. Lewis and the United Mine Workers of America won a critical victory a week later when the justices agreed to consider the question of whether the Norris-LaGuardia Act applied to negotiations between a union and a company's owner when the owner was the federal government.

Spectators, lawyers, and journalists occupied every seat in the Supreme Court during three and a half hours of oral arguments in the case of *United*

States v. United Mine Workers of America. Attorney General Clark opened the proceedings by presenting the government's version of the facts to the Court. Assistant Attorney General John F. Sonnett argued the administration's legal position and answered the justice's questions.

Because the Supreme Court is a court of appeal, it generally does not question the facts in the trial record. Clark's decision to read the facts to the justices while leaving the heavy lifting of arguing the case to his assistant was a curious one that lent credence to criticism that he was a legal lightweight unfit to be attorney general, much less to assume the Supreme Court seat to which Truman later nominated him. UMW attorney Welty K. Hopkins remarked to the justices that Clark's argument "sounded like a political speech."[19]

Assistant Attorney General Sonnett and UMW counsel Hopkins were besieged with questions from the justices. Frankfurter, Black, Jackson, and Douglas were the most active questioners, while Vinson asked few questions.[20] The chief justice knew where he stood, and despite being new to the Court, he also knew that the complex case, which presented four distinct but related questions of law, would be decided in what promised to be a lively conference.

* * *

Six days later, on January 20, 1947, it quickly became clear at the conference that no majority existed on any of the major questions: whether the Norris-LaGuardia Act applied to the government; whether Lewis and the UMW could be held in contempt of court even if the act did not apply to the government; whether the trial judge had improperly commingled civil and criminal intent; and, lastly, whether the district court had imposed excessive fines on the union, its leader, or both.[21] Vinson urged his brethren to rule in the government's favor on every count. Lewis, he said, was "getting too big for his britches."[22] But the conference adjourned without a single issue being resolved.

During the following weeks, several justices worked to persuade others. Vinson was determined to maintain the bare five-to-four majority vote in favor of the government's position on the primary issue, holding that the Norris-LaGuardia Act applied only to private corporate owners and was inapplicable to the federal government. He was happy when a seven-vote majority emerged to rule that the district court's order holding Lewis and the union in contempt was valid regardless of whether the

Norris-LaGuardia Act applied to the government. On the remaining issues, the Court was closely divided and votes remained in flux.

The most contentious debate centered on whether the district court
had imposed excessive fines on Lewis and the union. Vinson argued that
Lewis's $10,000 fine should stand. He could compromise on the fine levied
against the UMW, but on Lewis's culpability the chief would not yield.
Vinson met daily with Frankfurter, Jackson, Burton, and Reed to negotiate the fines. Douglas wondered "how our Court had the power to set a
fine in a criminal case which it never heard at the trial level."[23] But every
associate justice believed that the $3.5 million fine set against the union
was excessive.

Vinson successfully held together a five-justice majority to sustain the
fine against Lewis and on every other issue except the contempt question,
on which he maintained a stronger seven-justice majority. Only Frank
Murphy and Wiley Rutledge dissented. Black, Reed, Douglas, and Burton
joined Vinson in holding that the Norris-LaGuardia Act did not apply to
the federal government.[24] Reed and Burton, Truman's first Court nominee,
voted with Vinson on every question in the case. In doing so they gave a
glimpse of the center-right coalition that would take form after Truman
named Tom Clark and Sherman Minton to the Court.

* * *

For nearly fifteen years, the Supreme Court had issued decisions only
on Mondays.[25] Every Monday morning since the Lewis and union case's
mid-January oral argument, more than three hundred spectators had filled
the Court's hallways, hoping for a decision. By now it was March. On
Thursday, March 6, 1947, just thirty or so people were seated in the Court
when Vinson announced that he would read the majority opinion in the
case of *United States v. the United Mine Workers*.[26] Murmurs reverberated in
the courtroom before several spectators dashed out to notify attorneys, reporters, and others that the Court was rendering its decision in the closely
watched case.

"In October, 1946, the United States was in possession of, and operating, the major portion of the country's bituminous coal mines," the chief
justice read from his seat in the center of the dais. Lawyers and journalists
began flooding the courtroom until no seats or standing room remained.[27]
"The United States had taken possession of the mines," Vinson continued,

"pursuant to Executive Order 9728 of May 21, 1946." In contrast to the steel seizure case that was still years away, there was no dispute here as to the president's power to seize the coal mines: "Section Three of the [War Labor Disputes] Act authorizes the seizure of facilities necessary for the war effort if and when the President finds and proclaims that strikes or other labor disturbances are interrupting the operation of such facilities."[28]

Court adjourned for lunch at two-thirty that afternoon, reconvening a short time later for the justices to continue reading from their concurring, partially dissenting, and fully dissenting opinions on the case. Enough words were spoken, the Associated Press reported, to "fill a medium-sized book."[29]

In the end, the Supreme Court upheld the injunction against Lewis and the UMW and also upheld the contempt-of-court rulings against them. That the Court split five to four on the substantive legal questions accentuated the fact that they voted seven to two in favor of upholding Lewis's $10,000 fine. Some of the justices might have regretted Vinson's in-conference statement that Lewis was "getting too big for his britches," but it appeared that they agreed with him. "For the first time," Douglas recalled, "I saw passion sweeping my Brethren and sending them pell-mell to a public stand against John Lewis."[30]

Whatever fervor the justices might have felt paled in comparison to that expressed by senators and congressional representatives of both parties as they praised the Court's decision. Vinson was not alone in his assessment of Lewis. Democratic senator Burnet Maybank of South Carolina happily proclaimed, "The outrageous treatment the country has received at the hands of John L. Lewis is at an end," while New York Republican congressman Kenneth Keating extolled the Supreme Court's decision as an overdue message: "I hope it will have a good effect in showing defiant labor leaders—such as Mr. Lewis has shown himself to be—that government is still supreme."[31] As Douglas noticed, "Washington, D.C. seemed to heave a sigh of relief when Vinson lowered the boom on John L. Lewis."[32]

Lewis, who was scheduled to testify before a Senate committee the following day regarding unrelated labor legislation, issued no immediate statement.[33] Men of the UMW proclaimed that they were "shocked" and "surprised" that the Court ruled against them on every count. Some raised the legitimate prospect that the union might disregard even the Supreme

Court's orders. "Are we going out again?" Pennsylvania miners wondered aloud. They vowed to follow Lewis if he ordered them back out to strike. "If John L. Lewis told us to go on strike tomorrow, we would go out even if it meant going to prison for twenty years." One Allegheny Valley miner declared, "This isn't going to stop any strikes. I think this makes matters worse. I'm looking for some real trouble now."[34] But Lewis and the unions heeded the Court's ruling.

Truman was visiting Baylor University in Waco, Texas, when he received news of the ruling. White House press secretary Charles Ross told reporters that the president was "gratified that the Supreme Court had sustained the Government's position."[35]

If, as Truman's close advisor Clark Clifford believed, the president's successful challenging of John Lewis marked the moment he emerged from Roosevelt's considerable shadow, then Vinson's assembling a majority to support the administration's side on every issue in the *United Mine Workers* case marked the point when the chief justice took hold of the reins of the Supreme Court. Vinson argued, voted, and wrote to sustain the lower court's rulings because the law and facts as he understood them demanded that he do so.

In upholding the lower court's decision, Vinson and the Court sustained every action the Truman administration had taken against Lewis and the union he led. As one reporter wrote, except for reducing the fine imposed on the union, "The decision was a complete victory for the Government."[36] Legal scholar and Vinson confidant C. Herman Pritchett declared that March 6, 1947, the day the Court issued its decision in *United States v. United Mine Workers of America*, was the day "the Roosevelt Court came to an end."[37]

CHAPTER THIRTEEN

A Civil Service

HARRY TRUMAN DID NOT WANT his presidency limited to the term to which Franklin Delano Roosevelt had been elected. After more than a year in office, he wanted to be elected president—to *be* president—in his own right. By Thanksgiving of 1946, however, the prospect of his being nominated for president by his own party, much less winning a general election for the office, seemed remote. He was so unpopular that it would even be difficult for a Democrat *not* named Harry Truman to succeed him as president.[1]

In New York, Republican governor Thomas Dewey had just been reelected by the widest margin in the state's history. He had connected with voters who, so soon after the Roosevelt era, were not inclined to support Republican candidates. For example, Truman's decision to lift price controls on meat compelled many working-class African American New Yorkers to vote Republican. As one Black columnist wrote, soaring meat prices "dealt a body blow to Negro consumers, staggering at the bottom of the economic ladder. It is among Negroes that Republicans have the highest hopes of creating dissatisfaction."[2] Republicans distributed pamphlets in Harlem featuring a photograph of Dewey with former heavyweight boxing champion Joe Louis.

Dewey planned to run for president for the third time in 1948. He expected congressional Republicans to spend the next two years butting heads with the unpopular Democratic president, setting the stage for him to win the Republican nomination and the White House.[3] In fact, Dewey was the favorite to win, regardless of who was the Democratic nominee.[4]

Truman knew that if he had any realistic hope of winning the 1948 presidential election he had a great deal of work to do. Republican candidates had earned the votes of many African Americans in 1946—he would challenge them for those votes. His political foes charged his administration with general incompetence—he would run a tighter ship.

Finally, congressional Republicans had gained ground by accusing him of allowing Communists to infiltrate the federal government. On this count he would prove them wrong. But to do so, he would need his attorney general's help and, eventually, assistance from the man he had recently named chief justice of the United States.

* * *

On March 21, 1947, Truman signed Executive Order 9835 to establish the Federal Employees Loyalty and Security Program. "I am not worried about the Communist Party taking over the government of the United States," he declared, "but I am against a person, whose loyalty is not to the government of the United States, holding a government job."[5]

The new program applied to 2.2 million federal employees in every agency of the executive branch. Only members of Congress, their aides, and judiciary branch employees were exempt. Truman's order stipulated that executive branch civil servants and applicants were to be investigated. In sweeping language, the order mandated that a person was to be considered "disloyal" if the investigation revealed that he or she was a member or had

affiliation with or sympathetic association with any foreign or domestic association, movement, group or combination of persons designated by the Attorney General as totalitarian, Fascist, Communist or subversive or as having adopted a policy of advocating or approving the commission of acts of force or violence to deny other persons their rights under the Constitution of the United States or as seeking to alter the form of Government of the United States by unconstitutional means.[6]

The order cast a wide net that alarmed even many Americans who were neither current nor prospective federal employees.

Under Truman's order, an agency loyalty board investigated civil servants, and one of fourteen regional loyalty boards investigated applicants. If an investigation revealed suspicious information, the FBI would conduct a full field investigation on the person and present its findings to the agency or regional board. The FBI was not required to reveal the names of informants or witnesses, permitting anyone who accused employees or applicants of disloyalty to remain anonymous. Although the right to confront one's accuser had been a pillar of Western law for centuries, its notable absence from the loyalty review process spurred little opposition from Congress.[7] The standard was whether "reasonable grounds exist for belief that the person involved is disloyal to the Government of the United States."[8]

Employees whose loyalty was deemed questionable could appeal the determination to the politically appointed leaders of their agencies while applicants could appeal to the Loyalty Review Board. In either appeal, the allegedly disloyal individual had to refute anonymous accusations.

Truman himself acknowledged that the program "had a lot of flaws in it." He believed that two facts should control the program:

1. That although the loyalty of by far the overwhelming majority of all government employees was beyond question, the presence in the government service of any disloyal or subversive person constituted a threat to our democratic processes, and

2. That maximum protection must be afforded the United States against infiltration of disloyal persons into the ranks of its employees, *and* equal protection from unfounded accusation of disloyalty must be afforded the loyal employees of the government.[9]

Truman was not the first American president to institute a loyalty program for federal employees. Between 1930 and 1935, membership in the Communist Party of the United States of America increased from 7,500 to around 30,000.[10] Americans were so wary of Communist influence that state and federal legislators passed laws criminalizing membership in the Communist Party. In the summer of 1940, amid the looming prospect of war and evidence of widespread fascist and Communist subversion in some European governments, Franklin Roosevelt ordered the FBI to investigate federal employees if an employee's department leader requested it. More than a year later, Attorney General Francis Biddle authorized FBI agents to investigate federal employees suspected of participating in "subversive" activities, regardless of whether a department's senior official requested the investigation. Civil servants could be fired only upon documented evidence of subversive activity. The goal was to eliminate spies and those actively working to subvert the government.

Truman's loyalty program differed from Roosevelt's in two ways. First, it would investigate federal employees' political beliefs in addition to their activities. However, by restricting civil servants' right to engage in political activity or even to hold certain political views, Truman's loyalty program posed significant questions of constitutional law. By the time cases presenting these questions reached the Supreme Court, Truman would have named two more justices to it.

Second, the timing of Truman's order supported the perception that political considerations drove his decision to implement the program. Campaigning for Democrats less than a month before election day, on October 9, 1946, Attorney General Tom Clark declared, "The issue of Communism has been exaggerated and distorted by the Republican Party for political purposes. . . . It is so clear to me as beyond doubt that we face no danger of Communism in the United States so long as we assure the American people of an opportunity to make orderly progress toward social goals."[11] But the specter of the Iron Curtain after World War II changed the political atmosphere in a way that Truman seemed not to appreciate until after Republicans swept the 1946 midterm elections. As Republicans prepared to take control of Congress, Truman realized that if the executive branch did not establish a system to investigate civil servants, the Republican-led legislative branch would.

In fact, many who otherwise might have criticized Truman's executive order instead complimented it because they realized how harsh any politically palatable alternative would have been. As columnist Jerry Kluttz wrote, "All federal workers would have been subjected to something far worse by Congress if the president hadn't come through with his program." This was because "Democrats and Republicans are both to blame for trying to mix politics and loyalty—and the federal worker stands to suffer for it." Kluttz reported that members of both the House and Senate were considering "knocking out the president's program because it provide[d] 'too many safeguards' for accused employees."[12]

Perhaps with this in mind, James Burns, president of the American Federation of Government Employees, pledged that members of his union would comply: "It is hard to understand why anyone would offer an objection to this type of [program]. Any program dedicated to eradicating disloyalty should receive the full cooperation of every employee." Despite whatever alarm the loyalty boards were causing in the federal workforce at large, "We in the AFGE assert that loyalty is a condition precedent not only to citizenship but also to employment in the government service. We welcome the loyalty program."[13]

Civil service commissioner Arthur Flemming assured, "The loyalty investigations will be a routine matter for the vast majority of federal employees." Interviewed alongside Flemming, FBI associate director Clyde Tollson assured, "There is no cause for hysteria except on the part of those who have something to conceal."[14]

International considerations also contributed to Truman's decision to implement the loyalty program. The United States' ability to help democratic allies defend themselves against Communist aggression would be compromised if Communists were able to stymie efforts from within the federal government. The loyalty program was in part a domestic manifestation of the administration's increasingly hard-line foreign policy.[15]

Truman's executive order differed from Roosevelt's in tone as well as substance. In November 1947 former First Lady Eleanor Roosevelt wrote Truman to express her dismay. She thought the Loyalty Review Board should consist of more women and fewer attorneys. But it was the board's very existence that compelled her to write: "My own reaction is anything but happy. I feel we have capitulated to our fear of Communism, and instead of fighting to improve Democracy, we are doing what the Soviets would do in trying to repress anything which we are afraid might not command public support, in order to insure acceptance of our own actions."

The president responded to Mrs. Roosevelt with a personal letter two weeks later. He reasserted his belief "that the overwhelming number of civil servants in the United States are not only faithful and loyal, but devoted patriots." He recognized the repugnancy of the loyalty program's inquiring into federal employees' privately held political beliefs, "but I became convinced that it was necessary not because as you say 'we were trying to repress anything we were afraid might not command public support,' but because there were indications of a small infiltration of seriously disloyal people into certain sensitive parts of the government."[16]

Members of Congress from both parties lauded Truman's order. Democrats privately hoped that the new program would help neutralize opponents' charges that their party countenanced Communist sympathizers. Democratic representative E. E. Cox of Georgia went so far as to say that issuing the order was "one of the smartest things [Truman] has ever done. He is acting realistically and is taking notice of the fact that people of the country are aroused over these Communists and subversives." One of Mississippi's Democratic congressmen declared about subversive federal employees, "We must get rid of them any way possible. There are still a lot of them on the payroll."[17]

Republicans congratulated Truman on pursuing a course of action they had been advocating, according to the new Speaker of the House, Joseph Martin, "for at least four years."[18] Martin was satisfied that "the President has finally awakened" to the threat posed by internal subversives.[19] The chair of the Republican National Committee proclaimed, "I am glad the president, however belatedly, has adopted this important part of the program supported by the Republican Party and its candidates in the 1946 campaign."[20]

Indeed, Truman's decision to establish the loyalty program lent credence to some Republicans' claims that the federal government had been infiltrated by Communists and Communist sympathizers. Wisconsin senator Joseph McCarthy, who owed his 1946 election win to stoking public fear of Communist subversives, declared, "The President's order is definitely needed now, since over the past number of years there has been a tremendous number of communistically inclined employees on the Federal payroll."[21]

Despite their praise for Truman's program, the Republican-led House of Representatives passed a bill weeks later to establish a more restrictive loyalty program. The House bill, which passed by a vote of 319 to 61, required agencies to investigate every single one of America's civil servants. It allowed them to be dismissed without a right to appeal the decision or an opportunity to confront their accusers.

The bill stoked lawmakers' passions. Democratic congressman Glen Johnson of Oklahoma thundered on the House floor, "In heaven's name, what more heinous label could be attached to a man than to say that he was disloyal to his own government?" When Johnson's Republican colleagues pointed out that their bill was similar in most aspects to Truman's executive order, he answered, "And that order is just as wrong in its way as in this bill. In order to get rid of Communists, let's don't do the same thing they do in communist Russia."[22]

By September 1948 the FBI had investigated and concluded that 2,110,521 civil servants were sufficiently loyal that no further inquiry was required, while 6,344 employees warranted additional investigation.[23] Eight hundred and eighty-three of these federal workers resigned rather than face further investigation.[24]

* * *

Outraged opponents of the loyalty program argued that federal law already prohibited federal employees from associating with a group advocating or seeking to overthrow the government. The United Public Workers Union vowed to defend the "democratic civil rights of government workers" in the fight against "witch hunts in Government service."[25] The American Civil Liberties Union proclaimed, "The greatest threat to civil liberties lies in the power given the Attorney General to designate, after investigation, organizations for blacklisting." After learning that it was among the ninety-one organizations deemed subversive when Attorney General Clark released his list on December 4, 1947, the Ku Klux Klan angrily echoed the ACLU's objection: "This is purely an arbitrary matter of Clark's department setting itself up as a Czar of this country."[26]

Groups as divergent as the ACLU and the KKK directed their ire not at the unpopular president who issued the executive order but instead at the attorney general charged with its implementation. They accurately surmised that Clark was more eager than Truman to expand the federal government's power under the guise of the loyalty program. They had good reason to focus on Clark.

In speeches Clark repeatedly claimed that Communists had infiltrated labor unions to force strikes that would destabilize the American economy. He suggested that Communist subversives were becoming lawyers so they could defend their fellow travelers in American courts. "We know," Clark announced in a speech before the Chicago Bar Association, "that there is a national and international conspiracy to divide our people, to discredit our institutions and to bring about disrespect for our government." The attorney general struck a foreboding note: "No country on earth, and no government, can long endure this vicious attack. I say to you that [subversives] are driving law enforcement in this country to the end of its patience."[27]

CHAPTER FOURTEEN

Truman at the Lincoln Memorial

HARRY TRUMAN'S AND FRED VINSON'S friendship did not fade after Vinson became chief justice. To the contrary, their friendship flourished once Vinson no longer served at the pleasure of the president. Their families became so close that Truman's daughter, Margaret, called the chief justice "Poppa Vin"; within the family, Truman called him "the Big Judge."[1] Vinson's wife, Roberta, was the only woman other than Bess and Margaret Truman whom anyone could remember visiting the Little White House on Key West. In Washington, the Vinsons hosted the Trumans for dinner at their Woodley Park apartment. Amid their tumultuous Washington lives, the men and their families found comfort in each other's company.

Fred Vinson was perhaps the only man in Washington whom Truman trusted completely. The chief justice, according to Truman, "was gifted with a sense of personal and political loyalty seldom found among the top men in Washington."[2] Because the president so valued Vinson's judgment as well as his friendship, he routinely sought his advice on matters pertaining both to policy and politics. As Truman scholar Richard Kirkendall put it, "Vinson, in a sense, remained a part of the administration."[3]

Late evenings often found the two friends talking to each other on the telephone, discussing domestic policy, politics, and international affairs. "It used to be said that the man having the most influence with the President of the United States," began one *New York Times* article, "was the last one to see him before he went to bed. It is different today. Now it is the man who talks to him long after the last caller has left the White House and the President is presumably tucked away for the night. That man is Fred M. Vinson, Chief Justice of the United States."[4] Truman and Vinson did not publicize their colloquies but neither did they keep them secret. Vinson's trips to the Little White House on Key West were a matter of public record.

Today such a relationship between the president and chief justice would be considered highly inappropriate. Until the middle of the twentieth century, however, it was not uncommon for presidents to consult with justices regarding political affairs. Throughout the twentieth century, Supreme Court justices advised presidents, suggested legislation to Congress, or accepted appointments to governmental tribunals.[5] Justices Louis D. Brandeis, Felix Frankfurter, and William O. Douglas continued to advise Roosevelt after their confirmations to the Court. But Roosevelt was not close friends with them, certainly not to the point of treating them like family.

Beginning in the 1970s justices became ostentatiously wary of which declarations they applauded during the president's annual State of the Union address, lest their impartiality on future rulings be questioned.[6] If a chief justice today were to advise the president on federal policy or campaign politics, there likely would be calls for the impeachment of at least one of them.

* * *

One of the reasons Truman and Vinson became such close friends was that they both loved playing poker. For the president, poker was more than mere recreation. It was a comforting constant in his life. His Aunt Ida and Uncle Harry had taught him how to play cards on their farm back in the 1890s, and he remained an avid player for the rest of his life. As an Army captain during the Great War, he played with his men, and continued playing with them after the war, often gathering in a third-floor room at 101 North Main Street in Independence, Missouri.

After being elected senator, Truman relished his trips back home to Missouri in no small part because he was able to play poker with his Army friends. Win or lose, he found comfort in the game. As one of his fellow players explained, playing poker was Truman's "only means of relaxation—that and walking. Never did anything else."[7] Indeed, he remained a devoted player through his active retirement years.

When Truman was sworn in as president, his poker buddies in Washington and Missouri presumed that his playing days were over, at least while he was president. They were wrong. On May 26, 1946, six weeks after taking office, the president and Mrs. Truman took their first public outing. They attended a dinner with some current and former members of Congress at the Burning Tree Club in Bethesda, Maryland, and after dinner, a poker game got started. Truman heartily joined the table—and did well.

Days later, word spread among his closest friends and advisors that the games would continue. Truman's White House naval aide regretfully told him that he neither drank nor played cards. That young officer was quickly replaced with another officer who did drink and play cards: Clark Clifford, who would go on to advise several presidents over the coming decades and become a Washington legend in his own right.[8]

Truman refused to allow poker games in the White House. Air Force Major General Donald Dawson, a White House aide at the time, recalled, "Boss never would host his poker games at the White House since he felt strongly that a game involving money was off limits for that great house."[9] Washington games were held at a hotel, on the presidential yacht *Williamsburg*, or at Clifford's home. On long voyages to and from Europe, he played with reporters but made sure no photographs were taken. Perhaps Truman's rules were based in part on the amount of money usually at stake in his games. Visiting players sometimes were surprised to learn that hundreds of dollars were bet around the table. If a player lost a good deal of money, however, he was invited to replenish his stack from the healthy pot. "He never wanted anyone to get hurt in a poker game," recalled reporter Robert G. Nixon.[10]

By this time, Truman was so well-versed in playing poker that he had mastered obscure and difficult variations of the game. One newsman who played with him recalled that the president "knew some of the wildest games that I have ever heard of. . . . There was one that I'll never forget. It was a seven-card game called 'seven card, low hole card wild, high low.'" If one held "a pair of deuces as low hole cards, nothing can undercut you. You are a lucky man on that hand. If you have a pair of treys or a pair of anything else, and you have matching cards up, you may think that you have three or four wild cards but the last card that's dealt down can turn out to be a deuce, undercutting the treys and you're dead. Your hand is worthless."[11]

Treasury Secretary Vinson quickly became Truman's favorite poker companion. The president rarely played without him. In fact, Truman so loved playing poker with Vinson that he invented a variation of the game and named it "Vinson." And Truman was the only one who was good at playing Vinson. One player explained that the game was hard to understand: "It's low ball, high ball, I never did understand. [Truman] was pretty good at it, because nobody else understood what we were doing. So every time we played Vinson, he would win." Because the games were dealer's choice, "about every time he was dealer, he'd say, 'Well, we're going to play Vinson now.'"[12]

Along with Vinson, Truman's poker game regulars included Secretary of Agriculture Clinton Anderson, Missouri businessman and future secretary of the Air Force Stuart Symington, and Truman's old Army buddy and White House aide Brigadier General Harry Vaughan. Texas congressman Lyndon Johnson eagerly joined the games whenever possible, but, to the other players' annoyance, he was more interested in talking politics than in playing the game.[13]

The single phrase most associated with Truman is a reference to dealing poker cards. U.S. Marshal Fred Canfil of the western district of Missouri was one of Truman's many friends. Shortly after Truman became president, Canfil commissioned the inmates at the Federal Reformatory in El Reno, Oklahoma, to make a foot-long, two-inch-tall wooden sign, which Canfil mailed to the president on October 2, 1945. On one side it read, "I'm from MISSOURI," and on the other it read, "The BUCK STOPS here!"

Truman placed the sign on his desk, where it remained for most of his presidency. The "buck" referred to a knife with a buckhorn handle used during the frontier era to indicate whose turn it was to deal the cards. If a player did not want to deal, he handed the knife to another player—that is, he passed the buck. Truman declared that, as president, he could not pass the buck. He made the sign famous by referring to it in speeches, including his farewell address in which he told the American people, "The president—whoever he is—has to decide. He can't pass the buck to anybody. No one else can do the deciding for him. That's his job."[14]

* * *

On the political front, the 1946 midterm elections were so disastrous for Truman that they freed him. As some Democratic leaders called on him to resign, voters began to doubt that he could win his party's nomination, much less the presidency in 1948. The likelihood of him losing was so great that it afforded him a freedom rarely enjoyed by any president.

In his weakened political state, he could not rely on support from congressional Democrats. Republicans had gained so many seats in the midterm elections that whatever Democratic votes he could muster would hardly matter. Truman's ability to pursue his agenda through legislation was all but closed.

He had never hesitated to use his executive powers to achieve policy goals. Truman had issued executive orders to address both foreign and domestic crises. But these orders, like the one seizing the coal mines in 1946, were issued pursuant to powers accorded to him by laws: Congress had expressly empowered him to take those actions.

After the 1946 midterm elections, with no viable legislative paths left in Congress, Truman felt compelled—and empowered—to issue executive orders pursuant to the president's inherent constitutional powers as he understood them. And he expected federal district and appellate courts, which seemed to accept an expansive breadth of presidential authority during World War II, to uphold his actions.

Along with issuing executive orders, Truman prepared in this new political environment to pursue his agenda through the judiciary. Attorney General Tom Clark had assembled a staff of seasoned attorneys at the Justice Department who were able and eager to pursue the administration's agenda through the judicial process. This was particularly true in Truman's growing determination to end legally enforced racial segregation. Clark later recounted, "Sometimes we'd get to talking and he would tell me about, how when he was growing up—about the discrimination aginst the blacks, and how they couldn't get to first base, and everybody used them and things of that kind, you know. He was going to try to do something about it, that's what he told me."[15]

Perhaps the only good news for Truman in the 1946 elections was that many African American voters in northern states supported Democratic candidates, despite earnest competition from Republicans. White House aide David Niles trumpeted, "The Negro vote in New York City was decisively pro-Democrat." Republican governor Thomas E. Dewey, a pro–civil rights politician whom pundits expected to run for president, failed to win a single voting district in Harlem. But this could change as Republicans courted African American voters. NAACP chairman Walter White focused on the midterm elections as a harbinger of the upcoming presidential election, noting, "In seventeen northern and border states with a combined electoral vote of 281 it should be remembered by both major parties [that] the Negro vote could swing the balance of power."[16]

* * *

On June 29, 1947, Clark joined a small group that accompanied Truman to the steps of the Lincoln Memorial, where he became the first president to address the NAACP. When Truman accepted White's invitation to speak, he asked White to provide a memorandum "emphasizing the points you think I ought to emphasize."[17] Truman intended to deliver a speech of substance, not platitudes, and radio stations around the world prepared to air it live.

America was still a nation divided. Twenty states required all public accommodations to be segregated while only eighteen states outlawed racial discrimination of public facilities.[18] The nation's capital was a harshly segregated city. African and Carribean diplomats visiting on official business were routinely shocked to be refused service at downtown restaurants.

More than ten thousand spectators gathered at the Lincoln Memorial, appreciating the magnitude of the moment. Joining the president on the dais were Eleanor Roosevelt, Republican senator Wayne Morse of Oregon, Justice Hugo Black, and Chief Justice Fred Vinson. Dressed in a light-toned double-breasted suit accented with his trademark picket-fence folded pocketsquare, Truman rose to the podium at 4:30 p.m.

After greeting Roosevelt, White, and members of Congress, Truman delivered a speech that was as substantial as it was short: "I should like to talk to you briefly about civil rights and human freedom. It is my deep conviction that we have reached a turning point in the long history of our country's efforts to guarantee freedom and equality to all our citizens. Recent events in the United States and abroad have made us realize that it is more important today than ever before to ensure that all Americans enjoy these rights." He paused for emphasis. "When I say all Americans I mean all Americans."[19]

Audience members applauded enthusiastically. An NAACP statement later described the address as "the most comprehensive and forthright statement on the rights of minorities in a democracy and the duty of the government to secure safeguards that has ever been made by a President of the United States."[20]

That the chief justice and senior associate justice sat behind Truman as he spoke was no small gesture. The only presidential speech justices typically attended was the annual State of the Union address. But Vinson's and Black's decision to sit behind Truman as he delivered his first major civil rights address signaled to all Americans that the federal government at last intended to address the constitutional divide left unresolved by the Civil War and Reconstruction. And it suggested to members of Congress that this work could be done despite their intransigence.

To be sure, when Truman declared that the nation "can no longer afford the luxury of a leisurely attack upon prejudice and discrimination," he was speaking to congressional leaders of both parties as much as he was to the millions of White Americans listening on their radios. "Our national government must show the way," he continued. "This is a difficult and complex undertaking. Federal laws and administrative machineries must be improved and expanded. We must provide the government with better tools to do the job. . . . We must strive to advance civil rights wherever it lies within our power."[21]

CHAPTER FIFTEEN

Shelley v. Kraemer
The Judicial Revolution Begins

SEVEN MONTHS BEFORE TRUMAN BECAME the first president to address the NAACP and just weeks after the Republican landslide in the 1946 midterm elections, Truman signed Executive Order 9808 to establish the Presidential Committee on Civil Rights. Attorney General Clark had privately counseled him to establish the committee, believing that it "would be of the utmost value in the task of preserving civil rights."[1] The multiracial committee consisted of fifteen leaders from the fields of law, business, education, labor, and religion, with General Electric Corporation president Charles E. Wilson serving as its chairman.[2] Truman later explained, "I created this Committee with a feeling of urgency. No sooner were we finished with [World War II] than racial and religious intolerance began to appear and threaten the very things we had just fought for."[3] He expected concrete, assertive recommendations from the committee.

Committee members were progressives or moderates but otherwise comprised a diverse lot. As one White House aide recalled, "We were so meticulous to get balance that we wound up with two of everything: two women, two southerners, two business [leaders], two labor [leaders]." Staffers privately took to calling it the "Noah's Ark Committee."[4] The president personally thanked members for agreeing to serve on the committee, telling them, "You have a vitally important job. . . . You may get more brickbats than bouquets. Your willingness to undertake the job shows that your hearts are in the right place."[5]

Truman's executive order empowered the committee to thoroughly investigate how state-enforced racism affected the lives of all Americans. Twelve full-time staff members worked for the committee, which met and held hearings from December 1946 through October 1947. Federal employees asked to testify before the committee were required to comply. FBI director J. Edgar Hoover testified that at one prison of which he knew,

"It was seldom that a Negro man or women [sic] was incarcerated who was not given a severe beating, which started off with a pistol whipping and ended with a rubber hose."[6]

* * *

On October 29, 1947, four months after his historic NAACP address, Truman received the 178-page report of the Presidential Committee on Civil Rights. Entitled *To Secure These Rights*, the report accutely captured the president's vision. After laying bare the physical, emotional, and "moral dry rot" that institutionalized racism inflicted on Americans, the report set forth nearly three dozen recommendations, each centered on one of what it deemed "four basic rights":

1. The Right to Safety and Security of the Person
2. The Right to Citizenship and its Privileges
3. The Right to Freedom of Conscience and Expression
4. The Right to Equality of Opportunity.[7]

To secure each of these rights, the report recommended several actions, including:

- Eliminating segregation in the armed forces;
- Enacting federal legislation to ban racially restrictive covenants;
- Making police brutality a criminal offense;
- Enacting state or federal legislation to outlaw poll taxes;
- Converting the Justice Department's Civil Rights section into a fully funded, permanent division; and
- Eliminating segregation in federal facilities and the public schools in Washington, DC.[8]

When Truman accepted the report, he became, in the words of journalist Carl Rowan, "the nation's first president to say unequivocally that the federal government has the primary responsibility to secure the basic civil rights of minority group citizens." White southerners responded by inundating the White House with angry letters and telegrams like the one from Mrs. M. R. Baker of Virginia, who wrote, "If you do away with segregation, allow negro children in white schools, churches, etc. you might as well drop a few bombs on us and not prolong the agony. Just come down here (southern Va.) and live awhile and you'll see why we are right."[9]

But Truman believed they were wrong. His Committee on Civil Rights had delivered just the sort of substantive recommendations he wanted. As Clark later explained, *To Secure These Rights* became "a blueprint of most everything that's been done in the area of civil rights since that time."[10] One day after Truman accepted the report, senior officials at the Department of Justice decided to file an *amicus curiae* brief in support of the NAACP's position challenging racially restrictive covenants in the Supreme Court case *Shelley v. Kraemer.*[11]

* * *

To Secure These Rights attacked racist restrictive covenants as strongly as it condemned segregation in the armed forces and police brutality, noting that approximately 80 percent of Chicago's homes were subject to such covenants.[12] The Supreme Court had ruled in 1917 that local ordinances mandating racial segregation unconstitutionally violated private property rights.[13] Therefore, to maintain racially segregated neighborhoods, White property owners began including racist restrictive covenants in their real estate contracts.

J. D. and Ethel Shelley moved with the Great Migration from Mississippi to St. Louis in 1939. Mr. Shelley found work in Missouri at a munitions factory preparing for the anticipated war effort. By 1944 the Shelleys had saved enough to make a down payment on a home in which to raise their six children. They bought and took possession of 4600 Labadie Avenue on October 9, 1945. They had never met the sellers and were unaware of any racist restrictive covenants on the property. So the Shelleys were shocked to be served the very next day with a lawsuit demanding that they vacate their new home.

The plaintiffs, the Kraemer family, lived ten blocks away from the Shelleys. The Kraemers' lawsuit was funded by the Marcus Avenue Homeowners' Association. Their complaint contended that the Shelleys' contract was void because a covenant executed in 1911 declared that the house could not be "occupied by any person not of the Caucasian race."[14]

The African American real estate agents who negotiated the Shelleys' purchase of the home through a straw buyer (and at a considerable profit) financed the family's defense. They retained George Vaughn, a prominent African American attorney in St. Louis whose parents were born into slavery. Vaughn launched a vigorous, multipronged defense. Specifically, he asserted that the covenant was defective because it had not been signed by all property owners. Second, the racist covenant violated the federal Constitution, the Missouri Constitution, and the 1866 Civil Rights Act. Lastly, because numerous African American families had moved into the neighborhood since 1911, the covenant was void due to substantially changed conditions.

After a two-day trial, the court ruled in the Shelleys' favor, accepting their argument that the restrictive covenant was invalid because it was not signed by all the necessary parties. The Supreme Court of Missouri reversed the trial court's decision, holding that the covenant was valid because it had been signed by all required parties when originally executed in 1911. Missouri's Supreme Court dispensed with the Shelleys' public policy arguments as well, noting that such agreements were generally enforceable in the state.[15]

To Secure These Rights recommended that states enact laws declaring such covenants unenforceable and that Congress pass a similar law for the District of Columbia. As a secondary option, the report called on the Department of Justice to file an *amicus curiae* brief asking the Supreme Court to declare restrictive covenants unconstitutional. With Truman's approval, Clark decided to file such a brief, telling the solicitor general's office, "We're going in."[16]

The Truman administration's brief was one of numerous *amicus* briefs filed in support of the NAACP's position. The National Bar Association, the Anti-Defamation League, the National Lawyers Guild, the American Indian Association, and the American Jewish Congress were among the prominent organizations who joined Truman's Justice Department to argue that racist restrictive covenants were unconstitutional.[17]

The Supreme Court consolidated *Shelley v. Kraemer* with other cases challenging racially restrictive covenants and scheduled oral arguments for January 15 and 16, 1948.

* * *

A couple of days before oral arguments, on January 12, 1948, the Court issued a unanimous *per curiam* opinion in *Sipuel v. Board of Regents of the University of Oklahoma*, just four days after hearing arguments in that case.

Ada Lois Sipuel was an Oklahoma resident who had been rejected from the University of Oklahoma College of Law because the school refused to admit African Americans. The school claimed that it was bound by state law: the State of Oklahoma levied a five-hundred-dollar fine on anyone who taught Black and White students in the same classroom.

NAACP attorney Thurgood Marshall, who would argue one of the *Shelley* cases just a few days later, presented one of his finest Court arguments in *Sipuel*. The justices' questioning suggested that most of them supported his position—at least so far as it came to admitting Sipuel to law school.

For the first time, however, Marshall and his legal team were asking the Court to overturn *Plessy v. Ferguson*, to declare that state-sponsored segregation violated the federal Constitution. It was a daring question to place before the Court. If a majority ruled to uphold *Plessy*, it would deal a potentially fatal blow to African Americans' legal campaign. The justices could expressly affirm *Plessy* while still finding a way to rule in Sipuel's favor. Nonetheless, Marshall decided that now was time to ask the Court to confront *Plessy*.

In a letter Marshall assured his mentor Charles Hamilton Houston that he did "not suggest this lightly. Several factors favor a charge at *Plessy*, with a view to presenting our case to the Supreme Court during the 1948 term. First, this is the best bench we will get for some time." He contended that Reed, Douglas, Murphy, Black, Rutledge, and the chief justice were likely to provide six votes to overturn *Plessy*. Second, in a point that unsuspectingly foreshadowed the future Eisenhower administration's ambivalence toward *Brown v. Board of Education*, Marshall wrote, "Harry Truman is a genuine anti-segregationist." He could be counted on to enforce a Supreme Court decision ordering desegregation.[18] And so in their briefs and at oral arguments, attorneys for the petitioners urged the Court to overturn *Plessy v. Ferguson*.

The justices were unwilling to do so. But they clearly did not think much of the arguments set forth by Oklahoma assistant attorney general Fred Hansen. The *Washington Post* reported that at oral argument, "Counsel for the State of Oklahoma took a severe hazing from the Supreme Court. . . . The justices asked sharply—again and again—why did Ada Lois Sipuel, a Negro girl, have to come clear to the Supreme Court to get into the State law school, which is open to students of other races."[19]

Sipuel likely generated the least amount of discussion among the justices of any desegregation case before or since. Vinson convened the conference on January 10, 1948, and said simply, "I reverse." Black echoed, "I reverse."

Kentucky-native Stanley Reed, who dined with his wife each night at one of Washington's Whites-only restaurants because they did not cook, almost timidly registered his concern. "This case is not that easy," he said. "I am not in sympathy with what the Court has been doing in this field. I pass."

Douglas summarized the Court's thinking when he said, "I reverse. Admit her to the Oklahoma Law School." Jackson agreed: "I hope that we can dispose of it in a *per curiam* [opinion] on Monday. I reverse."[20]

Four days after hearing oral arguments in *Sipuel v. Board of Regents of the University of Oklahoma*, the Court issued a *per curiam* opinion reversing the ruling issued by the Oklahoma Supreme Court. The short opinion did not address Sipuel's contention that *Plessy v. Ferguson* should be overturned. Instead, it cited *Missouri ex rel. Gaines v. Canada*, an earlier case won by Houston and Marshall, to affirm that Sipuel was "entitled to secure legal education afforded by a state institution. To this time, it has been denied her although, during the same period, many white applicants have been afforded legal education by the State. The State must provide it for her in conformity with the equal protection clause of the Fourteenth Amendment, and provide it as soon as it does for applicants of any other group."[21] *Sipuel* presented a welcome but curious victory for civil rights advocates because the decision did not forbid state-enforced racial segregation.

In a historic Supreme Court calendar month, Houston and Marshall would have another opportunity just a few days later to argue that government-enforced segregation violated the federal constitution. This time they would be joined in brief and at argument by Justice Department attorneys. And the courtroom drama would begin before a word was spoken.

* * *

Silently, Justices Wiley Rutledge, Robert Jackson, and Stanley Reed rose from their chairs and left the courtroom. Their homes were subject to racist restrictive covenants. "It shows how deep the case cuts," Houston later told reporters, "when one-third of the nation's highest court disqualifies itself."[22] Everyone—litigants, justices, and observers—now worried that four of the six justices to hear the case would decide it with a majority that was a minority of the full Court.

Solicitor General Philip Perlman rose on behalf of the Truman administration. Often called "the tenth justice," the solicitor general's argument carried weight as the expressed legal position of the executive branch of government. The Justice Department's brief unequivocally stated, "The Government is of the view that judicial enforcement of racial restrictive covenants on real property is incompatible with the spirit and letter of the Constitution and laws of the United States." The brief noted that, while African Americans have suffered the most from restrictive covenants, courts have routinely enforced covenants "directed against Indians, Jews, Chinese, Japanese, Mexicans, Hawaiians, Puerto Ricans, Filipinos and 'non-Caucasians.'"[23] Perlman delivered a masterful performance. Racist restrictive covenants, he told the justices, "should be relegated to the limbo of other things as dead as slavery."[24] He implored the Court to declare the covenants unconstitutional and contrary to public policy.

Behind him in the gallery sat many Black Washingtonians who had waited in the January cold for hours before the Court's doors opened to garner seats at the argument. Feeling their eyes on his back, Perlman argued, "They have been told time and again by this Court that this is a government of laws and not of men and that all men are equal before the law. They wait—millions of them—outside this courtroom door, to learn whether these great maxims really apply to them."[25]

George Vaughn, who had represented the Shelleys since the lawsuit's beginning, rose next to address the Court. Vaughn presented a fiery argument that laid bare his passion about the case, contending that judicial enforcement of the racist covenants amounted to state action and violated the Civil Rights Act of 1866. He declared that the covenants were "the Achilles' heel" of American democracy.[26] Reaching his crescendo, Vaughn bellowed, "And Moses looked out across the River Jordan and across the Mississippi River and said, 'Let my people Goooooooooooo!'" He rapped the podium with his knuckles. "As the Negro knocks at America's door, he cries: 'Let me come sit by the fire! I helped build the house!'"[27]

Silence filled the courtroom. Perlman, Houston, Marshall, and the other petitioners' attorneys stared straight ahead. None of the justices dared ask Vaughn a question.

Gerald Seegars, the Kraemers' attorney, rose next and asked the Court to disregard the sociological arguments offered by opposing counsel. "This is a lawsuit, this is a court of law," he offered, "and the problems before the Court are legal ones." Seegars conceded that many African Americans lived in deplorable housing conditions but, he insisted, the judiciary lacked the power and responsibility for resolving that predicament. Racial discrimination could not "be solved by judicial decrees and the current housing problem is no justification for a judicial amendment to the constitution."[28]

Thurgood Marshall and Loren Miller rose next to address the Court. By now, having argued and won several landmark cases for the NAACP, Marshall had developed a rapport with the justices. They often saved their most probing questions for him because they trusted his intellectual candor. Today, Marshall not only argued that racist restrictive covenants violated the 14th Amendment but he presented social science evidence illustrating the deleterious effects they wreaked on communities.

Frankfurter interrupted him: "What's the relevance of all this material? If you are right about the legal proposition, the sociological material merely shows how it works. If you're wrong, the material doesn't do you any good."

Marshall replied that pertinent sociological evidence warranted the Court's consideration, particularly in the District of Columbia case in which the state action theory was inapplicable because the District was not a state. Despite the fact that Marshall was representing the Michigan appellants, Frankfurter agreed that the relevant social science could be important to the District of Columbia case and allowed the future Supreme Court justice to proceed.[29] When Houston later presented sociological evidence while arguing for the DC plaintiffs, Frankfurter, who was Houston's former law professor, declared, "This goes to the inequities of the case."[30]

During the months between oral arguments and the Court's announcing its decision, Vinson worked to assemble not just a majority but unanimity among the six justices who heard the case. Voiding the racially restrictive addendums attached to the deeds of millions of homes across the country would be no small act. He decided to write the majority opinion, believing that such a significant ruling should be delivered by the chief justice. "If you can get unanimous action," Burton wrote to him after the conference, "it will be a major contribution to the vitality of the Fourteenth Amendment, the Civil Rights Act, the general subject of interracial justice and the strength of the court as the 'living voice of the Constitution.'"[31]

* * *

The Supreme Court announced its decision in the covenant cases, along with several other rulings, on May 4, 1948. While justices read the opinions of the other cases, Vinson, as Walter White recalled, "sat relaxed in his leather chair stroking the side of his nose with a finger in characteristic fashion and chatting occasionally with Hugo Black." Vinson's demeanor suddenly changed as he gathered the papers in his hands, leaned forward, and took a deep breath. He would be announcing the next decision.[32]

"These cases present for our consideration," Vinson began in his smoke-gristle baritone, "questions relating to the validity of court enforcement of private agreements, generally described as restrictive covenants, which have as their purpose the exclusion of persons of designated race or color from the ownership or occupancy of real property. Basic constitutional issues of obvious importance have been raised." After summarizing the facts and procedural history, he announced, "We hold that, in granting judicial enforcement of the restrictive covenants in these cases, the States have denied petitioners the equal protection of the laws and that, therefore, the action of the state courts cannot stand."[33]

Because Washington, DC, was (and remains) something of a federal colony and not a state, the Fourteenth Amendment did not apply there. The Court nonetheless ruled for the District of Columbia plaintiffs, holding that the Civil Rights Act of 1866, which Congress drafted in conjunction with the Fourteenth Amendment, prohibited racially restrictive covenants. "That statute by its terms," Vinson wrote, "requires that all citizens of the United States shall have the same right 'as is enjoyed by white citizens to inherit, purchase, lease, sell, hold and convey real and personal property.'"[34]

The Court did not rule that the covenants themselves were unconstitutional because private discrimination at the time was legal. Rather, it held that the racist private agreements were legally unenforceable—that is, meaningless. The Court also ruled that covenants based on religious discrimination were also unenforceable. And, importantly, the decisions were unanimous: all six justices who heard the cases ruled that the enforcement of racially restrictive covenants was unconstitutional. Thurgood Marshall told reporters that the ruling gave "thousands of prospective home buyers throughout the United States new courage and hope in the American form of government."[35]

1. Supreme Court justices pictured in the front row, left to right, are Felix Frankfurter, Hugo Black, Fred Vinson, Stanley Reed, and William O. Douglas. Justices pictured in the back row, left to right, are Tom Clark, Robert H. Jackson, Harold H. Burton, and Sherman Minton, ca. 1950. Photograph by Ackad Photographers. Courtesy of the Harry S. Truman Library and Museum, Independence, MO

2. President Harry S. Truman leaves after delivering a speech at the NAACP conference at the Lincoln Memorial. He is accompanied by (front row) Eleanor Roosevelt and Walter White, president of the NAACP, June 29, 1947. Photograph by Abbie Rowe, National Park Service. Courtesy of the Harry S. Truman Library and Museum, Independence, MO

3. A political cartoon by Jim Berryman entitled "All You Have to Do Is Pull It Together Again, Fred!" The cartoon addresses the appointment of Fred M. Vinson to become chief justice of the United States. Published ca. June 1946 by the *Washington Evening Star*. Courtesy of the Harry S. Truman Library and Museum, Independence, MO

4. The crowd on the south lawn of the White House, celebrating Fred M. Vinson's swearing-in as chief justice, June 24, 1946. Photograph by Abbie Rowe. Courtesy of the National Archives and Research Administration, Washington, DC

5. Dr. Luther H. Evans (left) watches Chief Justice Vinson and President Truman help to seal the enclosure containing the final leaf of the U.S. Constitution at a dedication ceremony held at the Library of Congress on Constitution Day, September 17, 1951. Courtesy of the Charters of Freedom Photographic Collection, National Institute of Standards and Technology Digital Collections, Gaithersburg, MD

6. Tom Clark being sworn in as an associate justice of the Supreme Court by Chief Justice Vinson, as President Truman and others observe in the White House Rose Garden, August 24, 1949. Photograph by Abbie Rowe. Courtesy of the National Archives and Research Administration, Washington, DC

7. Charles Sawyer is shown with his hand raised as he is sworn in as secretary of commerce by Justice Harold Burton. In the background are, left to right, Postmaster General Jesse Donaldson, unidentified, Attorney General Tom Clark, Secretary of State George Marshall, Secretary of the Treasury John W. Snyder, and Secretary of the Navy John L. Sullivan, May 6, 1948. Courtesy of the Harry S. Truman Library and Museum, Independence, MO

8. Indiana senator Sherman Minton in his office at the Capitol, June 11, 1940. Photograph by Harris & Ewing. Courtesy of Prints and Photographs Division, Library of Congress, Washington, DC

CHAPTER SIXTEEN

Justice Douglas and the 1948 Presidential Election

AFTER THE REPUBLICAN LANDSLIDE IN the 1946 midterm elections, Justice William O. Douglas became something of a stalking horse to Truman's chances of garnering the 1948 Democratic presidential nomination. In time, Douglas's simmering presidential ambitions would collide with Truman's seemingly dismal election hopes to force a showdown between two men who were at the time literally and figuratively thousands of miles apart.

* * *

July 9, 1948, began as a rare good day for Harry Truman's election prospects. For the third and final time, retired Army general Dwight D. Eisenhower declared that he would not become a candidate in the 1948 presidential election. Eisenhower, who was serving as president of Columbia University, sent a telegram to Democratic senator Claude Pepper of Florida that read in part: "Under no conditions will I be in the position of repudiating or even seeming to swerve from the letter or spirit of my prior announcements. I will not violate my own conception of my appropriate sphere of duty. No matter under what terms, conditions or premises a proposal might be couched, I would refuse to accept the nomination."[1]

Pepper released the telegram to the public, announcing that, in accord with Eisenhower's clearly expressed wishes, Pepper would not nominate him at the Democratic National Convention. Unbeknownst to Pepper and the public, Eisenhower's statement had been drafted by Army Secretary Kenneth Royall and Truman advisor Clark Clifford. With Truman's blessing, Clifford had privately beseeched Eisenhower to issue a statement to foreclose the possibility of his being nominated for president.[2] Eisenhower, who sought to end relentless speculation about his plans, agreed to do so.

Pepper told reporters that he had not decided whom he would support for the Democratic nomination but offered that Justice William O. Douglas would make a "great president." He added that he of course would support Truman if he won the nomination.[3]

New York City mayor William O'Dwyer and other prominent Democrats agreed that their "Draft Eisenhower" campaign was over. Unlike Pepper, however, they pledged their support to Truman before the convention. No one seemed to consider the possibility that Eisenhower might be a Republican. The general's refusal to consider accepting the Democratic nomination for president cleared the way for Truman to win his party's nomination on the first ballot.[4] To the dismay of most Democratic Party leaders, Truman had made it clear that he planned to accept the nomination, telling one fellow Missourian that he "was not brought up to run from a fight."[5] Truman deeply wanted to become what he plainly called "an elected president."[6]

Many Democratic delegates believed that Douglas could wrest the nomination from Truman, but he would have to resign his seat on the Court and campaign hard—neither of which Douglas wanted to do. Party insiders like former Roosevelt confidant Tommy "the Cork" Corcoran and Texas congressman Lyndon Johnson had all but given up on Douglas. As his Columbia Law School classmate federal judge Simon Rifkind put it, Douglas wanted to be president but "he just wanted the office handed to him."[7]

* * *

William O. Douglas was a man in a hurry when he was nominated and confirmed to the Supreme Court of the United States at the age of forty. Raised in poverty in Yakima, Washington, in 1925 Douglas graduated from Columbia, where he became a professor after a couple years of unsuccessful legal practice. In 1928 he began teaching at Yale Law School and remained there until joining the Securities and Exchange Commission in 1934. Douglas's Senate confirmation hearings, held four days after Franklin Roosevelt nominated him to the Supreme Court in 1939, lasted five minutes.[8]

From his earliest days on the Court, Douglas chafed at the sequestered professional life of a justice. Justice Hugo Black's law clerk and future acting U.S. solicitor general Walter Dellinger asked Douglas during the 1968–69 term whether, if given the chance to do it all over again, he would accept the Supreme Court nomination.

"Absolutely not!" Douglas roared. When another law clerk asked why not, he replied, "Because the Court as an institution is too peripheral, too much in the backwater on the Court. You're too far out of the action here."

But, the puzzled clerks wondered, what about the landmark cases that had revolutionized the nation? Justices united at the vanguard to support desegregation, free speech, and religious liberty.

"They're irrelevant. All of the action is elsewhere. All of the ability to affect action is elsewhere." Dellinger concluded, as many already had, that Douglas wanted to be president.[9] But by that time, the window on Douglas's political possibilities had closed.

* * *

Back in 1944, however, as Franklin Roosevelt prepared to run for an unprecedented fourth term as president, Douglas's political star was very much on the rise. He had served admirably as chairman of the Securities and Exchange Commission before becoming a Supreme Court justice, known for being unafraid to trust his individualist, western perspective on issues such as privacy and civil liberties. As Roosevelt's own physical decline deepened, he touted Douglas's political potiential, telling his advisors that Douglas had "the following of the liberal left wing of the American people; the same kind of people whom [outgoing Vice President Henry] Wallace had." Moreover, and perhaps more impressively to the patrician president, Douglas possessed "practical experience from the backwoods of the Northwest as a logger." The justice's rise from rural poverty to the Supreme Court would have undeniable "appeal at the polls."[10]

Despite being the president's first choice as a running mate, Douglas lost the 1944 Democratic nomination for vice president to Missouri senator Harry S. Truman. Roosevelt deferred to party powerbrokers who believed that Douglas, who had never held elective office and reveled in his libertine lifestyle, would prove to be at least as unpredictable as the vice president they were trying to replace.

Losing the Democratic nomination for vice president in 1944 was a devastating blow to Douglas. He wanted to be president and knew that Roosevelt was unlikely to survive another four years in office. Douglas's confidant Eliot Janeway admitted, "He really wanted it [in 1944] because he knew the situation with Roosevelt's health. Everyone did."[11] Truman's advisor Clark Clifford was good friends with Douglas, and he "had no doubt" that "Douglas wanted to be President." For years Douglas remained bitter that Roosevelt had not selected him to be vice president in 1944.[12] That would have been the sure bet he wanted to relinquish his lifetime tenure on the Court.

Economic considerations weighed heavily on Douglas's decision-making. Unlike Roosevelt or Truman, Douglas had grown up poor. As an adult, he struggled to support his wife, two children, and a traveling lifestyle on his government salary. His wife, Mildred, openly fretted that he would be unable to earn a living if he resigned from the Court to run for office and lost. Douglas remained keenly interested in becoming president but refused to relinquish his lifetime Court appointment to take a chance on a political campaign.

* * *

In February 1946, Truman invited Douglas to the White House for a leisurely lunch. They discussed the nation's natural resources and environment in considerable detail. Recognizing that Douglas was active in conservation efforts, Truman asked him to replace Harold Ickes as secretary of the interior. Douglas declined the offer before presenting the president with something of a counteroffer: He would leave the Supreme Court—and presumably not run against Truman in 1948—if the president made him secretary of state. This suggestion, according to Douglas, "was met with stony silence."[13]

Two and a half years later, on July 9, 1948, Douglas announced from his fishing cabin in Wallowa, Oregon, "I am not a candidate, have never been a candidate and don't plan to be a candidate." A reporter asked if he would accept the nomination if drafted. "I have no comment on that," Douglas demurred, still interested in winning the Democratic nomination so long as he did not have to campaign for it.[14] The fact that Truman had campaigned in western states just weeks earlier indicated that Douglas would have to fight for the nomination if he decided to run.

* * *

More than three thousand miles away at the Democratic National Convention in Philadelphia, party chairman J. Howard McGrath telephoned Truman to inform him that the party's powerbrokers could not agree on a vice-presidential candidate. Most of them either favored

Douglas or agreed not to oppose his candidacy. McGrath was asking the president to call Douglas and ask him to accept the nomination.

Truman asked Clark Clifford, who was a friend of Douglas's, to call the justice and ask him to join the ticket. Clifford was to impress upon him that Truman needed his help and really could win the election.

Back in Oregon, the National Forest Service alerted Douglas that he was needed on the telephone. He trekked to a telephone that he later described as "rather ancient and rickety, the telephone line being strung through many miles of forests and suspended from trees."[15]

After Clifford talked to Douglas, Truman asked, "How did he sound about it?"

"Dubious." Clifford told the president that he believed Douglas would decline the offer.

"Well, he respects Mrs. Roosevelt, so why don't you call her and ask if she will try and persuade Douglas to take the offer."[16]

Eleanor Roosevelt agreed to urge Douglas to accept the nomination for vice president. "I feel you are the best judge of where your services are most valuable," she wrote in a telegraph to one of the men her husband had nominated to the Court, "but you would be of great value and give some confidence in the party to liberals if you would accept. My confidence in your good judgment prevents my urging you to do anything but I want you to know that your acceptance would give hope to many for the future of a liberal Democratic Party."[17] Douglas remained noncommittal.

Frustrated and incredulous, Truman decided to call Douglas himself. Over the crackling phone line, Truman asked him to accept the Democratic nomination for vice president and become his running mate. Douglas asked if he could take the weekend to think about it. Truman agreed.

As the hours passed, Truman grew uncharacteristically anxious. He called Douglas twice more urging him to accept. Knowing how Douglas had revered Roosevelt, Truman told him, "I'm doing what FDR did to me. [You owe] it to the country to accept."[18] Douglas left the woods for a luxury hotel in Portland, where he claimed to be "in prayerful consideration of [Truman's] offer."[19]

Douglas waited until Monday, opening day of the Democratic National Convention, to relay his response. "I am very sorry," he told the president, "but I have decided not to get into politics. I do not think I should use the Court as a steppingstone."

"I am disappointed," Truman replied. "That's too bad."[20]

In his memoir, Douglas claimed, "In spite of the gloomy prediction of Truman's chances, I thought at the time he could and would win."[21] Almost certainly, this was untrue. Days after rejecting Truman's offer, Douglas told a close friend, "Truman isn't going to win anyway."[22] Douglas would not have declined to run on a national ticket that he thought would win. Long enamored with politics and bored with the slow pace of life on the bench, he entertained the notion of running for president not only in 1948 but again in 1952.[23] Neither time was he willing to relinquish his lifetime appointment in order to campaign for the nomination, and neither time did his candidacy gain any traction at the Democratic National Convention.

* * *

After Douglas's political aspirations collapsed, restlessness consumed his personal life. He married four women and divorced three of them in thirteen years. While in his mid-sixties he married a twenty-two-year-old and then a twenty-three-year-old, drank heavily, and, with the help of ghostwriters, produced thirty books, the sales of which helped him remain current on his considerable alimony payments.

Truman never believed Douglas's explanation. "Douglas says he can't quit the Supreme Court," he confided to his journal hours after talking to the justice. "Says no to my request that he take second place on the ticket with me. I'm inclined to give some credence to Tommy Corcoran's crack to Burt Wheeler that Douglas had said he could not be a number two man to a number two man."[24]

Shortly after Truman's extraordinary victory in November 1948, former Interior Secretary Harold Ickes told the president that Douglas remained interested in leaving the Court to serve as secretary of state. The president sharply retorted, "I used to like Bill Douglas but I am through with him. . . . I called him from Philadelphia to ask him to run for the Vice President. But he was afraid that I was not going to win and he declined to run. In politics a man has to take some chances and he would not take any."[25]

Years later Clifford's recollection buttressed Truman's real-time assessment of Douglas's motives. According to Clifford, Douglas "regarded

Harry Truman as an unlikely and accidental Chief Executive" who was unlikely to win election in his own right in 1948. Like Truman, Clifford wholly rejected Douglas's explanation for declining the vice-presidential nomination: "His rejection was based, in my opinion, almost entirely on the assumption that the Democratic ticket had no chance to win in November."[26] By the time William Douglas retired in 1975, he had served on the Court for more than thirty-five years—longer than any other justice.

CHAPTER SEVENTEEN

The Vinson Mission

ON SUNDAY, OCTOBER 3, 1948, one month before the presidential election, President Truman invited Chief Justice Vinson to the White House to discuss an urgent matter. Upon arriving, Vinson was ushered into the West Wing to meet privately with the president. He listened silently as Truman explained his proposal.

The United States and the Soviet Union were engaged in complex negotiations on the peaceful maintenance and use of atomic energy. Vinson knew from newspaper accounts that delegates to the United Nations were conducting most negotiations. Truman told him that a UN conference in Paris had just ended. The parties could not agree on a method of inspecting each others' atomic energy facilities. American negotiators were beginning to doubt that any enforceable agreement on atomic energy control could be reached. In their view, Truman told Vinson, Soviet negotiators seemed determined to prevent just such an agreement from being reached.

With UN negotiations at an impasse and all established diplomatic channels having failed, Truman believed that the parties had nearly "exhaust[ed] all traditional avenues of negotiation." It had become clear to him that, in the present framework, "the Russians would not trust either us or themselves to talk freely and frankly."[1] Diplomatic progress among the professional diplomats seemed unlikely.

So Truman asked Vinson to travel to Moscow to meet with Soviet premier Joseph Stalin to resolve the stalemate. It was a matter of national security and global nuclear safety. Truman compared the proposed mission to a trip taken by the lord chief justice of England and Wales, Viscount Reading, who traveled to the United States at the close of World War I to help smooth the strained relations between the two countries. As Truman remembered it, Viscount Reading's American mission was successful because of the lord chief justice's stature, his personal bearing, and the fact that he was removed from his nation's political and diplomatic operations. Truman believed that the mission he was proposing to Vinson would succeed for the same reasons.[2]

Truman offered advice to Vinson about how to succeed even while still trying to convince him to accept the assignment. "Play it by ear," he told his friend. The atomic stalemate appeared to Truman to be but a problem of trust. He wanted Vinson "to go to Moscow and see if he could not get Stalin to open up." Truman "had a feeling that Stalin might get over some of his inhibitions if he were to talk with our own chief justice."[3]

Vinson sat in stunned silence. Whether he thought Truman was proposing this trip out of political desperation, diplomatic naiveté, or some unfortunate combination of both, the chief justice considered it a bad idea. He did not want to go.

* * *

The Vinson mission idea had been hatched by two young Truman campaign staffers who were concerned both with Truman's dismal political prospects and with America's deteriorating relations with the Soviet Union. They privately suggested to appointments secretary Matt Connelly that the president dispatch the chief justice to Moscow to meet privately with Stalin. Connelly bypassed the White House, the State Department, and campaign senior advisors to present the prospect directly to Truman, who immediately embraced the idea.

As soon as they learned of the plan, Clark Clifford and other close advisors desperately tried to change Truman's mind. The idea of inserting the chief justice into delicate international negotiations about which he knew little more than an ordinary American citizen sparked "enormous tensions" among the president's closest aides.[4] In the end, however, the president would not be dissuaded.[5] Truman held immeasurable faith in Vinson's abilities. He was convinced that the present environment of distrust between the West and the Communist bloc necessitated "a totally new approach with the right man to make it."[6]

* * *

Quickly filling the silence, Truman assured Vinson that his mission would not interfere with official diplomatic efforts being led by Secretary of State George Marshall, the retired five-star Army general whose reputation exceeded Truman's and Vinson's both at home and abroad. Marshall was in Paris working to resolve the UN stalemate. Truman intended to secure support from Marshall for the proposed meeting and then convince America's allies that it was in their best interests as well. If Marshall agreed to it, then European diplomats would likely fall in line. Truman intended to telephone Marshall in Paris. He assured Vinson that this was a mere formality, saying, "I am sure that he will be for it, as he is always for any constructive move to advance the cause of peace."[7] The president would soon learn just how wrong he was about Marshall's response.

When Vinson finally spoke, he expressed his reservations delicately but firmly. Disregarding for now the question of whether the president's request was inspired by political or diplomatic necessity, Vinson considered the matter not as Truman's confidant but as the chief justice of the United States. Truman had made clear that it was Vinson's position as chief justice that compelled him to believe that Vinson would be successful where other gifted men in government had failed. Confirmed to a lifetime appointment, the chief justice was politically responsible to no one. Had Vinson not been chief justice, then Truman, as much as he respected Vinson, would not have asked him to travel to Moscow. This fact was enough for Vinson to decline Truman's invitation.

Vinson reminded Truman that, along with his predecessor, Harlan Fiske Stone, he had taken a hard stance against justices accepting government assignments beyond their judicial duties. It would be hypocritical for him to travel to Moscow to meet with Stalin. In fact, it would be improper for the chief justice to meet with any foreign leader at the president's behest. Particularly with the presidential election one month away, as Truman later put it, Vinson argued that he "could not break his own rule."[8]

When Vinson finished, it was the president's turn to sit in silence, which he did, expectantly.

In retrospect, it seems that Vinson's extensive experience in government might have hindered his judgment at this crucial moment. Unlike earlier chief justices such as John Marshall, Roger Taney, and Charles Evan Hughes, Vinson, in this hour at least, seemed not to have believed himself to be the leader of a coequal branch of government. If he did, then his answer belied his belief when, after a long pause, he replied, "Mr. President, as chief justice I must decline to undertake this mission to Moscow. But if you make it as a presidential request, I shall have a clear duty to comply."

"I am sorry, Fred, to do this to you, but in the interest of the country and the peace of the world I am compelled to request you to go."

"I'll be ready in a few days."[9]

* * *

Truman was anxious to dispatch Vinson to Moscow as soon as possible. He instructed White House press secretary Charlie Ross to request free airtime from the major broadcast networks for a nonpolitical presidential address. With the election less than a month away, network executives were skeptical and pressed for some information on the president's speech. Ross confidentially informed them of Vinson's planned mission to Moscow. They agreed to cede their airwaves to the president.

Amazingly, Truman requested television airtime before consulting with Secretary of State Marshall. The president reached Marshall in Paris and realized during an intense teletyped conference that he had made a mistake. The most respected and popular member of his cabinet was incredulous. Marshall declared that Truman should have consulted him before meeting with Vinson, much less authorizing White House officials to negotiate with television executives. He explained that his proposed meeting would directly affect the multinational efforts he and his staff were leading in France. Western nations were presenting the Soviets with a united front that the proposed unilateral meeting threatened to crack.

Truman agreed to cancel the Vinson mission. Realizing how deeply he had offended Marshall, whom he not only respected but admired, he asked the retired general to return to Washington to discuss the matter in person. Truman would leave the campaign trail, sacrificing personal campaign time in the critical states of Pennsylvania, New Jersey, and his opponent's home state of New York, so that he and Marshall could meet in person.[10] Although Truman arrived back in Washington just a half hour before his secretary of state's plane was scheduled to land, he made the exceptional gesture of greeting Marshall at National Airport.[11] Marshall arrived at 10:10 in the morning after having flown home on the plane normally reserved for the president.[12]

* * *

By then, however, news of Vinson's planned private meeting with Stalin had spread beyond the few network executives whom White House officials had told. On October 8, reporters revealed that Truman, against the vehement objections of his closest advisors, had been planning to dispatch Vinson to Moscow to meet privately with Stalin in a dramatic attempt to resolve postwar disputes between the West and the Soviet bloc. Television executives confirmed that they had agreed to grant Truman one half-hour of free airtime but stressed that he would have been speaking as president and not as a candidate.[13] When correspondents asked Vinson whether reports of the mission were true, the chief justice said only, "I have made no such engagement."[14]

Just before six o'clock the following evening, after Truman had met twice with Marshall and Undersecretary of State Robert A. Lovett, the White House released a statement in which the president announced that he had canceled the Vinson mission to Moscow. "Secretary Marshall described to me the situation which we faced in Paris," his statement read, "and, in light of his report and the possibilities of misunderstanding to which any unilateral action, however desirable otherwise, could lead at present, I decided not to take this step."[15]

The statement did little to calm nerves in federal Washington or in Western capitals abroad.[16] Nearly everyone agreed that the president of the United States should not have needed to meet with the secretary of state to realize that the mission was a terrible idea. Marshall personally received six teletyped reports from America's allies expressing their displeasure. "They are keyed up to a very high degree," he recognized.[17] The *Guardian* newspaper captured England's national sentiment in an editorial quoted by American newspapers: "Mr. Truman [acted] irresponsibly by all the diplomatic rules and the rules of good faith between allies, but his excellent intentions are not questioned, much as his insight into Russian (and allied) psychology may be."[18]

Soviet media provided a lonely and unwelcome defense of the Vinson mission. State-sponsored journalists charged Marshall's State Department with having "openly sabotaged a direct attempt by President Truman to reopen direct talks with the Soviet Union through a special ambassador." Suspicious of the United Nations negotiations, leaders in Moscow welcomed a unilateral meeting with the United States. Russian reporters charged Western powers with using the United Nations "as a stage for anti-Soviet agitation."[19]

Marshall was correct in noting that the Kremlin had been trying in vain to crack the Western powers' united front at the Paris negotiations. In news of Vinson's aborted mission, the Soviets saw an opportunity to exploit what appeared to be a separation between members of the same branch of government in the most powerful Western nation at the table. To this end, Soviets alleged that the cleavage in the Truman administration was not confined to a personal feud between Marshall and Truman. Rather, the rift was between the entire U.S. government and the State Department, whose personnel "agitate for a new war against the Soviet Union, who consider the atomic bomb the key for their domination of the globe, who frustrate the Council of Foreign Ministers."[20]

Marshall denied reports of a rift between him and the president, claiming that there was "no foundation" to them. He reminded journalists that such unsubstantiated reports were not without effect. They "can do no good and certainly do a great deal of harm," he declared, "and I deplore them."[21]

Career diplomats working in Paris were acutely unnerved by the abandoned mission. They worried, as one State Department official told the *New York Times*, that Truman's campaign staff would continue to meddle in international affairs. American diplomats worried that, as the election approached, the campaign would grow more desperate, until Truman embarked on a plan that would be, as one official described, "even worse than the Vinson scheme."[22] Despite concerns at the State Department, Vinson's canceled mission to Moscow died a relatively quiet death in the kinetic postwar diplomatic world.

What astonished Democratic Party operatives was that the mission died a similarly quiet political death. With less than one month remaining before America's first presidential election since the Allies' victory in World War II, the Republican ticket of Thomas Dewey and Earl Warren pointedly refused to take issue with Truman's idea of dispatching the chief justice to meet with Joseph Stalin. Truman confidante Clark Clifford considered the proposed Vinson mission to be "the worst mistake of the Truman campaign," the sort of major "mistake which could have cost [Truman] the election—had Dewey exploited it."[23] But when news of the mission broke, Dewey refused to even comment on what appeared to be the biggest foreign relations blunder of Truman's presidency.[24]

Conversely, South Carolina governor and States' Rights Democratic Party presidential candidate Strom Thurmond wasted no time in chastising the president. He alleged that the ill-fated plan "conclusively proves that [Truman] is incompetent to handle our foreign relations and that his incompetency endangers the peace of the world." It seemed clear to Thurmond that the idea "was hatched up by the political guard of the White House as a spectacular move to bolster the president's sagging campaign."[25]

In October 1948 Dewey led Truman in every reliable poll. The man whom most Americans expected to be elected president in a month decided that exploiting Truman's mistake would buttress Soviet claims of disunity within the United States' government.[26] An internal Dewey campaign memorandum dated October 12 expressed senior advisors' belief that Truman's mistake was its own best evidence of the president's ineptitude: it was "an error of judgment of such proportions that it could alone be sufficient to swing the election, if the contest were in doubt."[27] Republican strategists saw little to gain by attacking Truman on the failed plan.

Dewey was content to make oblique references to Vinson's assignment. In Pittsburgh, he pledged to lead a government that would "unfailingly back up the work of [our] representatives in the United Nations." At events in Erie, Pennsylvania, and Rochester, New York, Dewey told supporters, "We need a government that knows where it is going. We must build a foreign policy which stands firmly and consistently upon the rock of freedom, which supports our friends wherever they are, and supports our representatives all over the world, unfailingly and strongly." Unfortunately for him, Dewey's criticism was too polite by half because, to the dismay of his campaign workers, most audience members seemed oblivious to the fact that he was drawing a constrast with the president.[28]

In Kentucky, Dewey clarified his attacks on Truman's ability to lead America into the new postwar world order. "Your sons and mine," he proclaimed in Lexington, "have a right to know that they have a government that not only wants peace but knows how to work for peace; a president who will consistently, day in and day out, support the people who are working for peace as our official representatives without undercutting them anywhere."[29] Dewey still refrained from directly assailing the Vinson mission as the lapse in judgment that most observers considered it to be. Dewey's campaign advisors were so confident of victory that they treated Truman's foreign policy blunder as if their candidate already had been elected.

To be fair, one can hardly blame them for feeling confident of victory in October 1948. The *Baltimore Sun* reported that Dewey's "election [was] as much assured as that of any candidate has ever been at this stage in an American political campaign."[30] Nationally syndicated columnist Thomas L. Stokes urged the president to "just stay home," because "if Truman is reelected he will thereby become the miracle man of this crazy era."[31] Even the State Department's *Voice of America* radio broadcast, which was beamed across Western Europe and Communist-controlled Eastern Europe, was telling listeners that Dewey would probably win the presidential election. According to every reliable poll, *Voice of America* newscasters reported, Dewey "holds a substantial lead over the President."[32]

Perhaps Governor Dewey would have been well-served to listen to *Voice of America*, which, after reporting on his remarkable lead, reminded listeners, "But nothing is certain—least of all an election in a democratic country."[33] In Lexington, Kentucky, journalists described the crowds at Dewey's campaign events as "considerably smaller than those that welcomed President Truman about ten days ago." In Louisville, for example, Dewey attracted roughly fifteen thousand supporters while Truman addressed a crowd of forty thousand.[34]

*　*　*

Over the course of what became known as his Whistlestop Tour, Truman traveled 31,700 miles and spoke to 352 audiences. He kept a meticulous routine aboard the armored presidential train car *Ferdinand Magellan*. The president awoke between five and six each morning and enjoyed a breakfast of eggs, toast, orange juice, and coffee while reviewing notes for the day's speeches and meetings. If there was time after breakfast, he stepped off the train to take a walk with a couple of aides and several Secret Service agents. In one sentence, *Time* magazine captured a typical day in the president's extraordinary schedule: "Between breakfast and midnight that day, Harry Truman traveled 500 miles by train, 141 by automobile and bus, made 11 speeches in 15 different towns, changed his clothes eight times, and met 250 politicians, labor leaders, and civic dignitaries."[35] Truman's daily campaign schedule would be frenetic even by twenty-first-century standards.

On October 29, less than a week before election day, President Truman delivered a lively address to African American voters in Harlem's Dorrance Brooks Square after accepting an award from the Interdenominational Ministers' Alliance. Drawing a direct line from "the way in which the

Declaration of Independence was drawn up" to his own Committee on Civil Rights, Truman reminded voters that when Congress refused to act on the committee's recommendations, he "went ahead and did what the president can do, unaided by Congress." He issued an executive order desegregating the armed forces. He ordered the Department of Justice to join the legal battle to eliminate racially restrictive covenants because the "promise of equal rights and equal opportunity for all mankind . . . is among the highest purposes of government." In his opponent's home state, Truman closed with a rousing promise "to keep moving toward this goal with every ounce of strength and determination that I have."[36]

In Lansing, Michigan, more than 100,000 people packed into Cadillac Square to greet the president. "These are critical times for labor and for all who work," he told the enormous crowd. "There is great danger ahead. . . . If, in this next election, you get a Congress and an administration friendly to labor, you have much to hope for. If you get an administration and a Congress unfriendly to labor, you have much to fear, and you had better look out."[37]

Along with African Americans and White union workers, farmers were crucial voters in the electoral coalition Truman was fighting to assemble. He reminded farmers in New Mexico that thirteen times as many farms in their state had electricity as did in 1932. "If there is any farmer or miner or workingman who is foolish enough to want to turn the clock back," he insisted, "he ought to vote the Republican ticket. Otherwise, he had better vote for himself when he votes for me."[38]

Finally, on the eve of Election Day, Truman addressed the nation from his home in Missouri, telling radio listeners, "Now it is up to you, the people of this great Nation, to decide what kind of government you want—whether you want a government for all the people or government for just the privileged few." He acheived a plain-spoken eloquence: "Go to the polls tomorrow and vote your convictions, your hopes, and your faith—your faith in the future of a nation that, under God—can lead the world to freedom and peace."[39]

* * *

On election day, Truman defeated Republican Thomas Dewey, States' Rights Democrat Strom Thurmond, and Progressive Party candidate Henry Wallace in the biggest upset in American political history. He had won the presidency in his own right. Truman won 303 Electoral College votes compared to Dewey's 189 and Thurmond's 39. He won the popular vote by over 2 million ballots, winning states on both coasts and even in the South, where Thurmond had focused his campaign. (Wallace nearly matched Thurmond's 1,169,021 popular votes but, unlike the "Dixiecrat" candidate, did not carry any states.) Truman carried California despite the fact that Dewey's running mate, Earl Warren, was California's governor. Truman won Texas and Massachusetts, Georgia and Montana. His election victory was as resounding as it was historic.

Like all successful politicians, Harry Truman was lucky. His opponent's failure to capitalize on the canceled Vinson mission was perhaps the most underrated stroke of good luck in Truman's political career. To be sure, Truman completely outworked Dewey on the campaign trail, holding several events each day and taking strong stances on issues while Dewey seemed so intent on avoiding controversy and error that caution consumed his campaign. Regardless of what the polls indicated, it was political malpractice for Governors Dewey and Warren, in the final weeks of a national campaign, to fail to capitalize on the president's lapse in judgment. Decades later, Clark Clifford still believed that had Dewey and Warren done so, they very well might have won the election.[40]

In his second term, Harry Truman would nominate two more men to the Supreme Court, both of them longtime friends.

* * *

Despite the fact that the trip never happened, President Truman remained grateful to Chief Justice Vinson for having accepted the mission. In a 1950 letter to Bess, Truman wrote, "He didn't want to go, but he said, 'I'm your man to do what you want me to do for the welfare of the country.' How many Congressmen, Senators, even cabinet secretaries would have said that?"[41] The two close friends discounted the liabilities of loyalty in federal Washington.

CHAPTER EIGHTEEN

Justice Tom Clark

ON JULY 19, 1949, FIFTY-NINE-YEAR-OLD Justice Frank Murphy died of coronary thrombosis, a heart attack, succumbing to the disease that had plagued him for years. He had known for months that his end was growing near but, in the words of Chief Justice Vinson, Murphy had "walked in the great shadow—unafraid."[1] Murphy's brother George, a judge of the Recorder's Court in Detroit, was at his bedside at Henry Ford Hospital when William Francis Murphy died, just an hour after Father Henry Kenowski administered the sacrament of Anointing of the Sick.[2] Murphy's family, friends, and fellow justices knew how much his health had deteriorated but his death shocked most Americans. He had served on the Court since 1940.

A graduate of the University of Michigan Law School, Murphy was elected mayor of Detroit and governor of Michigan before Franklin Roosevelt tapped him to serve as attorney general of the United States. Murphy was a confirmed bachelor and a teetotaler during some of Washington's most bourbon and branchwater–soaked years. After Justice Pierce Butler's death, Roosevelt told Murphy that he intended to nominate him to the Court, but the attorney general demurred, claiming that he did not feel qualified to be a justice. Nevertheless, Butler had been a Catholic and the politically astute Roosevelt was intent on replacing him with Murphy, a similarly devout Catholic who had become an altar boy at age seven.

Murphy accepted the nomination but confided in a letter to his former parish priest, "I am not too happy about going on the Court. A better choice could have been made." Lest his misgivings be dismissed as a nominee's requisite humility, he added, "I fear that my work will be mediocre there while on the firing line where I have been trained to action I could do much better."[3] Frank Murphy was more gifted in politics than in jurisprudence and would not pretend otherwise.

On the day after Murphy's death, the *Washington Post*'s editors wrote, in an editorial extolling his "devotion to human rights and humanitarian spirit," that "his record might well have been more notable if he had not attempted to reconcile his humanitarianism with a judicial role."[4] At least one reader took issue with that assessment of Murphy's nine years of work on the Court. In doing so, the reader provided what remains perhaps the most precise assessment of Murphy's tenure. "The memory of Mr. Justice Murphy," Howard M. Schott of Washington, DC, wrote, "will serve ever to remind us that justice need not be tempered either with mercy or morality, but that it springs directly from them both."[5] Indeed, one of Murphy's finest moments on the Court was his dissenting opinion in the 1944 case *Korematsu v. United States*. In his first paragraph, he wrote that the Roosevelt administration's policy of forcing Americans of Japanese ancestry to live in camps was not only unconstitutional but "falls into the ugly abyss of racism."[6]

Throughout his tenure, however, rumors swirled that Murphy leaned on his law clerks to draft most of his opinions, so much so that others caustically referred to them with the honorific "Mr. Justice" before their last names.[7] Both Chief Justices Stone and Vinson were careful not to burden Murphy with writing more opinions than he—or his clerks—could bear.

Because Murphy had replaced Butler and was known for his religious observance, senators and pundits began to speak of a "Catholic seat" on the Court. At least one of his obituaries declared, "He was one of the nation's outstanding Catholic laymen."[8]

Before his death, Murphy disavowed any notion of a "Catholic seat" on the Court, saying, "As I see it, the view that one of a certain faith should be succeeded by another of like faith is entirely unworthy. . . . Members of the Supreme Court are not called upon or expected to represent any single interest group, area, or class of persons. They speak for the country as a whole."[9] Truman agreed and had no intention of allowing religion to play a role in his selection process. Until he nominated Murphy's replacement, however, nearly everyone presumed that the nominee would be Catholic.

When asked for thoughts on Murphy's passing, Attorney General Tom Clark told reporters that the Bill of Rights, in particular, was "close to the heart" of the late justice, who "never lost the opportunity to insist on the enforcement of its great guarantees of liberty."[10] Clark had no idea that Truman was considering him to take Murphy's place on the Court.

* * *

Just a few days after Murphy's death, the president summoned his attorney general to the White House. "Well," Truman told Clark, "I was just thinking about the vacancy up in the Court." Clark was well-prepared for the meeting, having prepared a short list of well-respected—and Catholic—lawyers and jurists. But before Clark could begin, Truman excitedly relayed his plan: "I am thinking of a package job and wished to know what you thought of it. You don't have to tell me today. I want you to go and talk to this man and see what you both think."[11]

When Clark had accepted Truman's nomination to become attorney general, Truman asked him to "pick out somebody for solicitor general who, in the event you go, I'll have another man—I won't have to look all over the country and wait around to get me another man to be attorney general."[12] Now Truman wanted to promote a former solicitor general to attorney general and nominate Clark to the Supreme Court. Senator J. Howard McGrath, a Rhode Island Democrat who had served a year as Truman's solicitor general on Clark's recommendation, would become attorney general. But McGrath was also serving as chairman of the Democratic National Committee—and he was Catholic. "Do you remember when I appointed you," Truman continued, "why I told you to get somebody [for solicitor general] who would be a good man to succeed you? And I think he would be, and I don't think it's good to have the chairman of the [Democratic National] Committee to be in an official [administration] position, so I'm going to put Bill Boyle in the chairmanship. I want you to go and talk to Howard and you all let me know."[13]

With the political press abuzz about the vacant "Catholic seat" on the Court, the Roman Catholic Senator McGrath was so devastated to learn that Truman had not selected him for the nomination that he refused the invitation to serve as attorney general. After reconsidering a few days later, McGrath agreed to take the position, resigning his Senate seat with the hope that his proven loyalty would earn him the nomination for the next Supreme Court vacancy.[14] With his self-styled "package job" complete, Truman announced at a press conference his intent to nominate

Attorney General Tom Clark to the Supreme Court and Senator Harold McGrath to lead the Department of Justice.

*　*　*

Believing that his and Clark's legal views were aligned, Vinson had urged Truman to nominate Clark. The chief justice was finding it more difficult than he expected to bridge the chasm between the Court's factions. Three factors combined to make unifying the Court so challenging.

First, and most important, the justices disagreed on fundamental questions of constitutional law. Roosevelt's nominees to the Court were unanimous only in their agreement that New Deal legislation was constitutional. Once that became settled doctrine, their philosophical unity evaporated.[15] In the post–New Deal era, there were three blocs on the Court: one of Black, Douglas, Murphy, and Rutledge; a second two-man block of Frankfurter and Jackson; and a third comprised of Reed, Burton, and Vinson. Before Vinson joined the Court, Reed and Burton tended to vote with Frankfurter and Jackson.

Second, as Jackson's Nuremberg missive made clear, some of the justices personally disliked each other so much that their disdain sometimes clouded their professional judgment. One of Jackson's law clerks admitted, "I think how he felt about Justice Douglas had some effect in some of his votes."[16] There was a period, according to one of Vinson's law clerks, when Frankfurter simply refused to sign onto a Vinson opinion.[17]

The third and most direct reason why Vinson proved unable to narrow the Court's divisions was that the Roosevelt appointees did not consider the man Truman had nominated as chief justice to be their intellectual peer. It was one of the few ideas on which they could agree. Just two weeks into Vinson's first term, Frankfurter asked Reed, Vinson's fellow Kentuckian, for his honest opinion of the new chief. Reed, who was not known to labor in the Court's intellectual vanguard, answered, "He is just like me, except that he is less well-educated and has not had as many opportunities."[18] When Douglas remarked, "Truman seemed to like picking mediocre men," he did not exempt the chief justice.[19] Frankfurter seemed to hold Vinson in remarkably low regard, describing him as "confident and easy-going and sure and shallow."[20]

The justices' assessment surprised few observers. In January 1947 Arthur Schlesinger, Jr., wrote in *Fortune* magazine, "It will be hard for

[Vinson] to cope intellectually with men like Black and Frankfurter: his mind does not move fast in the same way." If he was to reduce the number of swiping dissents and pointed concurrences, Vinson would have "to influence the Court by a certain massive instinct for practicality."[21]

Fortunately, Vinson possessed just such an instinct. He was a skilled retail politician and, like any successful federal politician of that era, was well versed in the art of patronage. On the Supreme Court there was no patronage—but there were opinions to be assigned. When the chief justice voted with the majority, he selected who wrote the majority opinion. When the chief justice voted with the minority, the most senior justice in the majority chose who wrote for the Court. Vinson voted with the majority in 86 percent of cases.[22] He exercised considerable control over the vast majority of opinions because he chose who wrote them.

Vinson continued Hughes's and Stone's practice of assigning opinions only to justices who were current on their work. Those with overdue opinions received no new assignments. Justices Frankfurter, Rutledge, and Burton were slow workers. Frankfurter particularly fell far behind on his work. Rather than try to complete his assigned opinions more quickly, Frankfurter focused his extraordinary energies into drafting concurring opinions when he voted with the majority. As a result, he had fewer opportunities to write for the Court than his intellect and work ethic otherwise would have commanded. From 1941 to 1954, during the tenures of Stone and Vinson, Frankfurter wrote more than twice as many concurring opinions as the next closest justice and dissented more than any other justice.[23] Burton was scarcely more efficient, often working in his office until well past midnight. Douglas, who was a remarkably efficient writer, described Burton as "painfully slow in his work."[24]

Unlike the previous two chief justices, Vinson habitually assigned the most significant and interesting cases to his colleagues. (The desegregation cases were notable exceptions.) Ending the practice of reserving the newspaper-headline cases for the chief justice garnered him goodwill on the Court. It allowed him to preserve majorities. Justices knew that Vinson was not inclined to assign major cases based on how closely their opinions hued to his. He instead selected writers according to their apparent ability to maintain the majority established at the conference. "For example," one of his clerks explained, "he would say now if I assign

Bill [Douglas] to this, then he'll write such and such an opinion and you might lose Jackson or Burton. So I think what I'll do is assign [it] to [Jackson] and Burton may be able to go along."[25]

He also sought to disperse the Court's most significant decisions as evenly as possible among all nine members. To this end, Vinson kept in his office a large nine-columned chart listing which opinions had been assigned to which justice and when each assignment was completed. His law clerks recalled, "In the vast bulk of cases, the Chief's sole motivation was the equitable sharing of the work load."[26] The slow-working justices impeded Vinson's effort to divide case assignments evenly. Black and Douglas were the fastest writers on the Court, and so, despite Vinson's ideological disagreement with the two liberals, he often assigned cases to them.

Not all of the justices appreciated Vinson's willingness to distribute the most important cases as evenly as possible. Frankfurter concluded that the chief justice was reluctant to "tak[e] the initiative on questions before the Court." By assigning the most consequential cases to associate justices, Frankfurter believed, Vinson was abdicating his right and responsibility to employ the "intrinsic authority as the position of the chief justice gives."[27]

The only cases in which Vinson regularly exercised his prerogative as chief justice to write for the Court were the civil rights cases. He retained these opinions for himself. His successor, Earl Warren, would continue Vinson's practice of writing the civil rights decisions.

Aside from the cases affirming African Americans' constitutional rights, Vinson's opinions have largely receded from national memory. He served as chief justice for seven years. The paucity of his opinions betrayed a lack of interest in writing them. Indeed, it became something of an open secret in federal Washington that Vinson did not draft his opinions himself, preferring to assign the research and writing to his clerks after explaining to them his position on the legal questions involved. He then revised their drafts. The result was that Vinson's opinions varied widely in quality and craftsmanship.[28]

Judicial historians cite Vinson's dearth of written opinions as evidence that he was a substandard chief justice. Sometimes an entire term would pass without him assigning a significant case to himself. While there may be merit to the notion that the chief justice should write for the Court more often than Vinson did, this criticism ignores the important fact that Vinson almost invariably voted with the majority.[29] He therefore was able to choose who would write the Court's opinion in most cases. Writing was not where his talents or power lay. In Justices Black, Douglas, Frankfurter, and Jackson, he served alongside several of the most exceptional writers ever to serve on the Court, and Vinson assigned opinions to them as frequently as possible.

* * *

Public reaction to Tom Clark's nomination differed drastically from the reaction to Truman's first two nominees. While Harold Burton's selection was hailed as a show of bipartisanship by the new president and Vinson's nomination was praised as the elevation of a proven consensus-builder, Clark's nomination immediately sparked controversy. He received the support of his home state senators, Tom Connally and Lyndon Johnson of Texas, in addition to that of numerous federal judges and four former presidents of the American Bar Association.[30] But theirs were lonesome voices amid a chorus of concern about Clark's qualifications, record, and closeness to the president.

Some of Clark's harshest opponents were those who purported to know him best. In an article he wrote for the *New Republic*, Truman's former secretary of the interior, Harold Ickes, called his past cabinet colleague "a second-rate political hack who has known what backs to slap and when." Ickes charged that Clark was "an inconsequential lawyer" who was "the least able of the attorneys general." Serving as a Supreme Court justice "requires legal learning, wide vision and intellectual qualities that, if possessed by Mr. Clark, have never been capable of detection." O. John Rogge, who had served as assistant attorney general under Tom Clark, testified against his former boss at Clark's confirmation hearing. Rogge told members of the Senate Judiciary Committee that Clark possessed "neither the stature, integrity or ability" to be a Supreme Court justice.[31]

Despite the Truman administration's relatively positive record on civil rights, African American leaders were divided on Clark's confirmation. Actor and activist Paul Robeson found Clark's legal record troubling. "Attorney General Clark has winked at Jim Crow and white supremacy tyranny," he charged, "and has refused to take action against the lynchers and oppressors of the Negro people."[32] Robeson was among those who contended that Truman should have nominated an African American such as Harvard Law School alumni Charles Hamilton Houston or William Hastie.

William L. Patterson of the Civil Rights Congress testified before the judiciary committee, "Justice Taney held that a Negro held no rights that a white man was bound to respect. It is our belief that Tom Clark has accepted that dictum." Patterson then tilted his ire toward the president, who would not have won the 1948 election without the support of most African American voters: "The nomination of Tom Clark for the Supreme Court constituted a gratuitous insult thrown in the face of 15,000,000 Negro citizens, and a green light to their white-superiority infested enemies."[33] In his testimony, the national commander of the United Negro and Allied Veterans of America, George B. Murphy, Jr., echoed Patterson's concerns.[34]

Seeking to counter these voices, judiciary committee chairman Senator Pat McCarran of Nevada read into the record a letter from NAACP counsel Thurgood Marshall. By then Marshall was a widely respected constitutional lawyer known for leading the legal battle against segregation. Journalists reported that Truman was considering nominating him to the federal bench.[35] Marshall wrote to Clark, "All of us will miss you as Attorney General but are confident that you will carry with you your determination to enforce the Constitution and laws of this country without regard to race, creed or color. You have our sincerest best wishes."[36] McCarran also noted that Clark had recently received an award from the Washington, DC, branch of the NAACP.

Implicit in most criticisms of Truman's selection was dismay that the president had again decided to nominate one of his friends to the Court. Critics of Clark's nomination might have been apoplectic had they known the truth: at this point, Truman was considering *only* his personal friends to fill Supreme Court vacancies. After learning of Frank Murphy's death, Truman did not ask his aides to prepare a list of possible nominees nor did he bother to review the list of names Clark had personally assembled. Truman considered just two men: Tom Clark and Judge Sherman Minton of the U.S. Court of Appeals for the Seventh Circuit—each of whom had been Truman's friend since his days in the Senate.[37]

Even by Truman's exacting standards, Clark had proven to be an exceptionally loyal cabinet member. He strongly supported the administration's civil rights agenda as well as its government loyalty initiatives. During Truman's incredible 1948 campaign, Clark outworked every other cabinet member on the campaign trail, sometimes seeming like the only administration official aside from Truman who believed that the president would win.

Almost as important to Truman as Clark's loyalty was the fact that Chief Justice Vinson, whom Truman trusted absolutely, wanted Clark on the Court. Vinson trusted that Clark's legal perspective was similar to his own. It was clear by now that Fred Vinson would not become the unifying chief justice that Truman and litigators across the ideological spectrum had hoped he would. Under Vinson's stewardship the Court remained as sharply divided as it had been during Chief Justice Stone's tenure. The difference was that, in the wake of Robert Jackson's public letter from Germany, the justices' disagreements once again were kept private. The chief would welcome another needed, reliable vote, and he urged Truman to nominate Clark.[38]

* * *

Judge Sherman Minton arrived for a meeting with the president during the afternoon of July 26, 1949. For eight years, the Hoosier had performed well on the federal appellate bench. Surreptitiously entering through the west basement door to avoid being noticed by the press, fifty-eight-year-old Minton almost certainly expected to learn that his old friend planned to nominate him to take Murphy's place on the Court.

In the West Wing, Truman and Minton discussed several of the Court's recent decisions, with the judge confiding his belief that only Vinson and Black wrote consistently lucid opinions.

Truman then told Minton that he intended to nominate Tom Clark to the Court. He knew that Minton was hoping for the nomination and that the judge's name had been bandied about in newspaper columns portending to predict the nominee. He wanted to tell Minton personally that he had selected Clark.[39] Minton was deeply disappointed.

* * *

Despite the public furor, cries of cronyism, and unusually harsh testimony against the nominee, the Senate confirmed Tom Clark by a vote of seventy-three to eight. Republican senators decided against organizing a formal, party-line opposition to Clark's nomination. Senator Robert Taft explained that senators were free to vote against confirmation, "but we decided it was not a matter of party policy."[40]

Republican judiciary committee member Senator Homer Ferguson of Michigan, who called Clark's nomination "transparently political," wanted the committee to call Clark to testify but the committee did not.[41] Clark would have been the third Supreme Court nominee to testify before the judiciary committee after Harlan Fiske Stone in 1925 and Felix Frankfurter in 1939. Ferguson lambasted the committee's decision: "To confirm Mr. Clark by sharp parliamentary tactics can be neither in the public interest nor to Mr. Clark's benefit. As a justice of the Supreme Court he will forever be barred from replying to questions that should not remain unanswered."[42]

In the end, Ferguson and seven of his fellow Republicans voted against Clark's confirmation to protest the committee's refusal to call him to testify. Taft called the committee's decision not to summon Clark "utterly unjustifiable, arbitrary and outrageous." Vermont senator Ralph Flanders expressed his belief that Clark would make "an excellent judge" but also voted against confirmation to protest the committee's procedures.[43] These eight Republicans' votes against Clark suggested that future Supreme Court nominees would be called to testify before the Senate Judiciary Committee.

* * *

On August 24, 1949, an ebullient crowd of more than three hundred—including Clark's extended family members, friends, administration officials, and congressional leaders—gathered on the White House Rose Garden lawn. The eight Republican senators who had opposed Clark's confirmation attended to show that their opposition was not at all personal.[44] Washington's notorious August heat and humidity could not stifle the attendees' excitement.

Just after two o'clock in the afternoon, Tom C. Clark took his place on the White House steps with President Truman at his side.[45] Before Clark stood Chief Justice Vinson, wearing his judicial robe and holding the Bible.[46] Happily standing with the president and chief justice on the portico were Clark's wife, Mary; their sixteen-year-old daughter, Mimi; and Mimi's older brother, Ramsey, with his new bride, who, according to the society pages, wore a dress colored "the palest of aqua with a natural colored straw hat on her fair hair."[47]

The president, dressed in a smartly tailored suit and pressed pocket square, personally handed Clark his signed commission.[48] "For the last time, Mr. Attorney General," Truman said with a flourish, "I hand you a commission as justice of the Supreme Court of the United States. We have had a great attorney general for the last four years and we will have a great justice of the court from now on. I present to you your wonderful chief."

Vinson asked in his baritone, "Mr. Clark, are you ready to take the oath?"

"I am, sir."

Vinson then administered two oaths: the first in which Clark pledged to defend the Constitution and the second, the judicial oath, in which he swore to "administer justice without respect to persons and do equal right to the poor and to the rich."[49] The nation's newest Supreme Court justice lowered his right hand and turned away from the clicking cameras to kiss his wife and children.[50]

As was the case with Vinson, Truman's friendship with Clark did not end when the former attorney general joined the Court. Clark hosted Truman's birthday party at his home on May 8, 1952, three years after becoming a justice. "I don't know what I'd do for a birthday celebration," Truman wrote with gratitude, "if you didn't take care of it."[51]

CHAPTER NINETEEN

Justice Sherman Minton

ON SEPTEMBER 10, 1949, LESS than three weeks after Tom Clark was sworn in as an associate justice of the Supreme Court, Justice Wiley Rutledge died at the age of fifty-five. Roosevelt's last Court nominee had been in a coma at York Hospital for more than a week after suffering a stroke while vacationing in Maine. Supreme Court Marshal Thomas Waggaman accompanied Rutledge's body from Maine to Washington for his funeral at the Washington Unitarian Church he had attended.[1]

Although Americans have since grown accustomed to Court nominees who have scant experience actually practicing law, when Roosevelt nominated Rutledge, the nominee's lack of courtroom experience was presented as evidence that he was unqualified to be a justice. After graduating from the University of Colorado School of Law and practicing for two years, Rutledge became a law professor at the University of Colorado. He taught at various midwestern law schools for the next fifteen years before becoming the dean of the University of Iowa College of Law. His scholarly contributions consisted of a few book reviews and two law review articles.

"So far as I can learn," Republican senator William Langer of North Dakota professed on the Senate floor, "the nominee never practiced law and never even had been in a courtroom until he took his seat on the court of appeals in Washington a few years ago." Langer added, "The only justification that I can find for his appointment is that he comes from Iowa City, the home of [Roosevelt advisor] Harry Hopkins."[2]

As a law professor, Rutledge had spoken in favor of Roosevelt's 1937 judicial reform proposal. Two years later Roosevelt, acknowledging a political need to appoint someone to the federal bench who hailed from west of the Mississippi River, named Rutledge to the U.S. Court of Appeals for the District of Columbia. This failed to mollify midwestern and western senators, who rarely missed an opportunity to note that every Supreme

Court justice was from east of the Mississippi. (Perhaps on account of his time in New York City and New Haven, they considered William Douglas an easterner.) So when a Court vacancy opened four years later, Roosevelt again turned to Rutledge—this time nominating the forty-eight-year-old judge to the Supreme Court. "Wiley," Roosevelt said, confiding an open secret, "we had a number of candidates for the Court who were highly qualified, but they didn't have geography—you have that." On the official commission form, in his elegant, calligraphic penmanship, Roosevelt wrote Rutledge's name and, after it, wrote, "Iowa."[3] Days after Rutledge's death, the Associated Press recounted, "He was named both to the Circuit Court of Appeals and to the Supreme Court because a Westerner was needed."[4]

The Senate confirmed Rutledge by voice vote on February 8, 1943, less than a month after his nomination, and he took the oath of office a week later. As if to prove his mettle, Rutledge proved to be an indefatigable worker on the Court. He wrote 171 majority, concurring, and dissenting opinions in just six years.[5] The day after Rutledge's passing, Justice Jackson told reporters that his late colleague "literally overtaxed his strength by devotion to his work."[6] Chief Justice Vinson had served with Rutledge on the DC Court of Appeals as well as on the Supreme Court. "He was earnest, conscientious and an eminently able jurist," Vinson remembered, "whose death was a "severe loss to the country and to me personally."[7] Justice Douglas lamented Rutledge's death as "a personal loss, like a brother or member of the family."[8]

Douglas's sincere grief was professional as well as personal. Wiley Rutledge reliably voted with Justices Black, Douglas, and Murphy. Together they had comprised a moderate to liberal bloc that stood athwart an increasingly conservative Court. They also were able to provide the four votes necessary to grant certiorari to cases seeking Court review.

Rutledge voted with Murphy more than with any other member of the Court. They voted together 75 percent of the time.[9] Their deaths within weeks of each other in 1949 therefore had an immediate and substantial effect on the ideological makeup of the Court. Truman was able to dramatically change the Court not just because of whom he nominated but because of whom those nominees replaced.

* * *

When Truman announced his intention to nominate Tom Clark to the Supreme Court, he dismissed any intimation that religion might have or should have played a role in his selection: "If he is qualified, I wouldn't care what his faith is, whether it's Catholic, Baptist or Jewish."[10] Rutledge's death just a few weeks later nonetheless renewed speculation that Truman would nominate a Catholic to the Court. By replacing Rutledge with a Catholic jurist, he would have discharged the notion of a "Catholic seat" on the Court while preserving the ideal of Catholic representation among the justices. Roman Catholic attorney general J. Howard McGrath, once again and sooner than anyone expected, was among those presumed to be on the president's shortlist of potential nominees.[11]

Liberals sought assurances from the White House that the president would nominate a jurist with a proven progressive record, someone who likely would vote with Black and Douglas.[12] But their pleas were ineffective because Harry Truman had already decided on his nominee.

Truman had no intention of passing over Judge Sherman Minton for the second time in as many months, much less for the fourth time during his presidency. He hardly considered nominating anyone else, arriving at his decision less than a week after Rutledge's death.[13] At seven o'clock in the morning on the day of Wiley Rutledge's funeral, Truman reached Minton by telephone at his home in New Albany, Indiana. "Shay, I was figuring on naming you to the Supreme Court today. Will you accept?"[14]

Minton replied that he would. He was prepared for the call after reading in the newspapers the previous day that Truman planned to nominate him. The reports, based on anonymous tips from the White House, came to Minton as "a complete surprise."[15]

At his weekly news conference, Truman declared that he would nominate Minton to the Supreme Court. He then announced several lower court nominations before opening the floor for questions, but reporters asked none about any of the nominees.[16] The White House sent the official nomination papers to the Senate a few hours later.[17] Minton told reporters that he felt "profoundly grateful" to the president for nominating him and that he hoped "to prove worthy of such trust."[18]

* * *

Observers expressed surprise that Truman again had passed over Attorney General McGrath. The Democratic chairman of the Senate Judiciary Committee was so certain Truman would nominate McGrath that he indicated his approval of the nomination before departing for an overseas trip.[19] Minton's nomination indicated that the Court, for now at least, would continue to have no Catholic members. Minton listed no religion in his official federal biography.[20] His supporters were quick to note, however, that his wife and children were Catholics.[21]

It was Minton's political record and his friendship with Truman—not his faith—that posed obstacles to his confirmation. To be sure, his confirmation seemed secure, with Democrats controlling the Senate, which included thirty of Minton's former colleagues.[22] Democratic senator Millard Tydings of Maryland predicted, "The fact that the president went to the judiciary to find a capable appointee will, I think, meet with approval, both in Congress and out."[23]

But nearly every news account of Minton's nomination reminded Americans that, as a senator, Minton had been a firebrand who supported Roosevelt's so-called Court-packing plan. In strident terms, he had lambasted the Court's ostensible eagerness to strike down New Deal laws. "You can't offer a hungry man the Constitution!" he had shouted on the Senate floor. "You can't say to a man hunting a job, 'Here, have a Constitution.'"[24] The *Atlanta Daily World* recalled that Senator Minton had described the Court as "carrying the blight of the cold, dead hand."[25] The *Washington Post*'s front-page article was headlined, "He Favored Packing It—Minton Nominated for Supreme Court."[26] The *Baltimore Sun*'s headline read, "Judge Minton Named to Supreme Court, Former Indiana Senator Who Backed 'Court-Packing' Bill to Succeed Justice Rutledge."[27]

That Minton and Truman were friends caused many to liken Minton's nomination to Clark's. Giving short shrift to Minton's eight years as a federal appellate judge, editors at the *New York Times* wrote, "Once again the president seems to have allowed personal and political friendship to influence his choice, rather than a considered evaluation of judicial capacity."[28]

Republican senators indicated that Minton's political record necessitated further inquiry into his judicial philosophy, despite the fact that he had been a senator for six years and a federal appellate judge for eight. If Indiana's Republican senator William E. Jenner gave the word, Republicans were prepared to oppose Minton's nomination as a matter of party policy.[29] Senator Homer Ferguson of Michigan, a Republican member of the judiciary committee, was still smarting from being denied the opportunity to question then—Attorney General Clark before having to cast a vote on his nomination to the Supreme Court. "I think we should have full hearings to develop information about Minton's legal ability and about his background," Ferguson declared. "I don't know the man nor much about him."[30] Democratic senator Pat McCarran of Nevada countered that it was extremely rare for judicial nominees to testify before Congress and that, on the rare occasions when they had testified, it was usually at their own request.[31]

But Republicans' insistence on holding hearings prevailed—for the moment. On September 20, 1949, the Senate announced that hearings on Judge Sherman Minton's "qualifications" to serve as an associate justice of the Supreme Court of the United States would commence on Tuesday, September 27, and continue for as long as necessary. Senator Ferguson maintained that the hearings were appropriate to assess the nominee's "legal ability and background."[32]

Minton replied to the judiciary committee's invitation by letter. "I, of course, desire to cooperate fully with the committee at all times," he wrote, "but I feel that personal participation by the nominee in the committee proceedings relating to his nomination presents a serious question of propriety, particularly when I might be required to express my views on highly controversial and litigious issues affecting the court." Minton understood that senators' misgivings about his nomination stemmed largely from his vociferous support for Roosevelt's judicial reform plan during his single term in the senate. Presenting a theme that would be echoed more than fifty years later by chief justice nominee John G. Roberts, Minton explained, "When I was a young man playing baseball and football, I strongly supported my team. I was then a partisan. But later, when I refereed games, I had no team. I had no side. The same is true when I left the political arena and assumed the bench. Cases must be decided under applicable law and upon the record as to where the right lies."[33]

After considering Minton's letter, judiciary committee members voted to rescind their request that he testify. They recommended his nomination to the Senate by a vote of nine to two.[34] The next day, senators confirmed Minton's nomination, forty-eight to sixteen.[35]

The following day Minton visited the White House to thank the president for nominating him. Truman was watching game one of the World Series on television, and Minton settled in to watch some of it with him. New York Yankees right fielder Tommy Henrich stepped to the plate.

Minton got excited. "Here's one of the most dangerous hitters in baseball!" he told Truman. Henrich hammered the third pitch into the stands
for a homerun that won the game for the Yankees. "I expect," Minton later
told reporters waiting outside the White House, "that the president hopes
I know my law as well as my baseball."[36]

* * *

Roughly four hundred spectators attended Sherman Minton's swearing-in
ceremony in the White House Rose Garden. Justices of the Supreme Court;
members of the cabinet; ninety-two friends from Minton's hometown of
New Albany, Indiana; and forty members of the Indiana Bar Association
were among those gathered on the cool Wednesday morning of October
12, 1949.[37] As he had done for Clark just a few weeks earlier, Truman personally handed Minton his commission, saying into the microphone, "I've
got a duty to perform which is one of the most pleasurable in my political
career. There you are, Shay." Looking up at the crowd, the president announced, "I'm handing Mr. Justice Minton his commission as a member
of the greatest court in the world."[38]

Minton accepted the scroll, which he handed to his wife, Gertrude.
Holding a Bible, Chief Justice Vinson stepped forward to administer the
oaths. A few seconds later, Sherman "Shay" Minton officially became the
fourth justice Harry Truman had named to the Supreme Court, and even
including the nation's newest justice, no one appeared happier than the
president.

CHAPTER TWENTY

Civil Liberties and Loyalty

CHIEF JUSTICE VINSON OPENED THE Supreme Court's new term on October 3, 1949, by remembering Justices Frank Murphy and Wiley Rutledge. "Saddened by our losses," he said from the bench, "but inspired by the examples of devotion to duty which Mr. Justice Murphy and Mr. Justice Rutledge have provided for us, we turn to the work before us." When the Court issued its decisions months later, one Yale Law School professor wrote that "the work before us" to which Vinson referred appeared to consist largely of "rejecting the work and philosophy of the late justices."[1]

All four of Truman's appointees were on the Court. During the 1949–50 term, every major decision the Court handed down supported the administration's legal positions. Vinson's dissent rate dropped from 13 percent in his first three terms to just 4 percent.[2] The landmark cases decided during the opening years of the full Truman Court were significant because most of them concerned questions of civil rights or civil liberties. In the civil rights cases, the justices often reached unanimous decisions as they, led by the NAACP's legal team and Department of Justice appellate lawyers, began to steadily chip away at the legal vestiges of slavery in the American South.

In the civil liberties cases, however, the Court remained sharply divided. It was cleaved by questions such as whether the rights of freedom of speech and freedom of assembly extended to Communists and subversives who rejected the American form of government. Two legal observers wrote at the time that "the greatest single problem confronting the Supreme Court" was "the task of reconciling our traditional concepts of individual liberty, particularly freedom of expression, with the demands of national security."[3]

* * *

Just a few months before Vinson opened the 1949–50 term, on March 8, 1949, a World War II Army veteran and Syracuse University college student named Irving Feiner sought to advertise a political event taking place later that night at the Syracuse Hotel. He placed a wooden soapbox on the corner of South McBride and Harrison Streets in Syracuse, New York; attached a loudspeaker system to a parked car; and began railing for and against this and that in an attempt to spur interest in the meeting to be held a few hours later. Speaking in a "loud, high-pitched voice," Feiner gathered listeners to whom his friends handed leaflets. He declared that the mayor of Syracuse was a "champagne-sipping bum" and that Truman was also "a bum." The American Legion were "Gestapo Nazi agents" and large swaths of Syracuse were "run by corrupt politicians."[4]

Before long, his audience grew to more than seventy-five people: fellow students and professionals, women and men, and—as police officers, judges, and justices took pains to note—Black and White Americans alike. The integrated crowd spilled from the sidewalk into the intersection, forcing pedestrians to walk in the street and disrupting vehicular traffic. Some in the audience began to heckle Feiner. Before long, a nearby resident called the police. Officers named Flynn and Cook arrived and noticed that the crowd was growing agitated, with "angry muttering" and a little pushing and shoving. "Some were calm and some were not," Flynn observed. "They were discussing the speech pro and con."[5]

Feiner then spoke against racism. He argued that African Americans should "rise up in arms and fight" for equal rights. This caused some consternation in the crowd, and a man said to the officers, "If you don't get that son of a bitch off [the soapbox], I will go over and get him off there myself." Flynn approached Feiner and asked him to step down off the soapbox, but according to Flynn, Feiner "just looked and kept right on talking to the crowd." Twice more Flynn asked Feiner to step down before seizing him and placing him under arrest. "The law has arrived," Feiner announced into the microphone, "and I suppose they will take over now."[6]

Fiener was charged with disorderly conduct. At trial the judge assured Feiner that he had the right to disparage the mayor and the president and to speak into a microphone on the street corner. However, given the size of the crowd and the fact that some listeners had become hostile, "the officers were fully justified in feeling that a situation was developing which could very, very easily result in a serious disorder." For this reason, Feiner was convicted of disorderly conduct.[7] Feiner appealed his conviction, and his appeal eventually reached the Supreme Court of the United States.

* * *

Vinson wrote for a six-justice majority that upheld Feiner's conviction. The Court was wary of providing a "heckler's veto" to an individual's right to free speech: "We are well aware that the ordinary murmurings and objections of a hostile audience cannot be allowed to silence a speaker, and are also mindful of the possible danger of giving overzealous police officials complete discretion to break up otherwise lawful public meetings." The Court found that Feiner's speech exceeded the bounds of constitutional protection because he had "passe[d] the bounds of argument or persuasion and undertake[n] incitement to riot." Therefore, the Court declined to "reverse this conviction in the name of free speech."[8]

Vinson refused to recognize any distinction between a speaker who purposefully incites his audience to violence and a speaker whose audience threatens violence to silence him. As Douglas's dissent and countless commenters noted, the speaker most in need of First Amendment protection was the one whose audience would resort to violence to quiet him. As he often did—too often in the opinion of some of his brethren—Frankfurter voted with the majority but filed a concurring opinion joined by no other justices.

Black dissented, taking issue with the majority's complete acceptance of every one of the trial court's findings of fact. He declared that the Court's decision marked "a dark day for civil liberties in our Nation" because "a man making a lawful address is certainly not required to be silent merely because an officer directs it."[9]

Douglas wrote a dissent that was joined by newly appointed Justice Sherman Minton. Douglas and Minton conceded that a speaker may not lawfully incite a riot or purposefully breach the peace by using "fighting words." Feiner's case, however, presented neither incitement nor fighting words. Instead, it involved "an unsympathetic audience and the threat of one man to haul the speaker from the stage." Irving Feiner was the exact kind of speaker who "need[ed] police protection."[10]

Feiner's conviction had a lasting effect on his life. Syracuse University expelled him and every law school to which he had been accepted revoked its letter of admission. Decades later, Syracuse University readmitted Feiner to allow him to earn his degree, which he did in 1984. Two years before he died at the age of eighty-four, Irving Feiner presented a lecture at his belated alma mater on the topic of freedom of speech.[11]

* * *

That Minton joined Douglas's dissent was likely the only surprise in the *Feiner* ruling. Litigants and lawyers alike had quickly learned that the Court, fortified with the four Truman nominees, tended to uphold police actions and government restrictions on civil liberties. Between 1946 and 1953 the chief justice voted 83 percent of the time to deny a civil liberties claim; Harold Burton voted against civil liberties claimants 74 percent of the time; Tom Clark, 75 percent; and Sherman Minton, 87 percent.[12] Vinson and Minton voted together more than any other two justices.[13]

To be sure, their votes in civil liberties cases aligned not only with Truman administration policy but also with the national mood as the Iron Curtain dropped between Western nations and the Soviet bloc. Historian Robert G. McCloskey wrote that the "growing national awareness of the totalitarian threat in the years after 1945 generated a national mood toward 'subversion' that sometimes approached hysteria."[14] Truman implemented his federal employee loyalty program with bipartisan congressional support.

A majority of the Court at times seemed to dispose of civil liberties appeals with a facility that concerned many lawyers, elected officials, and certainly Justices Black and Douglas. Unlike the politicians who occupied the federal offices set forth in articles I and II of the Constitution, members of the Supreme Court were protected from the electorate's fevers and worries. But they too were living at the dawn of the Cold War, and the justices were not immune to Washington's winds.

* * *

Feiner was a noteworthy decision mostly because it solidified the Court's willingness to accept restrictions on civil liberties. Vinson's majority opinion laid another brick in a road started the previous year with *American Communications Association v. Douds* and *United States v. Rabinowitz*. As one law review article noted, these cases comprised a "broad jump to the right in respect to civil liberties [that] was the most important new development of the year."[15]

Douds arose from bipartisan congressional concern that members of the Communist Party were instigating some of the labor strikes that had severely hurt the American economy after World War II. Congress amended the Taft-Hartley Act to deny major benefits of the act to any labor organization unless each of its officers filed an affidavit with the National Labor Relations Board declaring "that he is not a member of the Communist party or affiliated with such party, and that he does not believe in, and is not a member of or support any organization that believes in or teaches the overthrow of the United States Government by force or by any illegal or unconstitutional methods."[16]

Congress intended the affidavit requirement to prevent so-called political strikes instigated by Communists in order to harm the American economy. Before voting to require the affidavits, Congress held hearings in which both corporate officers and labor leaders testified about strikes called at the direction of Communist Party leaders. Lawmakers were riveted by testimony of how Communists ordered strikes such as one at a Milwaukee plant manufacturing defense materials. Congress passed the affidavit requirement pursuant to its constitutional power to regulate interstate commerce, which could be disrupted by "political strikes."

Several unions filed suit, claiming that the affidavit requirement violated their members' First Amendment rights: it infringed on union officers' rights to hold whatever political views they wanted as well as to associate with whatever legal political groups they wanted, and it breached rank-and-file members' rights to elect their officers without government interference. As a practical matter, the unions argued, the requirement made it impossible for any member who could not sign such an affidavit to serve as an officer in his or her union.[17]

Vinson wrote for a five-to-one majority in *Douds*. He framed the Court's analysis around the fact that Congress instituted the affidavit requirement in an effort to stem the "political strikes" that were impeding interstate commerce. "There can be no doubt," he wrote, "that Congress may, under its constitutional power to regulate commerce among the several States, attempt to prevent political strikes and other kinds of direct action designed to burden and interrupt the free flow of commerce."[18]

Congress possessed nearly plenary power to regulate interstate commerce. By requiring union officers to submit sworn affidavits regarding their political beliefs and associations, however, "Congress has undeniably discouraged the lawful exercise of political freedoms as well." The anti-Communist affidavit requirement had the effect of "discouraging the exercise of political rights protected by the First Amendment. Men who hold union offices often have little choice but to renounce Communism or give up their offices." This created a "grave and difficult problem."[19]

But it was, as the Truman administration contended and the Court agreed, a problem that Congress had resolved. And the Court, unless faced with a clear violation of the Constitution, should not substitute its own judgment for that of those elected to office. Justices were obliged to construe statutes "so as to avoid the danger of unconstitutionality if it may be done in consonance with the legislative purpose."[20]

Within this framework of judicial restraint, Vinson purported to apply the "clear and present danger" test to the affidavit requirement. That test, established by Justices Louis Brandeis and Oliver Wendell Holmes, stood on the belief that the First Amendment guaranteed rights to speakers to promulgate and the public to hear the views of all people, even and perhaps especially unsettling views. But an individual's right to speak weakened when, as Vinson wrote, the speaker's "views are no longer merely views, but threaten, clearly and imminently, to ripen into conduct against which the public has a right to protect itself."[21]

Congress did not intend for the affidavit requirement to restrict speech, Vinson explained, but to guard "against what Congress has concluded [Communists] have done and are likely to do again." Congress intended for the affidavit requirement to protect interstate commerce from the threat of political strikes, not "to disturb or proscribe beliefs." Therefore, the Court held that the affidavit requirement "was compatible with the Federal Constitution, and may stand."[22]

Douglas, Clark, and Minton took no part in the *Douds* decision; Court rules did not require them to disclose why they recused themselves.

Frankfurter concurred and dissented in part, but he accepted the majority's decision to analyze the affidavit requirement within Congress's plenary authority to regulate interstate commerce. "It is too late in the day," he wrote, "to deny to Congress the power to promote industrial peace in all the far-flung range of interstate commerce." Congress was well within its constitutional rights "to restrict attempts to bring about another scheme of society, not through appeal to reason and the use of the ballot as democracy has been pursued throughout our history, but through an associated effort to disrupt industry." Demonstrating his fidelity to judicial restraint, Frankfurter made clear that he would prefer the affidavit requirement be adjusted to force union officers to disavow "actual membership in the Communist Party, or in an organization that is in fact a controlled cover for that Party or of active belief, as a matter of present policy, in the overthrow of the Government of the United States by force."[23] But Congress had not in this instance regulated membership, and Frankfurter would not vote to prevent the law from taking effect.

Jackson also concurred and dissented in part, opening his opinion with one of the characteristic flourishes that justified his reputation as one of the finest writers in Court history: "If the statute before us required labor union officers to forswear membership in the Republican Party, the Democratic Party or the Socialist Party, I suppose all agree that it would be unconstitutional. But why, if it is valid as to the Communist Party?" He then set forth the numerous ways in which Congress could have rationally concluded that the Communist Party fundamentally differed "from any other substantial party we have known, and hence may constitutionally be treated as something different in law." Expressly limiting his concurrence to the case against the Communist Party, Jackson agreed that the affidavit requirement was constitutional.[24]

Black completely rejected the affidavit requirement in his dissent. He declared, "Individual freedom and governmental thought-probing cannot live together," and this fact "should compel a holding that [the affidavit requirement] conflicts with the First Amendment." Presenting a theme that would echo in Jackson's *Feiner* dissent, Black wrote that a main purpose of the First Amendment was to protect those espousing unpopular views, "each member of the smallest and most unorthodox minority."[25]

The Court's *Douds* decision disappointed civil libertarians, many of whom viewed it as the most significant defeat for a free-speech claim in twenty years.[26] *Douds* indicated how far the Court would bend to uphold the government's action so long as the government was claiming to act in the interest of national security. On every question Vinson gave the government the benefit of the doubt.[27] Frankfurter's commitment to judicial restraint and Jackson's opposition to Communist influence led them to support the majority's ruling. With Douglas having recused himself from the case, Black stood alone in defending the plaintiffs' civil liberties.

That five of the six justices who heard the case decided that the anti-Communist oath was constitutional made clear where the Court stood on such questions. *Douds* undoubtedly was a victory for Vinson, who, even without the votes of two of his fellow Truman nominees, succeeded, as former Chief Justices Taft and Hughes would have said, in massing the Court.

Vinson's expansive career in all three branches of the federal government led him to believe that laws enacted by the two elected branches of government deserved considerable deference from members of the un-elected judiciary branch. Yale Law School professor Fred Rodell, Douglas's protégé, observed, "If ever a Court member's past life clearly tended him toward upholding whatever the federal government did or wanted to do, it was Vinson's."[28] As predisposed as Vinson seemed to uphold the federal government's actions, the Kentuckian remained skeptical of states' powers to restrict the rights of their citizens. This dichotomy would guide Vinson's increasingly active civil rights jurisprudence.

* * *

The new judicial reality in Washington was that the Court seemed to share the Truman administration's and Congress's concerns about Communist influence and infiltration. Police powers grew stronger almost as a corollary to officials' determination to stamp out both the actual threat and the larger threat they believed Communism posed in their time. Civil liberties became casualties in the worst way, not as destroyed targets but as collateral damage.

Police obtained a warrant to arrest Albert Rabinowitz after he sold four fraudulent stamps to an undercover agent. Officers arrested him in his small office and, without a search warrant but pursuant to his arrest, spent the next hour and a half searching his desk, safe, and file cabinets. In all they found 573 forged and altered postage stamps. Rabinowitz's motion to exclude evidence of the stamps was denied. He was convicted in a jury trial in which he presented no evidence.[29] His appeal eventually reached the Supreme Court, where the justices agreed to answer the question, "Were the 573 stamps, the fruits of this search, admissible in evidence?"

The Fourth Amendment states:

The right of the people to be secure in their persons, houses, papers, and effects, against unreasonable searches and seizures, shall not be violated, and no Warrants shall issue, but upon probable cause, supported by Oath or affirmation, and particularly describing the place to be searched, and the persons or things to be seized.

Because the Fourth Amendment prohibits "unreasonable searches and seizures," the common judicial question, of course, is what constitutes a reasonable or unreasonable search. The Court explained in *United States v. Rabinowitz* that what constitutes "a reasonable search is not to be determined by any fixed formula." Because the "Constitution does not define what are 'unreasonable searches,'" the "recurring questions of the reasonableness of searches must find resolution in the facts and circumstances of each case."[30]

Writing for a five-member Court majority consisting of himself, his three fellow Truman appointees, and Stanley Reed, Justice Sherman Minton asserted that, when pursuant to a valid arrest, the Court has "often recognized that there is a permissible area of search beyond the person proper." This was because "a limited search such as here conducted as incident to a lawful arrest was a reasonable search and therefore valid." Minton continued, "No one questions the right, without a search warrant, to search the person after a valid arrest. The right to search the person incident to arrest always has been recognized in this country and in England."[31] This ignored the fact that Rabinowitz was not protesting the search of his person but rather the police officers' ninety-minute search of his office after placing him under arrest.

The Court set forth five reasons why they denied Rabinowitz's claim that the search of his office was unreasonable: (1) The search was incident to a lawful arrest, (2) the place of search was a place of business open to the public and therefore also to officers, (3) the room was small and under Rabinowitz's control, (4) the search did not extend beyond this room, and (5) possession of the fraudulent stamps that were found constituted a crime. Moreover, even if the officers had had time to procure a search warrant, the five-justice majority ruled that they "were not bound to do so" because the search of Rabinowitz's office "was otherwise reasonable."[32]

Douglas took no part in the case but Black, Frankfurter, and Jackson dissented. Black urged the Court to adhere more closely to recently decided Fourth Amendment precedents. Doing so would provide clearer guidance to police officers, lawyers, and trial judges regarding what constituted a reasonable search.

Jackson joined Frankfurter's dissent, which decried the majority's willingness to accept that the extended search of Rabinowitz's office was reasonable because the police officers conducting the search possessed a valid arrest warrant. To allow officers to search an entire residential or office space pursuant to an arrest warrant was, Frankfurter argued, to make "a farce . . . of the whole Fourth Amendment."[33] If it did not clarify Fourth Amendment jurisprudence, the five-to-three decision in *Rabinowitz* did make clear that, in civil liberties cases, Stanley Reed would readily join the four Truman appointees to form a majority willing to sustain the government's actions.

* * *

As much as *Feiner*, *Douds*, and *Rabinowitz* indicated that the Court had joined the White House's rightward shift on civil liberties matters, no civil liberties case of the time captured the nation's attention like the 1951 case of *Dennis v. United States*. Even before it reached the Supreme Court, *Dennis* riveted Americans across the country.

In July 1948, Eugene Dennis, the general secretary of the Communist Party of the United States, and ten other party leaders were arrested and charged with violating two sections of the Smith Act, which made it illegal to advocate the violent overthrow of the federal government. The Communist Party had over the previous three years transformed its *modus operandi* from working within America's political system to advocating in newspapers and recruiting brochures for the violent overthrow of the federal government.[34] Dennis and his co-defendants were charged with knowingly and willfully conspiring to organize the Communist Party of the United States to teach and advocate for the violent overthrow of the U.S. government, and knowingly and willfully advocating the violent overthrow of the U.S. government.[35]

Dennis and his co-defendants were not charged with committing any act intended to bring down the federal government. Nor were they charged with conspiring to depose the government. They were charged with conspiring to organize a group to advocate overthrowing the government and with actually advocating for the overthrow of the government. Promoting the overthrow of the federal government or organizing a group to promote such a cause was prohibited by sections 2 and 3 of the Smith Act.

Judge Harold Medina, a former law professor and private practitioner who took an 85 percent pay cut at the age of fifty-nine to become a federal district judge, had been on the bench in the Southern District of New York for less than a year and a half when *United States v. Dennis* crashed into his courtroom. From the outset, the defendants' five attorneys appeared intent on making a spectacle of the proceedings. They openly disregarded rules of court decorum, wagging their fingers at Medina and even shouting at him. Profuse objections from both sides brought the trial to a standstill on nearly a daily basis. "You've called me corrupt and everything else you could think up," the exasperated judge told defense counsel at one point.[36]

Journalists from around the world reported daily on the case, providing a then-unprecedented level of media coverage for a criminal trial. Before long, Medina noticed that every day at 11:20 a.m. and 3:20 p.m., one of the defendants' attorneys accused him of lying from the bench. "What does the time element mean?" he asked.

A lawyer responded, "That is the deadline for the morning and afternoon editions" for the newspapers.[37]

The trial lasted nine months. At the time, it was the longest trial in American history, consisting of more than 5 million words of testimony.[38] In his jury instructions, which would come under close scrutiny in the months and years to follow, Medina told jurors that they could find the defendants guilty if the defendants intended "to overthrow the government by force and violence as speedily as circumstances permit."[39]

After the nine-month trial, the jury deliberated for less than one day before returning guilty verdicts for all defendants on all counts. Dennis and his co-defendants were sentenced to five years in prison and fined $10,000 each. They appealed their convictions.

The Communist defendants were not convicted of taking any action other than teaching and talking—activities presumably protected by the First Amendment. When their appeal reached the Supreme Court, it forced the justices to confront their differing opinions on how to balance an individual's right to free speech and federal laws enacted to protect national security.

Justice Oliver Wendell Holmes had established the prevailing limitation on free speech in 1919 when, writing for a unanimous court in *Schenck v. United States*, he declared that the question of whether or not speech was protected by the constitution was "whether the words used in such circumstances and are of such a nature as to create a clear and present danger that they will bring about the substantive evils that Congress has a right to prevent." To be clear, Holmes concluded, "It is a question of proximity and degree." This became known as the "clear and present danger test," most popularly described by Holmes himself in that same opinion when he wrote that the right to free speech "would not protect a man falsely shouting fire in a theater and causing a panic."[40]

Teaching and advocating for the future overthrow of the federal government would seem to qualify under the clear and present danger test as constitutionally protected speech. Prosecutors had not contended at trial that the *Dennis* defendants took any action intended to promptly bring down the government. But Judge Medina's jury instructions appeared to substitute intent for action. If the defendants intended to bring down the federal government "as speedily as circumstances permit," then they could be convicted—which they were—because their speech was not protected by the Constitution.

* * *

The Supreme Court upheld the Communists' convictions by a vote of six to two. Douglas recalled that the conference, held on December 9, 1950, "was largely *pro forma*." Most justices stated with little explanation that they would vote to affirm the lower court's decision. It appeared to Douglas that they "had their minds closed to argument or persuasion." He found "the brief nature of the discussion" to be "amazing."[41]

Despite its six-to-two majority, *Dennis* splintered the Court, laying bare the justices' diverging views on how to reach a constitutional balance between free speech and national security. Five of the eight justices filed opinions. Three of the four votes for the plurality opinion were Truman appointees, with Reed again joining Vinson, Minton, and Burton. In its coverage of the *Dennis* case, the *Nation* magazine derisively referred to "the Truman law firm of Vinson, Minton and Burton."[42] Frankfurter and Jackson wrote concurring opinions. Black and Douglas filed dissents. Clark, who as attorney general had argued that the Smith Act was an inadequate prosecutorial statute, did not participate.[43] There was no massing the Court—not this Court—in a civil liberties case such as *Dennis*.

Vinson's plurality opinion purported to apply the clear and present danger test but actually employed a test used by Judge Learned Hand, who wrote the *Dennis* opinion for the Second Circuit Court of Appeals. Hand's test asked "whether the gravity of the 'evil,' discounted by its improbability, justifies such invasion of free speech as is necessary to avoid the danger." Vinson concluded that the fall of the federal government presented such a "gravity of 'evil'" that the Constitution permitted a ban on teaching or advocating for it. The First Amendment's freedom of speech guarantee did not "mean that before the Government may act, it must wait until the *putsch* is about to executed, the plans have been laid and the signal is awaited."[44]

Black and Douglas in their dissents contended that applying the real clear and present danger test necessitated overturning the convictions. Because Black believed in an absolute right to freedom of speech, the clear and present danger test was mostly irrelevant to him. However, he argued, if the Court was going to employ the test, it should do so correctly. Although the majority professed to apply the test, as one legal scholar wrote, "*Dennis* marked the demise of the clear and present danger test."[45] Privately, Black and Douglas mocked Vinson's reasoning. After the chief justice circulated a draft opinion, Black derisively warned him that "the goblins are going to get you."[46]

Widespread praise for the Court's decision illustrated the strength of the nationwide anti-Communist fervor in which *Dennis* was adjudicated. At the dawn of the Cold War, many Americans believed that the Communist Party posed a threat to the republic. In March 1948 a mob in Columbus, Ohio, ransacked the home of a Communist Party leader days after a crowd dispersed a group of Communists distributing fliers in the city. Men in Rochester, New York, broke into a Communist Party meeting and sent attendees scattering.[47] The *Washington Post* editorial board called *Dennis* "the most important reconciliation of liberty and security in our time."[48]

* * *

After the Truman administration implemented its loyalty program for federal employees, many state and local governments across the country followed suit. The State of New York enacted Civil Service Law of New York §12-a, better known as the Feinberg Law, which called for the removal of any public school employee who belonged to an organization that advocated for the overthrow of the government by force, violence, or other unlawful means. The state published a list of organizations allegedly engaged in such activity. A public school employee or applicant's membership in one of the listed organizations constituted prima facie evidence for removal or disqualification, but only after a hearing in which he or she could be represented by counsel and appeal for judicial review. New York investigated more than 1,100 teachers and fired 378 of them. One teacher called out of her classroom for questioning, forty-year-old Minnie Gutride, went home after school and killed herself with oven gas.[49]

Among those fired was the chair of the math department at Straubenmuller Textile High School in Manhattan, a brilliant mathematician named Irving Adler. He had graduated *magna cum laude* from the City College of New York at the age of eighteen. Four years later he joined the American Communist Party. The school superintendent summoned Adler to his office to ask, "Are you now or have you ever been a member of the Communist Party?" Adler refused to answer and returned to his classroom.

Several weeks later Adler was called away from his students. "I was teaching a class," he recalled in 2009, "when the principal sent up a letter he had just received from the superintendent announcing my suspension, as of the close of day." He was fired shortly thereafter.[50]

Before he died at the age of ninety-nine at his home in Bennington, Vermont, Adler would write eighty-seven science and math books, most of them for children. His wildly popular books sold more than 4 million copies in nineteen languages. "There is no adventure more thrilling," Adler wrote, "than discovering the real wonders of the world we live in."[51] Decades earlier, however, he joined his fellow fired teachers in suing the Board of Education of the City of New York. Because plaintiffs were listed in alphabetical order, the case, which swiftly reached the Supreme Court of the United States, bore his name.

* * *

Adler v. Board of Education of the City of New York presented an opportunity for the Court to clarify the legal status of loyalty requirements for public employees. Critics decried the "guilt by association" basis on which New York's program relied, while supporters correctly noted that Communists were in fact seeking to infiltrate the government. New York required its loyalty attestation to be taken by all public school employees, regardless of their level of authority or interaction with students.

Minton wrote for a six-justice majority to uphold New York's Feinberg Law. In part because "school authorities have the right and the duty to screen the officials, teachers, and employees as to their fitness to maintain the integrity of the schools as a part of ordered society, [which] cannot be doubted," the Court found "no constitutional infirmity" in the law. Vinson, Burton, Clark, Jackson, and Reed joined Minton's opinion. They brushed aside appellants' guilt by association claims: "From time immemorial, one's reputation has been determined in part by the company he keeps. In the employment of officials and teachers of the school system, the state may very properly inquire into the company they keep, and we know of no rule," the Court asserted, "constitutional or otherwise, that prevents the state, when determining the fitness and loyalty of such persons, from considering the organizations and persons with whom they associate."[52]

Black, Douglas, and Frankfurter each wrote dissents. They raised points that, in the end, became law: in the 1967 case of *Keyishian v. Board of Regents*, the Supreme Court held that New York's loyalty oath requirements were unconstitutional.[53]

* * *

As the Court solidified its hardline jurisprudence on civil liberties during the Truman administration, it began, with increasing clarity and determination, to strike down race-based laws restricting Americans' civil rights. NAACP attorneys and the Justice Department beseeched the Court to overrule *Plessy v. Ferguson*, the 1896 Supreme Court case that allowed state-enforced racial segregation, but this the justices refused to do for now. Instead, in several cases over several years, they examined Jim Crow laws with growing suspicion. Both the Roosevelt and Truman appointees, who seemed to agree on little else, were united in their skepticism of government-enforced segregation. This suspicion contrasted sharply with the way most of them reviewed civil liberties cases, but, again, it aligned closely with the policies of the Truman administration.

CHAPTER TWENTY-ONE

The Path to *Brown*
First Steps

IN A 1952 CAMPAIGN SPEECH to rally support for Democratic Party presidential nominee Adlai Stevenson, President Truman told voters, "At my request, the Solicitor General of the United States went before the Supreme Court to argue that Negro citizens have the right to enter state colleges and universities." Referring to *Shelley v. Kraemer*, he continued, "At my request, the Solicitor General again went before the Supreme Court and argued against the vicious restrictive covenants that had prevented homes in many places from being sold to Negroes."[1] Realizing that racist southern Democrats in Congress would prevent any anti–Jim Crow legislation from becoming law, the Truman administration's Department of Justice had joined the NAACP's legal crusade in the courts.

Truman used DOJ to implement policy more than most of his predecessors, and he was more successful at it than most presidents before or since. This was especially true in civil liberties and civil rights cases. In the civil liberties cases, such as those involving free speech or alleged membership in the Communist Party, at least four members of the Supreme Court were inclined to vote in support of his administration's position.

In the civil rights cases, that number of votes was even higher. As one observer wrote, "The Vinson Court was keenly attentive to the president's concerns about civil rights reform. . . . As a result of the Court's and of Vinson's special receptivity, Truman was able to realize profound advances in regard to the civil rights of African Americans—advances that were simply impossible to achieve" with segregationists and their sympathizers in control of the Senate.[2]

Reaction to the Court's newly assertive civil rights jurisprudence was mixed. The *New York Times* reported on its front page after the Court's unanimous *Shelley* decision, "Negro and Jewish organizations and church

and labor groups hailed last night the ruling of the Supreme Court forbid-
ding use of the courts to enforce racially restrictive real estate covenants."
But the headline atop the front page of the *Washington Post* in the nation's
segregated capital city read, "Race Covenant Rule Disappoints Many."[3]
Neither the Court's growing suspicion of segregation nor the Department
of Justice's antipathy toward it emerged without political risk.

In this respect, Truman was immune. He had recently won the biggest
upset in presidential history and never again would run for office. He was
eager to enact legislation by working with Congress, but in an area where
Congress refused to act despite what he saw as a moral and geopolitical
imperative to do so, Truman decided to engage the judiciary. And so DOJ
lawyers joined the NAACP's attorneys to compel the Court to challenge
America to become what it already claimed to be.

* * *

Thurgood Marshall's victory in the Supreme Court case of *Sipuel v. Board
of Regents of the University of Oklahoma*, which compelled the the state
of Oklahoma to admit qualified African American students to its publicly funded graduate schools, encouraged several professional African
Americans to apply to Oklahoma's graduate schools. These applicants
were not seeking to become plaintiffs; they believed that the case already
had been won. If academically qualified, they would be admitted, pay
tuition, and attend classes.

Instead, Oklahoma continued to reject qualified African American
applicants on racist grounds. One of the rejected applicants was a sixty-
eight-year-old teacher named George McLaurin, who held a master's degree in education and sought a doctorate. NAACP attoneys approached
McLaurin to discuss a possible lawsuit.

Marshall later explained why he and his colleagues believed McLaurin
would make an ideal plaintiff:

> The Dixiecrats and the others said it was horrible. The only thing
> Negroes were trying to do, they said, was to get social equality. As
> a matter of fact, there would be intermarriage, they said. The latter
> theory was the reason we deliberately chose Professor McLaurin.
> We had eight people who had applied and who were eligible to be
> plaintiffs, but we deliberately picked Professor McLaurin because he

was sixty-eight years old and we didn't think he was going to marry or intermarry.[4]

On McLaurin's behalf, the NAACP Legal Defense and Education Fund filed a federal lawsuit against Oklahoma, asserting that the state was violating the Constitution as interpreted by the Supreme Court. The federal district court quickly agreed. It ruled that because Oklahoma offered no separate and equal graduate school of education for its African American citizens, the federal Constitution compelled the state university to admit McLaurin to its graduate program.

Oklahoma admitted McLaurin but would not allow him to sit with his fellow students. In each one of his classes, he was forced to sit just outside the doorway of the classroom. In the library he could sit only at one designated desk, which was placed behind a newspaper cart. In the cafeteria, McLaurin was forced to eat in a separate area at a predetermined hour when no other students were dining. The sixty-eight-year-old graduate student described the entire ordeal as "quite strange and humiliating."[5]

In its noxious treatment of McLaurin, Oklahoma unwittingly helped the NAACP lawyers steer his case to directly confront the issue of segregation. McLaurin had access to all the same educational assets as the White students but he could access them only by submitting to segregation's markers. He could attend the same classes, use the library, and dine in the cafeteria as long as he did so beneath the banner of segregation. McLaurin's attorneys filed suit again in federal court to protest his treatment. In response, the university permitted McLaurin to sit in the classroom with his White classmates, but his seat was encircled by a railing marked "Reserved for Colored." His fellow students, many of them at least forty years his junior, tore down the sign.[6]

By admitting McLaurin but segregating him from his White fellow students, Oklahoma brought into relief the very question the NAACP wanted to place before the Supreme Court: whether segregation itself violated the Constitution. As Marshall reported to his team of lawyers, "In this instance we have a class of students sitting down studying together, etc. and one student is ostracized from the immediate classroom and forced to study in a position of seclusion for the obvious purpose of humiliation, degrading and what have you." McLaurin had testified in federal district

court "that it is impossible for him to do his best work under these conditions and, as a matter of fact, he has threatened to withdraw for this
reason."[7] Oklahoma seemed to have fallen into a trap of its own making.

* * *

Just a few hours after Justice Sherman Minton took his oath of office,
the Federal Council of the Churches of Christ, on behalf of its 29 million
members, filed its first *amicus curiae* brief at the Supreme Court, asking the
justices to order the University of Texas School of Law to admit qualified
African American applicants. The Federal Council joined the certiorari
petition filed by Heman Marion Sweatt, a college-educated mail carrier
in Texas who had been denied admission to the University of Texas's
Whites-only law school. Sweatt was represented by Thurgood Marshall.
In joining the NAACP's petition for certiorari, the Federal Council argued
that "the right to enjoy and exercise the inalienable rights to which every
man is endowed by his Creator is not and cannot be confined to physical
existence. . . . Segregation in matters of the mind and spirit means second
class citizenship."[8]

Heman Sweatt personally knew how true those words were. After earn-
ing a bachelor's degree in biology, the only job the World War II veteran
could find was as a mail carrier. His supervisor, who was White, refused to
promote him to a desk job, spurring the bespectacled mailman to consider
a career in law. Sweatt believed the study and practice of law to be "a
basis for political interpretation, and knowledge of writing as a weapon of
expressive leadership." He was an educated, talented man whose succinct
lament was poetic: "Jim Crow America has so warped my life."[9] The Texan
applied to the University of Texas School of Law, but he was rejected because the school refused to admit African Americans. Sweatt filed suit in
federal court.

A surprising twist emerged in Sweatt's path to the Supreme Court.
District judge Roy C. Archer, adhering strictly to the Court's most recent
decisions in civil rights cases, ruled that the federal Constitution obligated the state of Texas to provide a separate but equal legal education for
its African American citizens. Because the Supreme Court had thus far
declined to overrule *Plessy v. Ferguson*, that case still controlled a state's
rights and obligations involved in segregating its residents by race. Judge
Archer gave Texas six months to open a law school for Black Texans.[10]

Governor Beauford H. Jester and the Texas legislature sprung into action. "Let us build for the Negro youth of this state," Jester implored lawmakers, "a university worthy of the name Texas."[11] Millions of dollars were proposed to establish a Texas State University for Negroes, with a law school to open immediately. The segregated, all-Black law school would temporarily be located in the basement of the University of Texas School of Law, which would remain all White.

State legislators lauded the governor's message because they, like he, understood what was at stake in the NAACP's latest round of litigation. They were not allocating millions of dollars to establish a law school for African Americans because they suddenly wanted an influx of Black lawyers in Texas. Instead, lawmakers recognized that law schools were but the vanguard of the NAACP's legal attack on segregated schools. A University of Texas professor of educational administration confessed, "I am unable to see how segregation could be constitutionally maintained below the college level if it is abolished at or above the college level." One lawmaker explained that his colleagues were faced with a choice of "passing this bill or permitting the destruction of segregation laws in all schools."[12]

Texas allocated $3 million to create Texas State University for Negroes. Three University of Texas law school professors would teach students in the soon-to-be-opened law school.

By boldly embracing *Plessy*'s separate but equal mandate, Texas did Sweatt a great favor: it forced the Court to confront the intangible effects of racist segregation. Lawmakers' $3 million appropriation indicated that they intended for their state's all-Black law school to be a legitimate, accredited law school. They sought to establish a separate and equal law school that would comply with *Plessy v. Ferguson* and every Supreme Court precedent since.

Texas's gambit was a gift to the NAACP and DOJ attorneys because, in order for the Court to rule for Sweatt, it would have to decide that the new law school could not be equal so long as Black applicants were excluded from the older, well-established University of Texas law school. This inquiry would not turn on the number of books in the library, seats in the classrooms, or any other brick-and-mortar comparison. It would turn on contrasts of intangible factors like reputation, prestige, and stigma.

Texas recruited eleven other states to join the defense of its previously unquestioned constitutional right to segregate its citizens by race. The attorneys general of Arkansas, Florida, Georgia, Kentucky, Louisiana, Mississippi, North Carolina, Oklahoma, South Carolina, Tennessee, and Virginia filed a forceful *amicus* brief. In it they cited numerous precedents upholding the constitutionality of racial segregation. They echoed a primary point made in Texas's brief, namely that none of the cases cited by Heman Sweatt's attorneys had held that "a state may not constitutionally provide separate education for its white and Negro students at separate schools where equal education is furnished to both groups."[13]

That so many southern states joined Texas to defend racial segregation demonstrated to the Truman administration, the NAACP, and the justices themselves how significant the *Sweatt* case was. The southern governments' unity suggested that they would consider a ruling declaring segregation unconstitutional, even in the limited context of public higher education, as an attack on their way of life. Southern politicians harbored no doubts about the threat posed by African American appellants' uninterrupted string of victories before the Supreme Court. The states' *amicus* brief was an announcement that the South was unified in fervent opposition to federal judicial action against segregation. The flagship universities of those eleven states issued a joint statement declaring that they would "close the schools to prevent wholesale violence" if the Court ruled in Sweatt's favor.[14]

Conversely, the American Veterans' Committee filed *amicus* briefs in both the *Sweatt* and *McLaurin* cases to remind the Court that Congress provided educational benefits for World War II veterans of any race who enrolled in a college or university by July 25, 1951. Congress mandated that veterans had to complete their education by July 25, 1956. The American Veterans' Committee charged that southern states' refusal to admit African American students "frustrates the Congressional purpose that all verterans should have equal opportunity to obtain the educational benefits" of the law. Their brief noted that qualified White students who applied to the University of Texas School of Law in 1946, when Sweatt had applied, were admitted, had graduated, and were practicing law, while thirty-seven-year-old Sweatt's application remained bogged down in litigation. George McLaurin's forced isolation outside the classroom was intended to "humiliate" the senior citizen with a "brand of inferiority." In its most progressive point, the committee's *amicus* brief contended that McLaurin's treatment harmed both him and his White classmates.[15]

One hundred eighty-eight law professors from forty-one schools filed an *amicus* brief on Sweatt's behalf. They argued that the framers of the Fourteenth Amendment "clearly understood" that segregation was incompatible with the "equal protection" guaranteed by the Constitution. "But in its decision in 1896 of *Plessy v. Ferguson*," the professors contended, "the Supreme Court abandoned the original conception of equal protection and adopted the legal fiction that segregation is not discriminatory."[16]

For his part, Thurgood Marshall made no secret of the NAACP's goal of, as he proclaimed to an integrated audience in Austin, Texas, "completely eliminating segregation from American life." This goal was neither new nor hidden but rather was "the job to which we're all dedicated."[17]

* * *

The Supreme Court granted *certiorai* in the cases of *Sweatt v. Painter* and *McLaurin v. Oklahoma State Regents for Higher Education*. Justices scheduled oral arguments for *Sweatt*, *McLaurin*, and *Henderson v. United States*, a case challenging segregated dining cars on interstate trains, for April 4, 1950.

CHAPTER TWENTY-TWO

The Path to *Brown*
Unanimous Progress

IN THE TRUMAN ADMINISTRATION, THE Department of Justice's consistent advocacy aligned with the president's belief that, so long as Congress remained recalcitrant, any progress in the field of civil rights would be won in the courts. Due to the magnitude of the constitutional questions presented, federal district court opinions served primarily to establish the factual records of cases both sides expected to be appealed. Appellate courts could serve to clarify or hone the legal issues but their rulings would not be the final word. Litigants, their lawyers, and nearly all observers expected questions of segregation's constitutionality to be answered by the Supreme Court, the body to which Harry Truman had named three associate justices and the chief justice. Richard Kluger, in his monumental book *Simple Justice*, wrote of the justices appointed by Truman, "It was not unthinkable that the politically attuned Justices he had selected felt they owed him their allegiance on racial questions."[1]

* * *

The *amicus* briefs filed by Truman's Justice Department unequivocally denounced segregation in terms so clear that they spoke to a wider audience than the nine justices of the Court. Indeed, the government's briefs were widely quoted in newspapers and radio reports. *Henderson, McLaurin*, and *Sweatt* were "significant" cases, the government argued, because "they test the vitality and strength of the democratic ideals to which the United States is dedicated." The Court's decision would have a "large influence in determining whether the foundations of our society shall continue to be undermined by the existence and acceptance of racial discrimination having the sanction of law."[2]

The Fourteenth Amendment prohibited any state from "deny[ing] to any person within its jurisdiction equal protection of the laws." Citing a line of cases stretching over seventy-five years, the Department of Justice argued that, with the exception of *Plessy*, the Court had construed the amendment "liberally so as to carry out its purposes, namely to establish complete equality in the fundamental enjoyment of human rights and to secure those rights against governmental discrimination based on race or color." The states' treatment of their African American citizens in the *Henderson*, *McLaurin*, and *Sweatt* cases comprised "an unwarranted deviation from the principle of equality under law which the Fourteenth Amendment explicitly incorporated in the fundamental charter of this country."[3]

* * *

Before oral arguments in the three cases, Tom Clark of Texas distributed a memorandum to his fellow justices. Because "these cases arise in 'my' part of the country," his memo began, "it is proper and I hope helpful to express some views concerning them." As a threshold matter, Clark advised against issuing any decision that would forbid segregation beyond "the cases . . . limited to their facts, i.e. graduate schools."[4]

The more pertinent task, Clark contended, was to reframe the Court's analysis of what constituted a substantially "equal" facility. He urged his fellow justices to forgo comparing the size of the graduate schools' libraries and professor-to-student ratios. Instead, they should assess the schools' intangible differences, such as alumni prominence and professors' reputations.

Clark listed several reasons why segregated graduate schools could not provide educational equality. These included the "higher standing" of the previously established all-White schools, the fact that it took time "to establish a professional school of top rank," and the importance of alumni professional networks.[5] Employing *Plessy*'s separate but equal test with this lens revealed that the segregated schools were not at all equal. "If some say this undermines *Plessy*," Clark concluded, "then let it fall, as have many Nineteenth Century oracles."[6]

Clark's memo provided the justices with the roadmap they needed to proceed as the wished. It showed how the Court could order the University of Texas to desegregate its law school and expand its civil rights jurisprudence without overruling *Plessy v. Ferguson*. To be sure, Clark declared that he "would not sign an opinion which approved *Plessy*." But neither would he advocate for one that overruled it. By turning their focus to the intangible inequities between the segregated law schools, the justices could, as Clark described, "undermine *Plessy.*"[7] The Court would move forward—but not too far. And it might be able to present the nation with another unanimous opinion.

* * *

"If I win," Heman Sweatt told reporters at a press conference, "I shall study for my law degree at the law school of the University of Texas."[8] But if the justices ruled against him, he would attend a law school in the North: "I do not intend to study any further in a segregated system." He noted that his mail delivery route was in a working-class White neighborhood where most of the men worked at the nearby railroad yards. "There has been no problem with them," Sweatt reported. "They discuss the case with me quite frequently and have been very encouraging."[9]

* * *

Spectators who spent the previous night camped out in front of the Supreme Court building to secure seats in the courtroom were rewarded with lively oral arguments.

Tradition held that if the attorney general chose to appear before the justices, they would not interrupt his or her arguments with questions. In his first Court presentation, Attorney General James Howard McGrath presented the Truman administration's legal policy. "Unless segregation is ended," McGrath argued, "a serious blow will be struck at our democracy before the world."[10] His words echoed sentiments expressed by Truman and civil rights advocates since African American soldiers had returned home from World War I. The president, who had commanded an all-White Army company in that conflict, believed that, at the dawn of what would become known as the Cold War, the United States' international standing was inextricably linked to how America treated its own citizens. "The top dog in the world which is over half colored," Truman quipped, "ought to clean his own house."[11] His attorney general now sought to hammer home this point as he argued that the separate but equal doctrine established by *Plessy* was "a contradiction in terms and an unwarranted departure from the Constitution."[12]

Even after his presentation, the justices declined to question McGrath, so he took his seat. Justice Jackson was unimpressed by the attorney general's appearance before the Court, telling a friend that McGrath's presentation "added nothing except to get into a position to capitalize on any advantages for the Administration."[13]

Solicitor General Philip Perlman, McGrath's subordinate, rose to the podium. Perlman hardly managed to say "May it please the Court" before he was assailed with questions. In his answers, Perlman made clear that Truman's Department of Justice stood united with the civil rights attorneys in asking the Court to confront *Plessy*—to decide whether state-mandated segregation violated the Constitution.

Thurgood Marshall, who argued the *Sweatt* case, was particularly incisive. He declared that the Court could not sidestep *Plessy* as it had in earlier desegregation cases because Texas was constructing a separate but purportedly equal law school for its Black citizens. The NAACP had been asking the Court "for thirty years" to rule on segregation. He rebuked predictions of violence set forth in Texas's brief, urging the justices "not to be intimidated by unspecified persons in undesignated places." So long as they behaved lawfully, White students' reactions did not concern Marshall: "We want to remove governmental restriction; if they want to, they can keep their prejudices."[14]

Pro-segregation advocates pointed to a public Washington, DC, swimming pool where violence erupted after the Truman administration ordered that the all-White facility be desegregated. Marshall responded by reading into the record a letter from Secretary of the Interior Julius Krug in which Krug affirmed that the pool would remain desegregated and that he was "confident there would be no violence."[15]

Texas's attorneys firmly contended that the drafters of the Fourteenth Amendment did not intend to prohibit segregation. How could they, the Texans argued, given that the amendment's framers accepted segregation in the nation's capital? Marshall responded that the legislative history of the Fourteenth Amendment "afforded arguments for both sides and it was not possible to make a clear-cut demonstration that the framers . . . intended either to permit or to forbid segregation."[16]

* * *

On April 8, 1950, Chief Justice Vinson convened the conference to discuss the *McLaurin* and *Sweatt* cases. Debate among the justices was even livelier than oral arguments. In his opening remarks about *McLaurin*, Vinson spoke plainly: "There is color discrimination in [Oklahoma's] treatment of Negroes. I reverse. McLaurin and the other twenty-three [students] are entitled to no discrimination. Negroes are entitled to enter the university without restriction if they are admitted at all."[17]

Perhaps viewing *McLaurin* as an obvious violation of the Court's recent decisions, Justice Black, speaking after Vinson, lept straight to *Sweatt*. "You can't set up a separate law school overnight that is equal to the old one," he argued. "The diplomas have different value." As in the other segregation cases, Black's argument, however predictable it might have become, carried significant weight because the most senior member of the Court was the only justice from the Deep South. Segregation was, Black explained, "a hangover from the days when the Negro was a slave." The Court's "premise in *Plessy* is not sound—it has been refuted by facts and by history." The Alabaman would vote to "reverse both *McLaurin* and Sweatt."[18]

The justices Truman had nominated to the Court agreed that George McLaurin should be permitted to attend classes without restriction or delay. "He is admitted [to the school]," Burton said. "He can't be in and not the same." Clark agreed. Minton figured, "If you admit him, it must be on an equal footing."[19]

The other, more senior justices generally agreed in the *McLaurin* case. Even Stanley Reed granted, "When you admit a person to school, [he] should have full freedom. . . . You must admit him on an equal basis."[20]

But turning to the *Sweatt* case, in which Texas was constructing a new, purportedly equal law school, the chief justice opened his remarks by recognizing the closer question: "Here they attempted to exercise the separate but equal doctrine. There is separate treatment." In response to the memorandum circulated by Justice Clark before oral arguments, Vinson said, "As matter of policy, no great harm would result from the mingling of races in professional schools. But I don't see how we can draw the line there. I can't distinguish professional and elementary schools." The chief justice said he would affirm the decision to ban Sweatt from the University of Texas.[21]

"I reverse," Black said.

"I would prefer to put it on the question of equality," Reed offered. "Every appeal raises this issue. Are the facilities equal? If we have to decide, I would say that the facilities were equal." Reed would join Vinson in affirming the the lower court's ruling.[22] Burton privately noted that Reed was arguing for the Court to expressly uphold *Plessy*'s separate but equal test.

Eager to embrace judicial restraint when the case involved civil rights or civil liberties, Frankfurter cautioned, "We should not go beyond what is necessary here. We should not go out and meet problems." He urged the others to resolve both cases within the confines of *Plessy*. As he often did when arguing against the NAACP's position, Frankfurter reminded everyone, "I was for ten years counsel for the NAACP." Here, again, the NAACP was asking the Court to overturn *Plessy*, but doing so, he contended, was unnecessary to resolve these cases. The record, particularly in *Sweatt*, clearly established inequality. "The Texas University law library has 65,000 volumes," Frankfurter noted, "compared to 20,000 volumes for the other school. This is not equality. I reverse [the lower court's ruling] on a separate and equal basis."

Realizing that a majority was forming around the idea of reversing on the basis of the schools' glaring inequality, Burton conceded, "I would be willing to say that it was not equal here, saving the broader question." But to be clear, he added, "I would like to overthrow the *Plessy* doctrine at the graduate level."[23]

Thurgood Marshall and his co-counsel had tacitly directed much of their argument toward Justice Clark. They correctly predicted that the proud University of Texas alumnus would reject his home state's argument that a newly created law school was equal to his alma mater. "It is ridiculous," Clark declared at the conference, "to say that [the new school] is equal. I don't think that they could build a school equal to the University of Texas." Even as he recognized the constitutional difficulty in doing so, Clark wanted the Court to hold that segregated graduate schools were unconstitutional but segregated elementary schools were not: "I don't want to affect elementary schools. It is important to have as many of us as possible in this opinion. I am willing to subscribe to the doctrine that in the Texas case the two schools were not equal."[24]

For the Court's most junior member, neither *McLaurin* nor *Sweatt* presented a difficult question. "It is an unreasonable classification, to refuse admission to graduate schools on racial grounds," Sherman Minton said, when at last it was his turn to speak. "I reverse."[25]

＊ ＊ ＊

Without recorded explanation, Vinson reversed his decision in the *Sweatt* case and assigned both the *McLaurin* and *Sweatt* opinions to himself. He assigned the *Henderson* transportation desegregation case to Burton. Vinson believed that the Court's word on the graduate school segregation cases should come from the chief justice. He also wanted to deliver a unanimous opinion to the American people. Elected officials, state attorneys general, civil rights attorneys, and judges across the nation needed a clear explication of the law to do their jobs. But more importantly, all Americans, particularly Black and White southerners, deserved to know that the justices were united on the segregation questions placed before them.

Reaching unanimity would be difficult to achieve, particularly as the NAACP and DOJ began directly calling on the Court to overturn the fifty-four-year-old precedent *Plessy v. Ferguson*. Vinson nonetheless would vie for all nine votes for his *McLaurin* and *Sweatt* opinions. His moderately progressive stance on the issues would, he hoped, move the Court's jurisprudence but not move it so far as to inspire dissent.

＊ ＊ ＊

Vinson circulated drafts of the *Sweatt* and *McLaurin* opinions, to which Reed and Frankfurter quickly suggested edits. Eager to keep Reed in the majority, Frankfurter urged Vinson to accept Reed's changes, contending that they were "after all, in the spirit of your opinions in that they seek to accomplish the desired result without needlessly stirring the kind of feelings that are felt even by truly liberal and high-minded southerners." (It seems clear that Frankfurter was referring only to "feelings that are felt by" White southerners.) The former Harvard Law School professor advised Vinson to keep his opinion as concise as possible: "The shorter the opinion, the more there is an appearance of unexcitement and inevitability about it, the better."[26]

Black offered support for the chief justice with whom he so often was at odds. After reviewing Vinson's draft *Sweatt* opinion, Black returned it with a note that read in part, "I sincerely hope it can obtain a unanimous approval. . . . Full Court acceptance of this and the *McLaurin* opinion should add force to our holdings."[27]

Again the NAACP and DOJ were asking the Court to overturn *Plessy*. And again, the Court would decline to do so. The decisions would be significant but not as groundbreaking as the NAACP and the Truman administration wanted them to be. This was, in no small part, how Vinson would garner unanimous support for his draft opinions in both cases.

* * *

On June 5, 1950, the Court announced its decisions in all three cases. In *Henderson v. the United States*, it ruled that the Interstate Commerce Act prohibited train companies from segregating passengers by race on interstate train lines.[28] Because this case turned on a statute rather than a constitutional argument, observers correctly understood *Henderson* as affirming existing law. Public attention focused on the education cases, *Sweatt v. Painter* and *McLaurin v. Oklahoma State Regents*.

The Supreme Court ordered the University of Texas School of Law to admit Heman Sweatt. But Vinson's opinion declined to address the "petitioner's contention that *Plessy v. Ferguson* should be re-examined in the light of contemporary knowledge respecting the purposes of the Fourteenth Amendment and the effects of racial segregation." In *McLaurin*, the Court ordered the University of Oklahoma to remove "state-imposed restrictions"—the markers segregating George McLaurin from his classmates—that rendered "his training unequal to that of his classmates."[29] As in *Sweatt*, the justices declined to address "petitioner's contention that *Plessy v. Ferguson* should be re-examined."[30] All three decisions were unanimous.

* * *

Sweatt's victory, though not as sweeping as he had hoped, reverberated throughout African American communities. Activist Maceo Smith later described the reaction: "The realization seems to be general that our struggle for freedom was really only begun when Heman Marion Sweatt received a favorable decision from the U.S. Supreme Court in June. Prior to the *Sweatt* victory, our fight was to gain a foothold, to make that first crack in the wall of oppression that surrounds us. The *Sweatt* victory was that foothold." The Court's ruling had vindicated African Americans' faith in what was possible: "Now we have before us the task of going to court again and again until the foothold becomes a walking room, until segregation is driven out of every Negro's life."[31]

Charles Lincoln Harper, president of the NAACP's Atlanta chapter, told reporters, "School officials of Georgia on all levels should take cognizance of these opinions and immediately provide equal school facilities for Negro youth, or the Negro people will have no other alternative than to invoke these decisions." He decried the continued existence of "these substandard Negro colleges operated by [the state]," as well as the different salary schedules for White and Black teachers and professors. White government officials "could save themselves embarassment and court costs by complying with the law without further delay."[32]

Some leaders in African American communities gave voice to the private disappointment felt by attorneys at the NAACP and the Department of Justice who had expressly asked the Court to overturn *Plessy v. Ferguson.* Dr. Benjamin E. Mays, the president of Morehouse College, pointed to the Court's dodges in each case: "The Supreme Court evaded the issue of segregation in ruling against a curtain or partition in dining cars [in *Henderson*]. It was done on the basis of interstate commerce law. . . . In the *Sweatt* case, the university was ordered to admit a Negro because the school at Houston is not as good as the law school at the University of Texas." Mays refused to acknowledge that the Court perhaps had gone furthest in *McLaurin*: "In the *McLaurin* case, the Supreme Court ruled against segregation at the University of Oklahoma because in segregating McLaurin, he was not provided equal education." Mays somberly concluded, "The U.S. Supreme Court has not ruled that segregation on the basis of color or race is discriminatory."[33]

In August 1952, two months after the Court's ruling, Heman Sweatt received a letter from the office of the registrar and dean of admissions at the University of Texas School of Law. Several Black-owned newspapers reprinted the short letter in its entirety: "On the basis of your B.A. degree from Wiley College and graduate work at the University of Michigan," Dean H. Y. McCown wrote, "you are eligible for admission to the law school."[34]

* * *

Southern White politicians were apoplectic and railed against the Court's rulings. Running for reelection, Georgia governor Herman Talmadge assured voters, "As long as I am governor, Negroes will not be admitted to white schools." His opponent, M. E. Thompson, promised that if he were elected, "There will be no Negroes attending white schools."[35]

In sharp contrast to the southern politicians, Truman praised the Court's decisions. Delivering Howard University's commencement address on June 13, 1952, the president extolled the Court's recent rulings, telling graduates, "Since the court decisions outlawing discrimination, more than a thousand Negro graduate and professional students have been accepted by 10 state universities that were closed to Negroes before. In the last 5 years," he added proudly, "legislation has been passed in 10 other States to abolish segregation or discrimination in schools and colleges."[36]

CHAPTER TWENTY-THREE

Caution in the Wind

DAYS AFTER THE COURT HANDED down the decisions, Thurgood Marshall wrote to a colleague that the *Henderson, McLaurin,* and *Sweatt* opinions were "replete with roadmarkings telling us where to go next."[1] He was terribly disappointed that the Court had again declined to overrule *Plessy,* but the Court also again had refused to affirm the nineteenth-century decision. Particularly in the *Sweatt* opinion, *Plessy* "ha[d] been gutted."[2] Answering the question of "where to go next" was the NAACP's first order of business.

Marshall called together forty-three attorneys and fourteen NAACP branch and state conference presidents. The group resolved that in all future education cases, their pleadings would "be aimed at obtaining education on a non-segregated basis and that no relief other than that will be acceptable."[3] With the *McLaurin* and *Sweatt* decisions in hand, Marshall contended, "We have at last obtained the opening wedge."[4]

* * *

After enrolling in the University of Texas School of Law, Heman Sweatt faced mortal threats and intimidation. A cross was burned next to his car. He fell ill and his marriage collapsed beneath the strain. Sweatt eventually failed courses and withdrew from law school.

As a practical matter, *Sweatt* and *McLaurin* delivered little impact. Colleges throughout the South remained all White; none were considering plans for gradual desegregation pursuant to the Supreme Court's rulings.[5]

Southern public officials nonetheless realized the threat posed by these decisions. Although the cases involved graduate schools, the coming fight would embroil primary and secondary schools, and here White southerners drew the line. In Black's home state of Alabama, the legislature passed a resolution condemning the Court's rulings and declaring that its public schools for children would remain segregated.[6] Led by Governor

Herman Talmadge, Georgia increased funding for its segregated schools for African Americans, seeking to at least feign compliance with *Plessy's* separate but equal mandate.[7]

Some of the justices shared the southern politicians' concerns. Desegregating graduate schools had become a proxy fight for both sides. Lawyers for the NAACP and the Truman administration signaled as much by directly—and repeatedly—asking the Court to overturn *Plessy*. Jackson wrote to a friend about the *McLaurin* and *Sweatt* cases, "Neither side had suggested any logical division" between graduate schools and elementary schools. "They all take the position that it is all or none. . . . That is the great hope of the one side and the great fear of the other."[8] Clark later said that, with the *Sweatt* and *McLaurin* opinions, "We implicitly overruled Plessy."[9]

Constitutional precedent, of course, cannot be overturned by implication. Truman's Department of Justice made clear that it would continue to call for the Court to confront *Plessy v. Ferguson* and declare racial segregation unconstitutional. The showdown that the Supreme Court had avoided for so many years could be avoided no longer.

* * *

In the summer and fall of 1951, the NAACP filed two appeals with the Supreme Court: *Briggs v. Elliot* and *Brown v. Board of Education of Topeka* sought to desegregate public schools in Clarendon County, South Carolina, and Topeka, Kansas, respectively. Granting *certiorai* and scheduling the cases in the regular order of business meant they would be argued and decided before the 1952 presidential election. By this time it appeared that the Court, though perhaps not unanimously, would rule that segregated public schools were unconstitutional. Therefore, as Frankfurter later explained to a group of law clerks, the justices wanted to forestall deciding the cases until after the elections, so that the Court's decision would not become political fodder in campaigns for every office from local school board to the presidency of the United States. The Court therefore took its time in responding to the *Briggs* and *Brown* petitions. Finally, on June 9, 1952, the Court noted probable jurisdiction and scheduled oral arguments for early October.[10]

On July 12, NAACP attorneys filed an appeal with the Supreme Court in the case of *Davis v. County School Board of Prince Edward County*, which arose in the Commonwealth of Virgina. News of the filing must have been music to the justices' ears: just a few days before they were scheduled to hear arguments in the *Briggs* and *Brown* desegregation cases, they noted probable jurisdiction in *Davis*, canceled the *Brown* and *Briggs* arguments, and scheduled all three cases to be heard on December 8, 1952—more than a month after Election Day.

There was a similar school desegregation case filed by African American families in Washington, DC, that was also winding its way through the courts. Chief Justice Vinson asked the clerk of the Supreme Court, Harold B. Wiley, to ask the plaintiffs' attorneys in that case to file an appeal directly with the Supreme Court. Vinson wanted the District of Columbia case argued along with the three others. The Washingtonians were still awaiting a hearing before the court of appeals, but they knew that the chief justice's request was as good as an order.[11] They filed a petition for *certiorari*, which the Court granted on November 10, 1952.

Three days later, Albert Young, Delaware's attorney general, filed a *certiorari* petition for two school desegregation cases in his state. When Wiley relayed Vinson's request that Young present oral arguments the same week as the other four school desegregation cases, Young objected, declaring that the proposed schedule did not provide enough time for him to properly brief the case. Wiley told Young that he could submit his briefs three weeks after oral arguments. But the Court would hear oral arguments in the Delaware cases along with the other four school desegregation cases, beginning on December 9.

* * *

Four days after hearing arguments, Vinson opened the conference on the school desegregation cases in a manner suggesting he had little intention of leading the Court on the momentous decisions before them. "I am not sure what we should do today," he said from his seat at the head of the conference table. "It is 3:30 p.m."[12]

He then embarked on a discussion of the five cases. In each one he expressed misgivings about ruling in favor of desegregation. "We face the complete abolition of the public school system in the South," Vinson warned. "It may be easy to say that the result is of no consequence to us, but I think that it is." He argued that southern states were working to make their schools for African American students equal to the schools for

White students, saying, "The schools here are not equal at the moment, but they are moving toward it. I am inclined toward giving these states the time to make their facilities equal." Amid his litany of reservations, Vinson proclaimed, "Boldness is essential, but wisdom is indispensable."[13] Some have pointed to this last statement, along with the pride Vinson took in his *McLaurin* and *Sweatt* opinions, as evidence that he was inclined to vote to hold segregation unconstitutional in these cases. Unfortunately, Vinson's own words and other justices' notes and recollections of the conference indicate this was not so.

Hugo Black dove straight to the practical realities he believed would arise in the wake of a ruling holding segregation unconstitutional. Black had represented Alabama in the Senate, where he filibustered antilynching legislation and briefly joined the Ku Klux Klan to benefit his political career. He was all but reborn on the Supreme Court, where by 1952 he was highly regarded as a progressive intellectual force. Black flatly told his brethren that there would "be serious incidents and some violence if the Court holds segregation unlawful." He correctly predicted that some southern states would "probably take evasive measures while purporting to obey [a desegregation order]." Southern White reaction "would be serious and drastic," and overturning *Plessy* "will mean trouble." Nonetheless, Black asserted, "I have to say that segregation *of itself* violates the Constitution, unless the long line of decisions and *stare decisis* prevents such a ruling. . . . I have to vote that way, to end segregation."[14]

Reed had been wary of the Court's desegregation decisions since at least 1948, when he expressed concern at the *Sipuel* conference. Faced now with the prospect of integrating children's classrooms, the Kentuckian spoke at some length. The fact was, as he saw it, "Negroes have not thoroughly assimilated." In a remarkable swipe at Thurgood Marshall, William Coleman, and other African American attorneys on the cases who happened to be light-skinned, Reed said, "There has been some amalgamation of the races, as shown by the counsel who appeared here. States are authorized to make up their own minds on this question. . . . There has been great, steady progress in the South in the advancement of the interests of the Negroes. States should be left to work out the problems for themselves. It is the right of the states to improve Negroes' status."[15]

Reed turned to a line of argument that charitably can be described as optimistic. "Segregation is gradually disappearing," he proclaimed. "This applies to both North and South." And because segregation was disappearing, he asked, "Why not let it go on? . . . Segregation in the border states will disappear in fifteen or twenty years. Ten years in Virginia perhaps. Ten years would make it really equal. Every year helps. In the Deep South, separate but equal schools must be allowed." Lest there be any mistake as to his position, Reed concluded, "I uphold segregation as constitutional."[16]

All the Court's decisions in the earlier desegregation cases had been unanimous. Reed's statement, in the wake of Vinson's remarks opening the conference, confirmed that a desegregation order in the primary school cases would be the ruling of a divided Court. If a majority of the Court declared segregation in public schools unconstitutional with a minority dissenting, White southerners' resistance might exceed that predicted by Black.

"We need an effective way to deal with this," Frankfurter asserted, "and we should set all these cases down for reargument on specific issues." He then spent some time explaining why he thought the cases should be reargued, but he likely already had the votes to delay deciding the cases.[17]

Minton disagreed with Frankfurter's suggestion that the justices schedule the cases for reargument. "The hour is late," the Court's junior justice announced. If the justices overturned *Plessy*, "There will be trouble, but this race grew up in trouble. The Negro is oppressed and has been in bondage for years after slavery was abolished. Segregation is *per se* unconstitutional. I am ready to vote now."[18]

Frankfurter estimated a five-to-four vote to overturn *Plessy*. Jackson believed there were five to seven votes to overturn, while Burton thought there was a six-vote majority to do so. Only Black, Burton, Douglas, and Minton had registered their intention to vote to overturn *Plessy*.[19] Faced with the likelihood of delivering a divided opinion on an enormously significant case, the justices unanimously voted to order that all five cases be reargued.

Frankfurter's clerks devised five questions for counsel to address in reargument. The justices edited the questions and sent them to the attorneys. Although broken into subparts and follow-up questions, the inquiries centered on two topics: the meaning and intent of the Fourteenth Amendment as it was drafted and ratified, and whether the Court possessed the authority to invalidate segregation under the Fourteenth Amendment or its equitable powers.[20] On June 8, 1953, the Court scheduled the cases for reargument on October 12.

By then, Truman was no longer president, and when the Court convened for oral arguments on October 12, 1953, Vinson would no longer be chief justice. Before *Brown*, the Supreme Court had delivered an uninterrupted line of unanimous decisions ordering neighborhoods and graduate schools to desegregate. With Truman's executive order desegregating the armed forces, the Court's decisions had conditioned the minds of all Americans to believe that integration was possible. Department of Justice attorneys had argued as forcefully for desegregation in the *Brown* cases as they had in *Hurd*, *Sipuel*, *Henderson*, *McLaurin*, and *Sweatt*. And yet when first faced with the five *Brown* cases, the Court was unable to achieve unanimity and, perhaps wisely, deferred ruling on the most significant litigation filed during the Truman administration.

CHAPTER TWENTY-FOUR

Monongahela River Valley Hope

SEVEN MONTHS BEFORE THE SUPREME Court heard the 1952 arguments in the school desegregation cases, President Truman delivered a television and radio address announcing his decision to seize the steel mills to avert an impending strike. He had signed Executive Order 10340 directing the secretary of commerce, Charles Sawyer, "to take possession of" the steel companies' plants, facilities, and any other property the secretary "may deem necessary in the interests of national defense." Truman's order instructed Sawyer "to operate or arrange for the operation of" the companies and to "determine and prescribe" the "conditions of employment" at them.[1]

Those directly affected by the executive order acted decisively in the first hours after Truman's speech. Philip Murray, president of both the Congress of Industrial Organizations (CIO) and the United Steelworkers, immediately issued a statement ordering his men back to work: "The Government having seized the steel plants, you are hereby directed to comply with the request of the president of the United States and to continue to work." He then assured the public, "As patriotic Americans, the United Steelworkers will comply with the president's request and continue to work for their Government."[2] Because the strike deadline was less than seventy minutes away, Murray could not rely on telegram and wire services to convey his message in time. He feverishly telephoned more than two-dozen district leaders to direct them to deliver his orders to their millworkers.

Murray's sense of urgency was well-founded. As jubilant as union members were about the president's decision to seize the steel mills, Harry S. Truman was not the man they had elected to tell them whether a strike was on or off. A few workers began arriving for their midnight shift at one Pennsylvania steel mill only to be turned back by their picketing

brethren, who told them, "We'll wait until we have orders from Murray."[3]
Steelworkers returned to the mills only at Murray's direction.

For all of the impending legal and political rancor in Washington, the
mills reopened peacefully. While the workers were greatly relieved and
executives were livid, calm prevailed. After a few days the mills would return to full production. In Youngstown, Ohio, the chairman of the Sharon
Steel Corporation announced that his company was operating under protest and without any waiver of its legal rights. "If these properties can be
seized in this manner," Henry A. Roemer angrily asserted, "it is high time
that the home-owning and home-loving property owners and owners of
other forms of business enterprises be awakened to the simple fact that
the American people are facing the most grave, the most serious and what
may prove to be the most tragic period of our history."[4]

* * *

Moments after Truman concluded his speech announcing the seizure,
Secretary of Commerce Charles Sawyer held a news conference in his office. He was the man suddenly in control of the nation's steel industry. An
experienced attorney and former lieutenant governor of Ohio, Sawyer had
been commerce secretary for almost four years. He was widely regarded
as more favorable to management and business than most members of the
administration.

Running the nation's steel industry from his government perch was a
job he told reporters he "neither requested nor wanted." During this time
of the Korean conflict, however, "when our men at the front are taking
orders in the face of great danger," Sawyer maintained that he "could do
no less. The president has given me what I realize is a difficult assignment.
I accept it." Sawyer answered questions with admirable candor. When one
journalist asked if the federal government could legally enter into a contract with the union, he replied, "I don't know." Another journalist asked
if Truman's seizure of an entire industry was tantamount to socialism. "I
would not consider it socialization," Sawyer answered. "I've been charged
with a good many things but I have not been charged with socialism."[5]

There were myriad logistical matters to settle. Sawyer surprised some
observers by appointing the steel company presidents to operate the now
government-owned mills.[6] He asked the executives to start keeping separate books for the time they were under government control, explaining
that the seizure was not intended "to make money for the government."

To whom did the company presidents now answer?

The men were now "responsible to me and to the board[s] of directors."

Could they declare stock dividends?

"Yes," Sawyer answered, before quickly adding, "Frankly I hadn't thought of that. My offhand opinion is that they could."

Could the secretary cite a specific constitutional provision to justify the president's seizure?

"No, I would rather leave that to the attorney general."

"Is it the general welfare clause?" a reporter persisted.

"It may not be confined to that."[7]

Whether Truman's executive order could find justification in that or any other constitutional clause was a question that would quickly be laid at the doorstep of the judiciary branch—specifically at the doorstep of one federal judge's home in a quiet neighborhood a few miles north of the White House.

* * *

Twenty-seven minutes after Truman's radio and television address, attorneys for the Republic Steel Corporation and the Youngstown Sheet & Tube Company rang the doorbell at the Washington, DC, home of federal district judge Walter M. Bastian.[8] They handed him a motion seeking both a temporary restraining order and an injunction to prevent Executive Order 10340 from taking effect. Judge Bastian scheduled oral arguments for 11:30 the following morning.[9] Their case would be heard by Bastian's colleague Alexander Holtzoff.

* * *

The morning after his speech announcing the steel seizure, before the federal district court hearing, Truman sent a message to Congress. Taking temporary control of the steel mills was, the president explained, an act he undertook "with the utmost reluctance. The idea of Government operation of the steel mills is thoroughly distasteful to me and I want to see it ended as soon as possible." But "the alternatives appeared to be even worse—so much worse that I could not accept them." He presented the federal government's alternatives as a choice between either shutting down the steel industry or agreeing to the steel executives' demand for a price increase so substantial it would inflict "incalculable damage" to the nation.

Truman all but ignored the Taft-Hartley Act, which Congress passed to deal with an extraordinary labor crisis such as this. Among other provisions, Taft-Hartley permitted the president to seek an eighty-day injunction to stop or prevent a strike. Labor leaders had opposed the act, and Truman had vetoed it, but Congress had overridden his veto.

Now, instead of invoking Taft-Hartley, Truman declared to the senators and representatives "that Government operation of the steel mills for a temporary period was the least undesirable of the courses of action that lay open." He invited Congress "to pass legislation establishing specific terms and conditions" under which the federal government would operate the steel mills. In the meantime, his administration would "keep the steel industry operating" while seeking to settle the industry's underlying labor dispute.[10] A few senators offered bills but none made it to the president's desk for signature. As far as Congress was concerned, Truman should have followed the law—the Taft-Hartley Act—which it had passed for emergencies just like this.

* * *

Roughly ten minutes after hearing oral arguments, federal district court judge Alexander Holtzoff summoned the parties back into his courtroom and called the court to order. He had made his decision. Hotlzoff explained that his primary concern was that an order granting the steel companies' motion for a temporary restraining order (TRO) would result in a federal district court disallowing an action of the president of the United States. It would, as he put it, "nullify and stop the carrying out" of a presidential executive order. This Holtzoff doubted his court had the power to do: "It is very doubtful, to say the least, where a Federal Court would have the authority to issue an injunction against the President of the United States."[11]

Even if he accepted the steel companies' contention that issuing a TRO would restrain only Commerce Secretary Sawyer from taking control of the steel industry, the effect of doing so would be to nullify Executive Order 10340. "The court should not do by indirection," Holtzoff explained, "what it could not do directly." He denied the steel corporations' motion. As the Associated Press reported, the Department of Justice attorney did not once cite any "specific authority" to support his argument that "the president had ample powers to take the action."[12]

* * *

Hours after winning his historic 1948 election, Harry Truman had confided to a friend, "Labor did it."[13] Whether organized labor played a larger role in

Truman's victory than African Americans' support or Strom Thurmond's Dixiecrat candidacy was debatable. As with most electoral victories—particularly upsets—Truman's triumph resulted from a combination of many factors, not all of which were under any candidate's control. But steel company executives embraced the idea that the president had seized their corporations because he owed the unions.

In a remarkable nationwide television and radio address delivered the night after Truman announced the seizure and hours after a federal district court declined to stop it, Clarence Randall, an executive chosen to speak for all steel companies, called Truman's seizure of the steel companies a "corrupt political deal" that "discharge[d] a political debt to the CIO." Randall responded to the president as stridently as any private citizen publicly ever had. Visibly angry, he asserted that the president had acted "without the slightest shadow of legal right. No law passed by Congress gave him this power. He knows this and speaks of general authority conferred on him by the Constitution. But I say, my friends, that the Constitution was adopted by our forefathers to prevent tyranny, not to create it."[14]

Randall incisively cut to the quick of the argument, turning to the very constitutional question that would reach the Supreme Court: "When he asked the Congress for power to seize private property, they said no. They gave him instead the Taft-Hartley Act, which he now spurns, and the power which they denied him he now has seized." Randall, perhaps unwittingly, had made a near-haiku of the reasoning behind what would become one of the most significant opinions ever written by a Supreme Court justice.

Randall's television and radio address struck a political nerve in federal Washington as well as with the public. Pennsylvania Republican representative Hugh D. Scott, Jr., echoed Randall's words when he charged that Truman was "engaged in paying a debt to the C.I.O. in as colorful, exciting and obvious way as possible." Seizing the steel mills was, Scott allowed, "a very shrewd political move."[15] Steel company executives not only bought radio and television airtime; they paid for newspaper advertisements promoting their position.

Given how strongly the editorial board of nearly every major newspaper and magazine in the country opposed Truman's actions, however, steel managers could have saved their money by letting the editors speak for them. The *Saturday Evening Post, Wall Street Journal, New York Daily News, Washington Post, New York Times, Nation* magazine, and *Time* magazine were among the publications that excoriated the president for exceeding what they viewed as the well-established bounds of the executive branch's constitutional authority. The *Detroit Free Press* cautioned that unless the courts or Congress stopped Truman, "our whole constitutional system is doomed to destruction," while the *New York Times* accused the president of attempting to create "a new regime of government by executive decree," which was incompatible "with our own democratic principle of government by laws and not by men."[16] Not seven years after the end of World War II, the *New York Daily News* blared an editorial headline reading, "Truman Does a Hitler."[17]

CIO president Philip Murray accused steel company executives of using their media campaign "to create strikes and disturbances" in the industry. In a speech at the National Press Club in Washington, DC, he charged the executives of launching "the greatest campaign of advertising against the president of the United States and the government in the history of the country."[18] Murray no doubt was concerned that the steelworkers, though relieved that the government takeover had averted a strike, remained restless about their wages, which at this point remained frozen.

Americans were closely divided on the question of whether the president had legally seized the steel mills. The Department of Justice received unsolicited legal advice from lawyers and laypeople on how to defend the seizure, while the Department of Commerce bore the brunt of angry letters opposing Truman's decision. White House officials claimed that their constituent mail was "running half and half." National polls indiciated that slightly more Americans approved of Truman's actions than disapproved. This roughly even split belied the fact that opinions divided along party lines, with most Democrats supporting his actions and most Republicans opposed to it.[19]

Perhaps reflecting this divide in public opinion, Congress held hearings on Truman's seizure of the steel mills but passed no legislation restricting or enabling his claimed right to commandeer the industry. The Senate Judiciary Committee formed a subcommittee to investigate whether the seizure was legal. The subcommittee's Democratic chairman admitted that the administration had ignored his request that an official appear to testify before the subcommittee. Upon further pressing, Solicitor General Philip Perlman explained that because the seizure was the subject of active litigation, "it would be inappropriate of me to make such a presentation at this time before a legislative body."[20]

Senator Robert Taft, who was embroiled in a crowded race for the Republican presidential nomination, declared that Truman's actions were "a valid case for impeachment" and that "impeachment should be considered by the House."[21] Democratic senator Estes Kefauver of Tennessee, who was running for his party's presidential nomination, called Taft's assertion "ridiculous." Campaigning in Boston, Kefauver explained, "My personal feeling is that executive seizure is dangerous and that concessions could have been made on both sides," but Truman "used his best judgment in the matter."[22] Democrat Hubert Humphrey chastised his fellow senators for not passing legislation to grant seizure powers to the president, proclaiming on the Senate floor, "Congress was perfectly willing to let the bodies of young men to be seized . . . [but seems] unwilling to give the president the power of seizure . . . so as to protect the bodies and hearts and lives and souls of those young men and their families by making sure that the arms for defense are ready and available."[23]

While Congress dithered and more steel companies filed suit against the government, Truman continued to make his case to the American public. But the more he spoke, the more he raised doubts over the legality of the seizure. Public skepticism grew as Truman insisted that the president, except where explicitly limited by the Constitution, possessed sweeping, nearly absolute powers to address national problems. A week after he issued the executive order, a journalist at a news conference asked, "Mr. President, if you can seize the steel mills under your inherent powers, can you, in your opinion, also seize the newspapers and/or the radio stations?" Without missing a beat, Truman replied, "Under similar circumstances, the president has to act for whatever is for the best of the country. That's the answer to your question." Three days later Truman doubled-down, declaring that the president "has very great inherent powers to meet great national emergencies." When asked if he recognized that substituting inherent, unspecified presidential powers for established written laws posed a "danger" to American liberties, he impatiently answered with a tautology: "Well, of course I do. . . . But when you meet an emergency in an emergency, you have to meet it."[24]

Congressional inaction to end the seizure raised the stakes of the federal court cases. White House officials had good reason to worry about the political effects of a judicial decision in the steel companies' favor. Republicans in the House of Representatives, emboldened by public alarm over the administration's argument that the president possessed sweeping powers to take control of virtually any business or industry if he deemed it necessary, announced that they were considering impeaching Truman. Republican leaders, however, were able to convince their caucus to wait until the courts ruled. "Nobody supported President Truman's position," Minority Leader Joseph Martin of Massachusetts told reporters after a meeting of House Republicans. "There is considerable sentiment for impeachment if the courts hold that [the seizure] was an illegal act."[25] Nine proposals, ranging from articles of impeachment to expressions of congressional disapproval, had already been referred to the House Judiciary Committee.

During the next two weeks, seven steel companies filed suit, seeking injunctions against Truman's order. All seven asserted that the president possessed no statutory or constitutional authority to seize their mills and therefore any government action taken pursuant to Executive Order 10340 was "invalid, unlawful and without effect."[26] In their prehearing brief, Department of Justice attorneys argued that the threat of a steel industry strike presented a national emergency which the president possessed inherent constitutional power to avert by seizing the mills. Second, they argued, the judiciary had no authority to forbid the executive branch from carrying out Executive Order 10340.

The Justice Department had no Senate-confirmed leader during this most critical time. Amid a cloud of ethical questions, Attorney General J. Howard McGrath had resigned just a few days before Truman seized the steel mills. Senators held off on holding a vote for federal judge James McGranery, Truman's nominee to replace McGrath, choosing to conduct the sort of lengthy, politically minded background investigation that is common in federal Washington today but in 1952 was rare. The practical result was that DOJ attorneys prepared the executive branch's arguments without an attorney general at the helm. The cases challenging the constitutionality of Executive Order 10340 were collectively assigned to Judge David A. Pine, who scheduled arguments on motions for preliminary injunctions for April 24, 1952.

* * *

A month before oral arguments, on March 29, dressed in a tuxedo for an event at the DC Armory for five thousand Democratic Party members who had paid at least a hundred dollars apiece to attend, Truman announced that he would not run for reelection. "I shall not be a candidate for reelection," he told the shocked crowd. "I have served my country long, and I think efficiently and honestly. I shall not accept a re-nomination. I do not feel that it is my duty to spend another four years in the White House." After a pause, the audience mustered the requisite cries of protest, over which Truman extolled "the things the Democratic Party has done, and the high ideals that have made it great."

Without doubt a good many of the donors gathered at the Armory that night were relieved Truman would not seek what would have amounted to a third term in office. His approval ratings hovered near 20 percent while the rates of inflation and unemployment continued to rise.[27] Americans had begun to view the Korean War, in which thousands of Americans had been killed and the Communists had twice ended truce negotiations, as an unnecessary and painfully costly war.

Truman had lost the New Hampshire Democratic Party primary to Senator Kefauver. It was doubtful whether the president could win the nomination of his own party, much less a general election. In the spring of 1952, when he seized the steel mills, Harry Truman was politically weaker than any American president had been in a generation.

On the very day he ordered the seizure of the steel mills, Truman replied to a letter from Justice Sherman Minton. About his decision not to seek reelection, the president wrote, "You and I have been 'through the mill.' Most politicians never know when to quit." Ever the keen political observer, he added, "All this 'weeping and wailing and so forth' convinces me that no mistake has been made."[28]

CHAPTER TWENTY-FIVE

The District Court Hearing

LAWYERS, JOURNALISTS, AND SPECTATORS PACKED the federal district courtroom, buzzing and twisting nervously before Judge David Pine's arrival. Twenty-one attorneys were to present on behalf of the seven steel companies. The federal government was represented by Department of Justice lawyers Holmes Baldridge, Marvin Taylor, and Samuel Slade. Reporters scoured the hallways for sources. Litigants and lawyers in other, unrelated cases found welcome distraction in the buzzing crowd.

In its remembrance of Pine, who died in 1970 at the age of seventy-eight, the *New York Times* asserted, "Judge Pine had developed his backbone over long and difficult years."[1] His father was a successful lawyer who, like many successful lawyers, died sooner than expected, and David was forced to drop out of high school in 1907 to support his family. Luck rewarded work as he eventually earned a law degree after attending night school at Georgetown. Pine served in the Army during World War I and returned home to work in private practice and later at the Department of Justice, where he rose to the rank of chief assistant U.S. attorney. On April 2, 1945, President Franklin Roosevelt named Pine and fourteen others to the U.S. District Court for the District of Columbia. Pine would serve there for twenty-five years and preside over thousands of cases, none of which would so affect the nation as the steel seizure case of 1952.

Pine was sixty years old when he heard oral arguments on the steel seizure case. One reporter described the married father of one daughter as "slightly stooped, with iron-gray hair and rimless spectacles [who] heard the hot arguments of Government and industry quietly." Spectators came to appreciate his patient, dry humor. When DOJ attorneys contended that the steel companies could afford to wait years for the courts to decide whether the seizure was constitutional, Pine retorted, "Why are they here, then?"[2]

Soon after the proceedings began, Judge Pine soon noticed a discrepancy between the steel companies' briefs and their arguments in court. In their briefs, plaintiffs' counsel argued that the secretary of commerce seizing their property pursuant to Executive Order 10340 was unlawful because the president lacked the authority to issue the order; therefore, the seizure should be enjoined. But here in court, the steel companies' lawyers, led by Theodore Kiendl of the prestigious New York City law firm of Davis, Polk, Wardwell, Sunderland, and Kiendl, argued only for a preliminary injunction to prevent Secretary of Commerce Charles Sawyer from changing the terms and conditions of the steelworkers' employment. Pine explained that if he granted that request, the seizure would continue under the current employment stipulations. If the seizure was in fact unlawful, then why should the court permit it to continue?

Bethlehem Steel's attorney, Bruce Bromley, quickly assessed the situation and broke with Kiendl, informing the court, "That is not all that Bethlehem Steel is asking for, Your Honor: we have filed a motion for a preliminary injunction and our position is 'the whole hog.'" Lawyers for the other steel companies, under questioning from Pine, agreed that they were seeking a declaration that the steel seizure was illegal. "I never look a gift horse in the face, Your Honor," said industry lawyer John Wilson.[3] Only Kiendl stuck to his argument asking that the steelworkers' contract terms remain in place during the seizure.

Pine then turned his attention to what he viewed as the question at hand: whether the president possessed the constitutional authority to seize the mills. Armco Steel Corporation's lead counsel, Charles Tuttle, deftly argued that Supreme Court precedent held that the Constitution granted judges the power to "determine judicially whether, first, the power [to seize the mills] existed at all; and second, whether the circumstances under which it is exercised have been lawful."[4] Tuttle asked the court to rule that the president had no constitutional power to seize the steel mills.

Assistant Attorney General Homer Baldridge rose to present the government's rebuttal. It did not go well. Baldridge declared that the government's "position is that there is no power in the Courts to restrain the president and . . . Secretary Sawyer is the alter ego of the president and not subject to [an] injunctive order of the Court."[5]

From where, Pine wondered, did the president obtain the power to order the seizure of the steel mills? No provision of the Constitution nor any act of Congress expressly authorized him to do so.

Baldridge replied that the president possessed a "broad residuum of power" that was "inherent" to the office.[6]

Pine asked whether, if the president summarily imprisoned someone and ordered his execution, the court could intervene to prevent the execution. When Baldridge appeared unable to answer, Pine answered his own question: "On the question of the deprivation of your rights, you have the Fifth Amendment; that is what protects you."[7]

Baldridge redirected his argument to the longstanding tenet that courts should not rule on a constitutional question if a case could be decided on any other grounds. Unfortunately for the government, Pine did not believe this case could be decided on other grounds because, as he saw it, the threshold question was a constitutional one: did Secretary Sawyer have the power to seize the steel mills?[8]

Baldridge argued that through the president, Sawyer did possess that constitutional authority. He told the court that "there is enough residual power in the executive to meet an emergency situation of this type when it comes up."

"I think that whatever decision I reach, Mr. Baldridge, I shall not adopt the view that there is anyone in this Government whose power is unlimited, as you seem to indicate."

Baldridge, rather than concede ground that appeared already lost, astonished the courtroom by pressing even further. He declared that the Constitution provided only two limits on presidential power: "One is the ballot box and the other is impeachment."[9]

Pine was incredulous. Was government counsel contending that the federal Constitution "limited the powers of the Congress and limited the powers of the judiciary, but it did not limit the powers of the Executive. Is that what you say?"

"That is the way we read Article II of the Constitution."[10]

"I have never heard that expressed in any authoritative case before."[11]

Baldridge's argument shocked those in the packed courtroom and millions of Americans who were following the court proceedings in the press. One White House official called Baldridge's overreach "the legal blunder of the century," which pushed for a theory of executive power "never dreamed of by anyone in the White House at any time."¹² The *Washington Evening Star* carried an article entitled "Baldridge Explains Baldridge on Powers of the Presidency," in which the assistant attorney general claimed that his argument had been "misunderstood."¹³ Justice Frankfurter later observed, "The government's argument in the district court was terrible."¹⁴

Truman's supporters on Capitol Hill were alarmed by the breadth of DOJ's claim to presidential power. Senator Hubert Humphrey relayed his concerns directly to the president, telling him in a telephone call that he and many of his colleagues were troubled by Baldridge's contention that the president possessed nearly unlimited powers in an emergency. "The president told me," Humphrey reported, "that he would rest his case with the courts of the land, which is an honorable and appropriate position."¹⁵ Truman's assurances to Humphrey belied remarks by Wage Stabilization Board chairman Nathan P. Feinsinger, who warned that there would be "trouble" if the court disallowed the seizure.¹⁶

Republican leaders in the House of Representatives continued to counsel patience to their caucus. They should wait for the courts to rule before advancing any of the impeachment or censure resolutions then pending in the judiciary committee. But Representative Paul Shafer of Michigan nonetheless introduced a new impeachment resolution as Judge Pine heard oral arguments. Shafer alleged that Truman had committed high crimes and misdemeanors by entering the Korean War without congressional authorization, firing U.S. Army General Douglas MacArthur, and unconstitutionally seizing the steel mills.¹⁷

* * *

The U.S. District Court for the District of Columbia issued its decision on April 29, 1952. After summarizing each side's arguments, Judge Pine wrote what he had explained to counsel at oral argument: "The fundamental issue is whether the seizure is or is not authorized by law. In my opinion, this issue should be decided first. . . . There is no express grant of power in the Constitution authorizing the President to direct this seizure." Nor was there, noted Pine, an act of Congress or any implied power empowering Truman to order the seizure. Rather, as the administration argued in its brief and at oral argument, Truman ordered the seizure pursuant to the president's "broad residuum of power," which was "inherent" to his office. "This contention," Pine wrote like an exasperated professor teaching first-year law students, "requires a discussion of basic fundamental principles of constitutional law."[18]

The federal government "was created by the ratification of the Constitution . . . which is the only source of power authorizing action by any branch of Government. It is a government of limited, enumerated and delegated powers." Pine stated the powers granted to the president in article II of the Constitution and declared, "Their mere enumeration shows the utter fallacy of defendant's claim." The president possessed no "inherent" powers. The administration's position suffered from an "utter and complete lack of authoritative support."[19] The president had no authority to order the secretary of commerce to seize the steel mills. Truman's executive order was illegal.

* * *

CIO and United Steelworkers president Philip Murray announced that a ruling "ousting the Government from possession of the steel mills leaves members of the union with no alternative but to cease work immediately in the absence of collective bargaining contracts."[20] Murray called the strike without conferring with other labor leaders or notifying the White House. When Secretary Sawyer learned of the strike, he had to call Murray for confirmation.[21] Less than one hour after Pine issued his ruling, local union officials conveyed the strike orders at U.S. Steel plants in Chicago, Pittsburgh, Baltimore, Cleveland, and Gary, Indiana.

Murray said that steelworkers would remain on strike until they received a contract based on the recommendations of the federal Wage Stabilization Board, which had advised a wage and benefits increase totaling twenty-six cents per hour. Steel company executives insisted that they could not afford this increase without being granted more than the three-dollar-per-ton price increase permitted under the stabilization rules.[22] Because it took two to three days to shut down a steel mill without damaging its equipment, Murray assured management, "Stand-by arrangements as usual will be negotiated at the local level."[23]

The strike posed immediate political, legal, and practical problems for Truman. He had told the nation that any interruption in steel production posed a national security risk. Now the very men who had benefited from his decision to seize the steel mills were interrupting steel production by walking off the job. Although Sawyer assured the public that he would take no action "which would run counter" to the district court's ruling, Truman had to end the strike as soon as possible.[24]

* * *

Pine's opinion reframed the national debate over Truman's decision to seize the steel mills. It turned America's focus away from the underlying labor dispute and toward questions of constitutional powers and law. Pine's assertion that the effects of a steelworkers' strike presented less danger to the public than the president's claim of near-unlimited power caused many reporters to question for the first time whether the administration had exaggerated the threat posed by the strike.

Senators from both parties praised Pine's decision, with South Dakota Democratic senator Burnet Maybank saying, "The people of America ought to be thankful for the judge's decision." Senate Republican leader Styles Bridges of New Hampshire proclaimed, "Judge Pine's decision completely vindicates the separation of powers provided in our Constitution. I do not see how an objective jurist could have ruled otherwise in rendering such a sweeping decision so promptly."[25] Senator Willis Smith, a Democrat from North Carolina, called the district court's decision "quite understandable to me" because he could find no lawful basis for Truman's executive order. Republican senator John Bricker of Ohio told reporters, "If the inherent powers theory had been sustained, the president could have declared an emergency, seized property and subjected the American people to tyrannical power at any time."[26]

Major newspapers printed Pine's opinion in its entirety, a rare move they would repeat two years later for the Supreme Court's *Brown v. Board of Education* decision. Joseph Evans of the *Wall Street Journal* accused the White House of "crying wolf."[27] Editors at the *Atlanta Constitution* extolled the "courageous Federal judge" who "looked beyond the immediate threat of the steel strike toward what he considered the more ominous, if long range danger of totalitarianism. . . . We commend him for his action."[28] An Associated Press reporter conveyed the conventional wisdom when he predicted, "It was almost certain that the ultimate decision would come from the Supreme Court after preliminary clashes through the lower courts."[29]

* * *

Truman and members of his administration were utterly unprepared for the district court's ruling. One White House official admitted anonymously, "We . . . never assumed for a moment that Judge Pine would . . . block the seizure entirely."[30] Future chief justice William Rehnquist, who was then a clerk for Justice Robert Jackson, later recounted, "The public reaction to [Pine's] ruling, as much as the ruling itself, suggested that the government was in more trouble in the case than might have originally been thought when it commenced, only three short weeks earlier."[31]

Murray's decision to immediately call a strike also surprised the White House. The administration needed to end the strike, and in the minds of many outside the White House, the most direct way to do so was to invoke the Taft-Hartley Act. Just hours after the steel workers walked out, one administration official anticipated, "Now that we have a strike, the cry for Taft-Hartley will be louder and louder. Demands from the Hill for Taft-Hartley began last night and the tempo will undoubtedly increase."[32] But invoking the Taft-Hartley Act would render the district court's decision moot and eliminate the administration's ability to appeal the ruling that the seizure was unconstitutional.

Indeed, congressional Republicans, led by Senator Taft, did call for Truman to invoke Taft's namesake law. Taft contended that Truman "should use the Taft-Hartley law and exhaust all other legislative remedies" before turning to Congress for emergency legislation to end the strike.[33]

At a news conference, reporters asked CIO president Philip Murray if he thought Truman might invoke the Taft-Hartley Act to end the strike. Murray's nonanswer indicated how firmly he and his union stood. "We believe we have complied meticulously with all provisions of the Act in every way," he replied. "We think we are in full compliance with it."[34]

Truman surprised no one by deciding against invoking the Taft-Hartley Act. Had he done so, not only would the district court opinion become ineligible for appeal but he would face bipartisan criticism for seizing the steel mills rather than employing the law in the first place. The public would conclude, as one White House official put it, that "the President was wrong in the first instance in asserting that we could not afford a shutdown [of the mills], wrong in not using Taft-Hartley and wrong in using a legal theory which the courts would not and did not support."[35]

Instead of implementing Taft-Hartley, the Truman administration would appeal directly to the Supreme Court and in the meantime ask the district court for a stay of its opinion pending its appeal.

Judge Pine rejected the Department of Justice's request for a stay. The administration appealed to the Court of Appeals for the District of Columbia Circuit, which agreed to hear the case *en banc*, meaning that a panel of nine judges, rather than the usual three-judge panel, would decide this very important appeal. After a contentious, three-hour hearing that focused more on the practical effects of the steel strike rather than the constitutional issues explored by the court below, the court of appeals granted the administration's request for a stay. The vote was five to four.

Philip Murray called off the strike, steelworkers returned to the mills, and DOJ attorneys prepared to file their appeal of Pine's ruling with the Supreme Court. They were surprised to learn that attorneys for the steel companies, despite having prevailed in district court, had already appealed the case to the Court.

CHAPTER TWENTY-SIX

The Supreme Court Hearing

ON MAY 3, 1952, SATURDAY morning, Truman summoned Philip Murray and the steel company chief executives to the White House for one last round of negotiations. He had lost patience with the parties' inability to settle their dispute. Coming to an agreement would provide each side with far more control over the terms of the steelworkers' contracts than would leaving matters to the courts. Truman decided to force their hand. With Commerce Secretary Sawyer at his side, he told the men that they had better come to an agreement here in the White House or his administration, which owned the steel mills pursuant to the court of appeal's ruling, would impose higher wages for the 650,000 steelworkers "on Monday morning or as soon as we can get ready."[1]

"I am sure you are aware," Truman continued, "that the government has been considering what are fair and reasonable wages for the employees during the period that the plants remain under government operation. Two weeks ago the secretary of commerce asked the Economic Stabilization Administration to prepare recommendations for changes in the terms and conditions of employment in the steel industry at this time."[2] Truman had received those recommendations and was prepared to implement them if the parties could not end their impasse.

To be sure, Truman assured all present that he no more wanted the federal government to set steelworkers' wages than he wanted it to be running private steel companies in the first place. This was why, with two petitions for *certiorari* pending at the Supreme Court, he had convened this meeting at the White House. "I didn't send for you just to make a speech," he said. "I sent for you for action and, gentlemen, I want it."[3] Despite his pro-union reputation, Truman made it clear that the parties would be better off negotiating an end to their dispute than letting the federal government decide matters: "If we have to take action, it will be something that is not satisfactory to either side."[4] With that, the president and Secretary Sawyer left the two sides to restart negotiations with newfound urgency.

By all accounts, with the threat of operating under whatever wages the government imposed, the parties immediately made progress on resolving their differences. By now, after months of discussions, each side understood the other's strengths and weaknesses—and knew that the other side recognized theirs. Early in the afternoon, with everyone absent from the room but two steel executives and Murray, the two sides agreed on the basic tenets of a new contract. Both sides felt relieved. The three men agreed to a short recess to obtain final approval from the other leaders in their camps. As they ambled into the hallway, they learned of the news tapping across the White House news ticker.

* * *

At their Saturday conference, the justices debated whether to hear the steel seizure case. This was no ordinary *certiorari* petition, because, as Vinson said to open the discussion, "the question is whether the court of appeals should be bypassed." Even in other extraordinary cases of national importance, the Court would not consider granting *certiorari* until after at least one—and usually more than one—federal circuit court of appeals had ruled on the case. But this case was different. "I have not been able to figure out the possibilities," Vinson admitted, "that would result from our not taking the case—the practical questions." He briefly summarized the appeal's substantive points before concluding, "I believe that we should grant cert and enter a stay."[5] Little did Vinson know that the practical result of their taking the case would be the collapse of negotiations at the White House.

Justices Black and Reed generally agreed that the Court should accept the case.

"I don't have that feeling of certainty," Frankfurter said. Given the progress being made at the White House between union and corporate leaders—of which the justices knew nothing—the former Harvard law professor's warning would later seem prescient: "What we may do may make this *more* difficult. My disposition runs against an eagerness to settle this." He recounted a few of the Court's most ambitious, disastrous decisions such as *Dred Scott v. Sanford* before concluding, "There is a heaviness of heart and history about rushing in. I would not take the case now. There is a stay [in effect] already, and the men will have to stay on the job."[6]

The justices voted seven to two to grant the steel companies' petition for *certiorari*. Frankfurter joined Burton in opposing the writ. They contended that the District of Columbia Circuit Court of Appeals should rule on the district court's constitutional law decision. "Little time will be lost," Burton wrote, "and none will be wasted in seeking [a court of appeals decision]." Burton noted in his personal journal that he agreed with the district court that the president lacked the authority to seize the steel mills. But he believed that Judge Daniel Pine should have granted the steel companies' request for a preliminary injunction to preserve the status quo rather than address the underlying constitutional questions raised by the seizure.[7]

Of great significance to the negotiations taking place at the White House, the Court unanimously ordered that the Truman administration refrain from making changes to "any term or condition of employment" without the express consent of the steel companies' executives.[8] The Court nullified Truman's wage increase threat.

* * *

As soon as company and labor leaders learned of the Court's order, negotiations ground to a halt. Perhaps out of respect for the fact that they were guests at the White House, the parties reconvened at ten o'clock the next morning. But they made no progress. No longer facing the threat of a Truman-imposed wage increase, steel company executives figured their better chances lay with the Supreme Court, even if most everyone expected the Court to rule in Truman's favor.

* * *

At noon on Monday, May 12, the Supreme Court was called to order. The lawyers' section was filled with more than forty people crammed into the steel companies' side. Nearly all seats in the courtroom were taken by steel company executives, union representatives, senior administration officials, and members of Congress, leaving few seats for journalists or interested members of the public.[9] Several of the justices' wives, who rarely attended hearings, were seated in the gallery. The Court relaxed its rules against standing in the courtroom to allow an additional two hundred spectators to crowd into the space. They stood along the walls while hundreds more waited in the crowded hallways outside the courtroom.[10]

The nine justices took their seats on the bench. They had allotted more than five hours for oral arguments, equally divided between the government and the steel companies. In addition, the Court granted the union attorneys time to argue as *amicus curaiae*, "friends of the court," because, although not a party to the case, the outcome clearly and directly would affect the union. This extraordinary amount of time devoted to oral argument demonstrated the seriousness with which the justices were treating this case. They typically granted each side sixty minutes for oral arguments and often reduced that allotment to thirty minutes each.

After the justices issued the order freezing the terms and conditions of their employment, the steelworkers' greatest concern was not that the Court would return control of the steel mills back to the companies; it was that the Court would remand the case back to the district court for a long, protracted trial on the merits of the seizure—while their wages and benefits remained frozen. Union leaders admitted that they had no strategy to deal with this worst-case scenario. They did not know how they would keep workers from walking off the job.[11]

Recognizing that their case at the district court level was hampered by having various lawyers presenting various arguments, the steel companies agreed to select one attorney to argue their case before the Supreme Court: John W. Davis, the former Woodrow Wilson administration solicitor general and the Democratic Party's nominee for president in 1924. This would be his 138th Supreme Court argument. Bruce Bromley and Theodore Kiendl joined the seventy-nine-year-old Davis at counsels' table for the steel industry.

Seated at counsel's table to their left were Solicitor General Philip Perlman and Holmes Baldridge, whose presence would soon become a matador's red cape to the justices. Seeing Baldridge appeared to remind them of the overreaching arguments he had made before Judge Pine. This afternoon, Perlman would pay for Baldridge's exuberance.

At 12:25 p.m., the steel seizure case was called and John Davis stepped to the lectern with a looseleaf notebook. He briefly recounted the origins of the labor dispute and the purpose of the Taft-Hartley Act before telling the Court, "There is no statutory framework into which this seizure can possibly fit." Standing before justices who jealously guarded their right to ask the questions, Davis rhetorically demanded,

> Is it or is it not an immutable principle that our government is one of limited powers? Is it or is it not an immutable principle that we have a choice tripartite system of legislation, execution and judgment? Is it or is it not an immutable principle that the powers of government are based on a government of laws and are not based on a government of man?[12]

Spectators standing along the walls would later complain that they could not hear the arguments because of the courtroom's lack of microphones and poor acoustics, but the justices listened with rapt attention. Law clerk William Rehnquist recalled that the justices "appeared to be almost in awe of Davis."[13]

Davis contended that Truman's decision to seize the steel mills ran afoul not only of the U.S. Constitution but of the Western liberal tradition on which the Constitution was based. The Truman administration's attempt to justify the seizure was but "a reassertion of the kingly prerogative, the struggle against which illumines all the pages of Anglo-Saxon history."[14] The steel corporations' advocate spoke for one hour and twenty-seven minutes during which the justices asked just three questions. Davis concluded with an emotional tremor in his voice as he quoted Thomas Jefferson: "In questions of power, let no more be said of confidence in man, but bind him down from mischief by chains of the Constitution."[15]

Finally his turn to rise, Solicitor General Perlman opened with a feint toward praising Davis's performance. "Your Honors have just listened to an eloquent argument," he acknowledged, "an argument that is designed to turn the minds of this court away from the facts in this case and away from the reasons which prompted the president of the United States to take the action that he did." Counsel for the steel companies had ignored "the condition of the world today . . . the struggle in which this nation is engaged . . . [and] the necessity, the vital necessity to keep the plants owned by the plaintiffs here in operation without interruption of any kind."[16] It swiftly became clear that Perlman sought to justify Truman's action not on the president's inherent constitutional powers but rather on the president's power to protect the nation in the face of immediate foreign threats. Unfortunately for the solicitor general, the justices who were skeptical of Truman's power to act were eager to engage on that precise point.

Douglas asked which section of the Constitution or which of the "many acts of Congress" or even treaties with other nations to which Perlman referred actually conferred upon the president the power to seize the steel mills.

Perlman answered that there was no specific provision designed for the crisis faced by the president the previous month but that Truman had acted to ensure that the government remained able to fulfill commitments Congress had made, including the NATO alliance treaty, the Mutual Security Act, and the Defense Production Act.

This answer left Douglas feeling "confused." Again he asked what constitutional provision or law empowered the president to seize the steel mills.

"I'm relying on every single law—"

"That doesn't help me."

"Let me finish, your honor. I'm relying on every single law passed in recent years." This included Congress's defense appropriations, billions of dollars that could not be spent if steel production ceased.

"Would you mind," Douglas asked testily, "giving me just one law this seizure helped to enforce?"

Yes, it helped to enforce the Defense Production Act.

Could the president seize farms if they failed to produce wheat?

No, he could not, because the executive branch's power to seize was limited to times of national emergency. "I've tried to say that this [seizure] was to meet an emergency in the absence of any other means, that the president had the authority to act under the circumstances that existed on April 8th."[17]

Perlman then reminded the Court that in June 1941, President Franklin Roosevelt had seized the North American Aviation plant. Justice Robert Jackson had served as Roosevelt's attorney general at the time. The Department of Justice's brief relied heavily on Jackson's written opinion to the president, and Perlman now turned to rely on it in oral argument.

"I have [recently] studied that case quite carefully," Jackson told Perlman from the bench, "because I wondered how much of this you would lay at my door." He asked if Perlman thought the government was "taking a good deal for granted" by citing the North American Aviation seizure, given how "different" the two cases were. When Perlman demurred, Jackson delineated the numerous ways in which the cases differed, including the fact that North American Aviation had contracted directly with the government to manufacture airplanes, and the aviation executives, unlike the steel industry executives seated in the courtroom today, had not opposed the president's actions.[18]

Justices Black, Frankfurter, and Burton then peppered Perlman with questions on Congress's role in the apparent emergency and why the president had disregarded the Taft-Hartley Act, which seemed tailor-made for this situation. Perlman replied by emphasizing that Congress had taken no action to limit or revoke the seizure and therefore it "could be inferred that Congress is content to let the president's actions stand."

"Where are the limitations?" Jackson wondered. "I suppose a seizure to reduce wages would be just as valid as a seizure to raise them. I just don't know where the end of this is."

"The end is always in this court," Perlman replied, in what might have been his first answer of the day that pleased the Court.[19]

Before the Court adjourned, scheduled to resume at noon the next day, the chief justice complained to Perlman that he was "bouncing around" in his argument without finishing any single subject.

The solicitor general revealed how much the Court's onslaught had wearied him when he answered, in a voice scarcely masking his frustration, that he was only trying to answer the justices' questions. He would be happy to finish discussion of one subject at a time.[20]

Arthur J. Goldberg, general counsel of the United Steelworkers of America, CIO, asked on a point of order if the Court expected to render its decision in the case before releasing opinions.

On rare occasions, the Court issued its decision on a significant case before the majority and minority opinions were ready for release. Jackson arguably stepped into the role of chief justice—the job he still coveted—when from the bench he assured Goldberg that no such decision would be forthcoming in this case. "Arguments just begin when counsel is through," he quipped to the lawyers' amusement. More seriously, Jackson said that the operative importance of the decision in this case might well lie in the opinions.[21]

* * *

That evening, Secretary Sawyer attended a reception at the White House. President Truman spotted him in the crowd and pulled him aside for a private conversation. How were the Supreme Court arguments going, Truman asked.

Sawyer replied that the justices had questioned Perlman harshly. They seemed skeptical of the Administration's position. Truman retorted that he would be "shocked, disappointed and disturbed" if the Court ruled against him.[22]

* * *

Court reconvened at noon the next day. After calling the case, Chief Justice Vinson, having just finished his lunch, "worked away industriously with a toothpick," as one reporter described it, while Solicitor General Perlman prepared to resume his oral argument.[23] He had less than twenty minutes of scheduled time remaining. "Your time has been fixed, Mr. Solicitor General," Vinson said. "You have had two-and-a-half hours. When the red light comes on, you may answer any questions that are pending."

Perlman nodded, began speaking, and in short order acknowledged the just-lit red light before him: "Well, I guess I'm finished."

"Oh no," Vinson replied. "I have a question. What do you have to say about Taft-Hartley?"

"I have a great deal to say about it, your honor."

"Well," Vinson gestured, toothpick in hand, "proceed then." Laughter filled the courtroom.[24]

Before Perlman could delve into his argument, however, Burton, Frankfurter, and Jackson resumed their sharp questioning. Justice Reed, who had remained silent the previous day, also joined in the spirited colloquy. In answering one of their questions, Perlman sought to return to his primary theme, albeit in more strident terms, arguing that the seizure was "the only manner in which the chief executive could assure the continued production of steel necessary for the whole war effort—and we are at war."

Jackson leaned forward on the bench. "Hasn't the president expressly disclaimed this and called [the Korean War] a 'police action?'"

"You can say without fear of contradiction—"

"That it looks like war and feels like war?"[25] He reminded Perlman that at a press conference on June 30, 1950, the president had emphatically told reporters, "We are not war" and insisted that the armed forces were engaged in "a police action."[26]

"That we are under war conditions."

"But yesterday," Frankfurter interjected, "in answering Justice Douglas, you emphasized that you are not using war powers. Now you say you are not exercising war powers but we are in a war."

"The executive order said the president was taking the step as commander in chief of the Army and Navy."

"But he is that during the most peaceful era in our country's history."

"Unfortunately," Perlman said, "we do not happen to be in such an era."[27]

The government's argument indicated, Frankfurter offered, that the president could dispatch agents to a citizen's farm and, without asking his permission, pick all the apples and cherries they needed.

"That's not the government's position," the solicitor general replied.

Frankfurter bristled. "Then I don't understand it."

"I'm sorry."

Vinson sought to come to Perlman's aid by noting, "We had seizures prior to Pearl Harbor that looked forward to preparedness." He turned to Perlman: "Your time has expired."[28]

John W. Davis rose to present the steel companies' rebuttal argument. Although he had nearly an hour of time left, he spoke briefly, again enjoying remarkable leeway from the justices and asking rhetorical questions without interruption. "What injury can be more irreparable," Davis implored, "than that which ousts the owner from his property and uses his funds?"[29] In response to the solicitor general's assertion that the steel companies were asking the Court to treat this as an ordinary case, Davis contended, "We, in this industry, are not living under normal conditions. We are faced with abnormal acts and . . . with a situation that, because of the extension of executive power—lacking legslative authority—we are deprived of our property and of our rights as citizens of the nation." He forcefully raised the ante of the government's argument: "The situation that is thus dictated is without paralllel in American history."[30]

Finally it was union counsel Arthur Goldberg's turn to rise. Having waited for hours while the government and steel company attorneys presented their cases over two days, Goldberg made clear that he had no intention of arguing the merits of Truman's seizure of the steel mills. He spoke more loudly than Perlman and Davis to ensure that the journalists and spectators standing along the walls could hear him clearly.

Justice Burton repeatedly asked him why the Taft-Hartley Act should not be employed. Goldberg astonished onlookers by pointing his finger at Burton as he answered. The national emergency arose, he argued, not on April 8, 1952, but on December 31, 1951, when the union members' contract expired. Union leaders notified management of their intent to strike pursuant to the Taft-Hartley Act. Everyone was surprised when the White House asked the union to defer its strike. Steelworkers acceded, believing that the Truman administration would help negotiate a new contract. "If the union," Goldberg assured, "after going the route of the president, was then confronted with Taft-Hartley, it would never again go the route of the president. Every intent of Congress was complied with. That, Mr. Justice Burton, is the answer to your question."[31]

Goldberg stressed that the steelworkers were no happier than management with their frozen, government-imposed wages and benefits, telling the Court, "We look upon the government-imposed settlement with disdain." Referring to the instant at the White House when union leaders and company executives learned that the Supreme Court had issued an injunction preventing the administration from changing the workers' wages, Goldberg said, "From that moment on, there was no bargaining."[32]

The chief justice, who was otherwise sympathetic to the union counsel's position, interjected, "You didn't get along with bargaining very well for days and weeks before that."[33] The Court adjourned shortly thereafter at 3:30 p.m.

CHAPTER TWENTY-SEVEN

Conference and Resolution

EVEN AFTER THE JUSTICES' BLISTERING questioning of Solicitor General Philip Perlman, his own halting performance, and the justices' awestruck deference to John W. Davis, most observers still believed that Truman would prevail in the steel seizure case. The Court would rule that he possessed the constitutional authority to seize the steel mills.

Six days after oral arguments, the Associated Press reported that the Court was likely to rule that the president did indeed possess the constitutional authority to seize the steel mills.[1] *Washington Post* columnist Drew Pearson noted that eight of the nine justices, before or after taking their seats on the bench, supported government seizures like the one ordered by Truman.[2] By one senator's count, the federal government had enacted thirty-eight seizures during World War II and ten since the war's end.[3] Until Judge Pine's decision, seizures had seemed to be an accepted item in the government's toolbox.

Harold Burton, Truman's first Supreme Court nominee, believed that his fellow Truman nominees Fred Vinson, Tom Clark, and Sherman Minton would be joined by Hugo Black and Stanley Reed in holding the seizure constitutional. Based on casual conversations with them, Burton figured that he was, as he put it, "largely alone in holding that the president was without power to seize the steel plants in the face of the Taft-Hartley Act providing a different procedure."[4]

In the wake of oral arguments, congressional Republicans declared that if the Supreme Court would not restrain the president, they would. Truman was not seeking reelection in the final months of his presidency, so public discussion of impeaching him had largely fallen by the wayside. Republicans instead focused on future presidents, with some leaders calling for a constitutional amendment.

Senator Wallace F. Bennett, a Republican from Utah, told the annual gathering of the American Steel Warehouse Association at the Waldorf-Astoria Hotel in New York City that if the Court upheld Judge Pine's decision denying the Truman administration's constitutional claims, then the matter would be closed. "But," he continued, "if the Supreme Court avoids the issue or reverses the Pine decision, I believe there will be passed a constitutional amendment which would define the powers of the president very definitely." Bennett emphasized before the five hundred steel company executives that the Republican Party appreciated their point of view: "It is my consideration that as a result of this steel situation, future legislation will limit rather than expand the right to strike. . . . This experience has definitely limited the Democratic Party, taking it far to the left, so that there will be many divisions within the party. As a result of [the steel seizure], there is an opportunity to change certain trends in America."[5]

* * *

After Tuesday's arguments, the conference for the steel seizure case was scheduled to begin at noon on Friday. Consistent with custom, five minutes before the conference convened, a buzzer sounded in each justice's chambers and throughout the building's first-floor hallway.[6] The justices made their way to the conference room, where Sherman Minton, as the junior justice, closed the door behind them.

Chief Justice Vinson opened the discussion: "To take either extreme position—that the president has either unlimited power or no power—is untenable. It runs in the face of the history of our government." He anticipated his brethren's retort by contending, "Arguments of prior seizures are not pertinent here. In many instance seizures have been pursuant to an act, but others have not been pursuant to an act. Here, we have a seizure ordered at 10:30 p.m. on the eve of the 12:01 strike deadline." Vinson cited Truman's sending a message to Congress the following morning, in which the president essentially told the legislature, "'The strike is going to be called, stopping [steel] production. I tried to work it out. . . . If I am wrong, tell me and provide a method for meeting this emergency and I will abide.' There could be," Vinson argued, "no criticism of this." He dismissed claims that Truman wrongfully disregarded the Taft-Hartley Act by reminding the Court, "John Davis admitted that the president was not compelled to go the Taft-Hartley route."[7]

Turning to the basis of the administration's defense, Vinson declared, "There is no doubt but that there is a war on and that the United States is preparing against it. That was the situation prior to World War II when Roosevelt seized the plants. Here the circumstances are clearer than in World War II." Ignoring the fact that Truman had not asked for and Congress had not provided a declaration of war, Vinson maintained that the president was "doing no more than carrying out his obligations to execute the laws. Hence it was the duty of the president, in seeing that the laws are enforced, to seize the mills. He must carry on that program. The United States has a right to defend itself and prepare itself for war."[8]

Here Vinson was attempting a preemptory strike against Douglas and Frankfurter, who had so effectively seized on Solicitor General Perlman's statement at oral argument that the nation was "at war." Just the day before the conference, however, Truman had pointedly refused to answer reporters' questions whether the nation was "at war," as his Department of Justice contended, or even whether the military was under "war conditions."[9] Because the commander in chief refused to say that the nation was at war, Vinson's declarations fell flat. But he persisted, arguing, "The stoppage of steel production would paralyze the war effort."[10]

In closing, Vinson returned to the message Truman had sent to Congress the morning after seizing the steel mills: "This is not a defiance of Congress. His letter to Congress was written in a spirit of humility and in a desire to solve the problem. He did not say that he did not have the power to seize. He did not say, 'I am seizing alone.' He wrote to Congress, 'I have done it; maybe it's wrong. If I was not right, let Congress choose the method.' Congress has done nothing. I affirm."[11]

Hugo Black, speaking next as the senior associate justice, complimented Vinson's remarks before saying, "I don't think that anyone's mind will be changed by what is said here. My view is that most of what Vinson said is irrelevant to my decision." Black turned to Vinson's claim that war justifed the seizure: "If Congress *had declared war*, then the president could do *everything* to produce war materials. . . . The question is whether the president had the power to seize without a statute. . . . The issue is whether the president can make laws. Here we have a labor dispute and lawmaking concerning it. That power, under the Constitution, is in the Congress." The former New Deal senator assured his brethren that he would say the same if Franklin Roosevelt were still president. "Controlling labor disputes, as here, is making law. My feeling as to the different branches of government is abhorrent to this. The president has two powers on legislation: he can recommend; and he can veto [or] execute. *There are no others.*"

Black closed by recognizing, "It is a serious thing for this Court, with no Army and only prestige, to tell the president what to do. . . . [But] this is not a case of the president tearing down the house in order to stop a fire. The conditions are not that serious."[12]

Stanley Reed struck a conservative and practical note: "I would hope that we *don't* reach the constitutional issue. Perhaps it can't be avoided. The elections [six months away] are coming at a bad time. Damages are here and they are irreparable." Reed urged the justices to limit their decision to the request for injunctive relief. But realizing that a majority might decide to rule on the merits of the case, he argued, "If we must act on the merits, I don't agree that the president's seizure power is limited to acts of Congress. History does not support such a conclusion." He briefly reviewed the history of several previous seizures before concluding, "There plainly is an emergency here. Steel is very important. *Newspapers or clothing, etcetera, not so—they are different. These are rules of necessity. Here, atomic enegery is involved. I would leave the president in control.*" Reed reiterated that he nonetheless wanted to avoid the constitutional question: "My preference is to put off the decision. I hope that the issue can be avoided and the case remanded for a hearing on a permanent injunction."[13]

Felix Frankfurter announced his desire for what several of his fellow justices and nearly every lower court judge, member of Congress, and practicing attorney certainly did not want: "I hope that nine opinions will be written. It is highly desirable that everyone writes." He returned to the chief justice's statement: "I agree with Vinson that there is no unlimited power of the president, or of Congress. The doctrine of separation of powers is wound into this case." The former Harvard law professor embarked on a lengthy summary of an article he had written twenty-five years ago about the separation of powers before concluding that Stanley Reed's plea to avoid the constitutional questions was untenable: "I strive like a beaver not to reach constitutional questions. The less this Court pronounces constitutional doctrine the better. But we cannot escape it here. . . . *Hence we must reach the separation of powers issue.*"[14]

Frankfurter joined Black in stressing that Congress had not declared war.

> President Truman cannot lump all of his powers together and thereby get authority: He cannot go to his war powers, *for no war was declared.* Only Congress can take that step. Speeches made by the president and secretary of state are not "war." Quasi-war powers? *No such thing.* . . . I differ a little from Black. If there had been no statutes on the books, in my opinion the president could have seized the steel mills, at least temporarily, in order to bring the matter to the attention of the Congress—a holding operation. . . . But that is not the case here. This was not a holding operation.[15]

He explored the history of presidential property seizures at some length, reading from an 1,100-page compilation of all emergency legislation from the colonial era until 1917. Truman was not obligated to employ the Taft-Hartley Act, Frankfurter insisted, but he was obligated to seek congressional approval before seizing the mills. "The power exercised here is not inherent in the office," Frankfurter explained. "I do not think that this power is inherent in the president by virtue of his duty to enforce the laws. As [former Justice Oliver Wendell] Holmes said, the duty of the president does not go beyond the laws of Congress and it does not require him to do more than Congress requires." Frankfurter closed with an offhand remark more concisely astute than the best lines of most majority opinions: "The 1787 Constitution was not meant for efficiency, but to preclude arbitrary power."[16]

Douglas was as brief as Frankfurter had been verbose: "Much has been said, but I am inclined to agree with Hugo. This is a legislative function in the nature of a condemnation for a short term." Because the seizure necessitated compensating the companies, "the power *must* be in the legislature, as it alone can appropriate funds." The proof of this was that "if Congress were to act, it would make the case moot."[17]

"I cannot add much," Jackson began. "This Court should not review whether there is an emergency. Stanley Reed might involve us in that. If the president declares an emergency, *I will take the president's judgment.* The question of how the president deals with an emergency is different.

How can he deal with it? Here," the former attorney general declared, "the Department of Justice has been demoralized. The crowd that wants to claim everything has taken over. The president is in an untenable situation. The government does claim inherent powers here!" In case his view of Truman's order was not clear, Jackson concluded, "The president can throw the Constitution overboard—but we can't. We can't sustain Perlman's argument without going beyond the Constitution."[18]

The three associate justices nominated by Truman spoke next, continuing in descending order of seniority. Harold Burton quickly dispensed with Reed's suggestion that the Court avoid the constitutional issues, arguing, "There is no reason to postpone a decision on the merits. This is a decision that requires policy-making and therefore it is for Congress to decide. Congress has the power to provide a remedy."[19]

Fifteen years before the Truman administration seized the steel mills, Burton, then the mayor of Cleveland, Ohio, had faced a similar situation. In May 1937 Cleveland's steel workers went on strike. Republic Steel Corporation refused to negotiate and, in an eerie premonition of the Berlin Airlift Truman would order almost a decade later, the company sought to airlift supplies to nonstriking workers barricaded inside its plants. Mayor Burton, realizing the hazards posed by the flights, revoked the company's airfield operating permit.[20]

Burton likely surprised his brethren by both the force and substance of his argument. "Here we have the Taft-Hartley Act. It was passed for this very purpose. Congress has almost said that there shall be no seizure. The legislative history indicates that Congress would provide for seizure after the Taft-Hartley remedy was exhausted." Reaching as dramatic a crescendo as the reserved Ohioan ever did, Burton concluded, "He has no power to seize apart from the statute. . . . The president has done an unauthorized act—*it was unlawful.*"[21]

Tom Clark spoke succinctly: "I am unwilling to say that the president has no power to act. . . . Congress has been careful as to the power it gave, and as to the limitations." Clark agreed with the consensus that the Court should not review whether an emergency existed at the time of Truman's order. As he saw it, that was immaterial to the question of whether the president acted within his constitutional authority: "I can't put this on a commander-in-chief basis, and it is not claimed to be. The commander-in-chief power has been declared with Japan, but this is not a declared war in Korea."[22]

"I am not as easy about this," Sherman Minton began. "I don't want a strike. The president did everything he could to avoid a strike." Minton bookended the conference by focusing, like Vinson when he opened the discussion, on the administration's national security justification for the seizure: "We have an acute emergency hanging over the world. The president seized the mills in self-defense of the nation. . . . Truman seized the plants because the defense of the country required it." Minton, who suffered from heart disease, became so agitated that he began pounding on the conference table:

> *This is not a legislative power—it is a defensive seizure. . . .* Nothing would be more tragic than our boys in Korea needing bullets and having none available because of this strike.
>
> The president can seize any property in an emergency. If Congress has not prohibited it and the Constitution has not, then the president need not stand by. He has the implied power to act in an emergency to defend the United States. His implied power goes back to his commander-in-chief status and his power to execute the laws.

Minton's passion flooded his argument. "Government either grows or it dies. . . . We have a living Constitution. The Taft-Hartley Act is not mandatory—it was not the only route. . . . The president gets his inherent power from the power to defend the nation in a day of peril."[23]

The justices voted. And four long hours after it began, the conference ended.

* * *

In the days after the conference, political leaders who supported and opposed Truman's actions prepared the nation for the likelihood that the Court would uphold his order as constitutional. The Maryland Civil Liberties Committee called Truman's seizure "un-American" and longed for the day when the United States was "the land where a man's property was his and not his government's."[24] Conversely, the Republican chairman of the House Judiciary Committee, Emanuel Celler, noted that, since the founding of the republic, federal judges had not restricted presidents from acting. They had not even sought to do so. "Frankly, indeed, never in history," Celler proclaimed on the House floor, "has any judge attempted successfully to restrain a president. He could not enforce his order against the wishes of the president."[25] According to a Gallup poll, 43 percent of Americans disapproved of Truman's order to seize the steel mills, while 35 percent approved and 22 percent had no opinion.[26]

The day after the justices' conference, the United Steelworkers of America CIO concluded its annual convention in Philadelphia. District leaders worried that any extension of the current wage freeze would result in widespread "wildcat strikes" not authorized by the union. All that kept many steelworkers on the job now, local leaders told their national representatives, was knowing that suddenly shutting down the blast furnaces would damage them so severely that they would be inoperable for at least a month.[27]

CHAPTER TWENTY-EIGHT

"Zone of Twilight"

JUSTICES READ THEIR OPINIONS FROM the bench only in highly significant cases or, when in dissent, to stress how strongly they disagree with the Court's ruling. They tend not to read their opinions verbatim and sometimes add commentary to emphasize a point. Invariably, they use the tones of their voices and demeanor to convey more than the printed words might.

The Supreme Court convened at noon on Monday, June 2, 1952, two weeks after hearing oral arguments in the steel seizure case. Chief Justice Vinson announced that, contrary to longstanding practice, the Court would delay announcing the attorneys newly admitted to practice before the Court until after the justices announced their opinions in the case of *Youngstown Sheet & Tube Co. v. Sawyer.* The chief justice asked Justice Black to read the Court's majority opinion.

Black's opinion had garnered six votes, but every justice who signed onto Black's opinion also wrote his own. Not only did this lessen the impact of the majority opinion but it made it difficult to discern why the majority reached its decision: the five concurring opinions filed by Justices Burton, Clark, Douglas, Frankfurter, and Jackson espoused rationales that substantially differed from the majority opinion. Decades later, many legal scholars have concluded that the majority agreed only that the president's seizure of the steel mills was unlawful.[1]

Conversely, Vinson drafted the sole dissent, which was joined by Minton and Reed. Minton had planned to draft his own dissent, which he discussed with Reed, when Vinson circulated his draft opinion. Neither Minton nor Reed agreed entirely with the chief justice's reasoning but they decided that a single, unified dissent would contrast more strongly with the numerous opinions in the fractured majority.[2]

Now, from the bench, Black read,

We are asked to decide whether the president was acting within his constitutional power when he issued an order directing the secretary of commerce to take possession of and operate most of the nation's steel mills. The mill owners argue that the president's order amounts to lawmaking, a legislative function which the Constitution has expressly confided to the Congress, and not to the president. The government's position is that the order was made on findings of the president that his action was necessary to avert a national catastrophe which would inevitably result from a stoppage of steel production, and that, in meeting this grave emergency, the president was acting within the aggregate of his constitutional powers as the Nation's Chief Executive and the Commander in Chief of the Armed Forces of the United States.

Here, after briefly summarizing each side's position, most majority opinions would announce the Court's decision. But Black instead embarked on a recitation of the facts that gave rise to the dispute, after which he framed the two issues as he saw them: *"First:* Should final determination of the constitutional validity of the President's order be made in this case which has proceeded no further than the preliminary injunction stage? *Second:* If so, is the seizure order within the constitutional power of the President?"[3] (These were the issues as Black saw them because the five justices who joined his opinion addressed different issues in their concurring opinions.) He succinctly dispensed with the first issue, agreeing with the district court that determining the damages incurred by the steel companies if the seizure were permitted to continue would be difficult.

Black then turned to the more complicated question of whether the president had lawfully ordered the seizure. Any power to do so, he wrote, "must stem either from an act of Congress or the Constitution itself." Because no law granted the president that power, "it must be found in some provision of the Constitution." Government counsel did not claim that the Constitution expressly granted this power to the president but rather "that presidential power should be implied from the aggregate of his powers under the Constitution."[4]

The Court rejected the Truman administration's argument that the president, as commander in chief of the Army and Navy, had the power "to take possession of private property in order to keep labor disputes from stopping production." Doing so was "a job for the Nation's lawmakers, not for its military authorities." Keeping with the foundation that Truman, by ordering the seizure, had enacted a law, the Court declared, "The President's order does not direct that a congressional policy be executed in a manner prescribed by Congress—it directs that a presidential policy be executed in a manner prescribed by the President."[5] This the Constitution did not allow. Congress alone was permitted to authorize the taking of private property for public use, regulate relationships between employers and employees, and assign wages and working conditions in certain sectors of the economy.

Black's majority opinion dismissed the point Truman would continue to stress years after leaving office: that previous presidents, dating back to the nineteenth century, had seized private property to sustain wartime production. Black noted that, even if this were so, Congress retained "exclusive constitutional authority to make laws necessary and proper to carry out the powers vested by the Constitution." Therefore, the Court ruled, "This seizure order cannot stand." The district court's ruling was affirmed.[6]

Justice Douglas's concurrence adhered most closely to Black's majority opinion, while Frankfurter's opinion sought to wrestle his vote with his commitment to judicial restraint. Burton's concurrence focused on the fact that Congress had "reserved to itself the right to determine where and when" to seize private property in an emergency. When Truman ordered Sawyer to seize the steel mills, he had "invaded the jurisdiction of Congress" and thereby violated the Constitution.[7]

Clark alone concurred in the Court's judgment but refused to sign its opinion, which he contended wrongly disregarded a president's inherent constitutional power to respond to a national emergency. In his opinion, Clark cited a line of cases in which the Court had upheld both the president's express and implicit constitutional powers. He nonetheless concluded that the Constitution obligated Truman to employ the Taft-Hartley Act, the Selective Service Act, or the Defense Production Act to compel the steel companies to maintain production during the nation's war effort.[8]

Justice Jackson's concurring opinion in *Youngstown Sheet & Tube Co. v. Sawyer* has endured as a judicial masterpiece. Even though no other justices signed onto it, Jackson's opinion became the most significant one, both legally and politically, to emerge from the steel seizure case. None of the concurring opinions nor the dissent matched Jackson's opinion for simplicity or eloquence.

Minton was incensed that Jackson, who as attorney general had justified Roosevelt's seizure of the North American Aviation plant, voted to prohibit Truman from exercising the same power. Minton personally confronted Jackson, demanding an explanation for the inconsistency. "I was attorney general then," Jackson replied easily, "and I'm a justice now."[9]

Jackson's explanation failed to mollify Minton. "The Korean War was on," Minton later explained, "and I couldn't think of anything worse than men on the firing line reaching back for munitions that weren't there. I believed that government had the right to defend itself in an emergency."[10]

Recognizing that Minton was expressing a concern borne by attorneys and Court observers nationwide, Jackson began his opinion with a reference to his service as Roosevelt's attorney general: "That comprehensive and undefined presidential powers hold both practical advantages and grave dangers for the country," he wrote, "will impress anyone who has served as legal adviser to a President in time of transition and public anxiety." To solve the perennial question of where a president's "comprehensive and undefined" powers might begin and end, Jackson declared, "Presidential powers are not fixed but fluctuate depending upon their disjunction or conjunction with those of Congress."[11] He then offered a three-part analytical framework in which to assess whether a presidential act was constitutional.

When a president acted pursuant to express or implied congressional authorization, his authority was "at its maximum." This was because, under these circumstances, the president acted with the weight of both his own constitutional powers and "all [the powers] that Congress can delegate."[12]

When a president acted with neither a grant nor denial of power from Congress, the president was relying solely on presidential powers and thus was "in a zone of twilight in which he and Congress may have concurrent authority, or in which its distribution is uncertain."[13]

Lastly, when a president took an action "incompatible with the express or implied will of Congress, his power is at its lowest ebb." This was because the judiciary could sustain the president's action "only by disabling Congress from acting upon the subject." Judges were obliged to closely scrutinize such actions because at stake was nothing less than "the equilibrium established by our constitutional system." Jackson decided that Truman's action fell into this third category and, after examining it under "the severe tests [of] this third grouping," found the president's actions to be unconstitutional.[14] Jackson's opinion was an explanatory meditation on the constitutional separation of powers.

When it was the chief justice's turn to read his dissenting opinion, he did not bother to hide his contempt for the majority's decision. One reporter wrote that Vinson spoke "with sarcasm and considerable scorn for his judicial brethren quite obvious to those in the crowded courtroom." This was in contrast to Black, who had spoken "in calm and measured tones."[15] Vinson blasted what he called the Court's "messenger-boy concept" of the presidency. When the nation faced an emergency, Vinson lamented, the president no longer could call on the "broad executive power granted by Article II [of the Constitution] . . . to avert disaster. Instead, the president must confine himself to sending a message to Congress recommending action. Under this messenger-boy concept of the office, the president cannot even act to preserve legislative programs from destruction so that Congress will have something left to act upon."[16]

In all, the justices took two and a half hours to read their opinions, finishing at 2:35 p.m., thirty-five minutes after the Court's usual two o'clock lunch recess. Journalists were quick to note that, as one reporter wrote, "Two of the justices named to the bench by President Truman, Justices Harold H. Burton and Tom Clark, voted against his act to bring about the 6–3 ruling."[17]

* * *

Years later Truman stressed the fact that the majority failed to agree on a single opinion to speak for the Court. "The diversity of views expressed in the six opinions of the majority," the former president wrote in his memoirs, "the lack of reference to authoritative precedent, the repeated reliance upon prior dissenting opinions, the complete disregard of the uncontroverted facts showing the gravity of the emergency . . . all serve to demonstrate how far afield one must go to affirm the order of the District Court." In a tacit rebuke that did not exclude the four men he appointed, Truman concluded, "I could not help but wonder what the decision might have been had there been on the Court a Holmes, a Hughes, a Brandeis, a Stone."[18]

Not surprisingly, Truman agreed with Vinson's dissent: "I think Chief Justice Vinson's dissenting opinion hit the nail right on the head and I am sure that someday his view will come to be recognized as the correct one."[19]

A President's Nadir

EFFECTS OF THE SUPREME COURT'S ruling were immediate and widespread. President Truman quickly directed Secretary of Commerce Sawyer to return the steel mills to their owners.[1] His message to Sawyer read,

Dear Mr. Secretary:

In view of today's decision by the Supreme Court, you are hereby directed to take appropriate steps to relinquish immediately possession of plants, facilities and other property of the steel companies which have been in the possession of the Government under Executive Order No. 10340 of April 8, 1952.

Sawyer executed Truman's order, and in every seized plant and office was posted a sign reading, "The Secretary of Commerce has authorized notice to whom it may concern that he is no longer in possession of this plant."[2] Before the chief justice had finished speaking—in fact, not long after he began and before Truman instructed Sawyer to relinquish the mills—steelworkers walked off the job and took to picket lines.[3] Steelworker CIO president Murray claimed that the Court's ruling left "the members of the United Steelworkers of America without the benefit of a collective bargaining agreement" and rendered all 650,000 workers with "no alternative" but to strike.[4] Government officials responded by ordering an immediate halt to deliveries from steel warehouses to manufacturers of consumer goods in order to preserve steel for military needs.[5]

Despite the fact that their workers had walked off the job, steel company executives were elated with the Court's ruling. Republic Steel president Charles White called it "the greatest Supreme Court decision of my lifetime." As far as the steelworkers's walkout was concerned, the strike was better "than further intrusion of government into private rights." Inland Steel president Clarene Randall agreed, proclaiming, "This is a great day for America. The whole country will take new hope for the future."[6]

Many Americans wondered if the White House had a plan to end the strike. "What will the president do about the steel strike?" one reporter asked White House press secretary Joseph Short.

"There is nothing beyond this letter [to Sawyer]," Short replied.[7]

Stock market investors reacted sharply both to the Court's ruling and to the strike, hurling steel stocks into a financial whiplash. Prices soared when Black announced the Court's ruling that the government seizure was illegal. Stock prices swiftly plummeted just a short time later when the steelworkers went on strike.[8]

Georgia Democratic congressman Carl Vinson warned, "Something's got to be done to assure the continued production of steel for the defense program. If steel falls down, the defense falls down. We can't allow that." Republican senator Irving Ives of New York told reporters, "I regret exceedingly that the strike of the steelworkers is being renewed." Unlike Congressman Vinson, Senator Ives did not echo the Truman administration's argument, but he added, "I feel strongly that an appopriate solution to the controversy can be found without resorting to a work stoppage in an industry so vital to the national safety."[9]

Bipartisan dismay over the steelworkers' strike was matched by both parties' satisfaction with the surprising ruling. "Hoo-ray!" shouted Senator Charles Tobey, a New Hampshire Republican, on hearing the news on the Senate floor. As the steel seizure had dragged on, Democratic senator Pat McCarran of Nevada, chair of the Senate Judiciary Committee, had introduced a bill to amend the Constitution to prevent any president from seizing private property without express legislative authority. Republican senator Homer Ferguson of Michigan obtained unanimous consent to retain McCarran's bill on the calender so senators could vote on it later if necessary. Senator Wayne Morse, a Republican from Oregon, had sponsored a bill granting the president power to seize a private company but providing Congress with authority to veto such a decision. A House judiciary subcommittee was considering at least a dozen measures to impeach, censure, or otherwise address President Truman directly.[10] The

Court's decision—for now, at least—relieved pressure on Congress to act on any of these controversial measures.

Many journalists and commentators shared the legislators' sense of relief at the Court's opinion. On news pages and in broadcasts nationwide, they denounced Chief Justice Vinson's dramatic assertion that the Court was relegating the president of the United States in times of emergency to the role of a "messenger-boy" whose sole option was to beseech Congress for help. This was, as more than one writer noted, simply not "a correct account of what was said in Mr. Justice Black's opinion or in any of the concurring opinions."[11] Reporters impressed upon their readers and listeners that, despite the unfortunate multitude of opinions handed down, a pillar of the justices' opinions was that the president cannot disregard federal legislation, even—perhaps especially—if he vetoed or disagreed with it.

* * *

President Truman was personally and politically devastated by the Court's decision. "I would, of course," he later wrote, "never conceal that the Supreme Court's decision, announced on June 2, was a deep disappointment to me." Secretary Sawyer recalled that a visibly emotional Truman concluded that the Court had not examined the case closely enough. Truman's memoirs lend credence to Sawyer's account, as Truman, writing as a private citizen retired from public life, continued to believe that the Court had disregarded crucial evidence:

> I am not a lawyer, and I leave the legal arguments to others. But as a layman, as an official of the government, and as a citizen, I have always found it difficult to understand how the Court could could take the affidavits of men like [Secretary of Defense Robert A.] Lovett, [Secretary of the Interior Oscar L.] Chapman, and many others, all of whom testified in great detail to the grave dangers that a steel shutdown would bring to the nation—affidavits that were neither contradicted nor even contested by the companies—and ignore them entirely.[12]

For two decades presidents had exercised power without judicial interference. As prominent steel seizure historian Maeva Marcus wrote,

Truman "took the Court's ruling as a personal rebuke."[13] In a letter he wrote but never mailed to Justice Douglas, the man he personally had asked to be his running mate in 1948, Truman expressed aggrieved regret:

> I am sorry that I didn't have an opportunity to discuss precedents with you before you came to the conclusion you did on that crazy decision that has tied up the country. . . . There was no decision by the majority although there were seven opinions against what was best for the country. I don't see how a Court made up of so-called liberals could do what the Court did to me.[14]

Perhaps Truman, whose political instincts were remarkably acute even by presidential standards, was right to view the decision as something of a personal affront. He never suggested that the six-justice majority reached its decision to spite him, but it was certainly possible that more than a couple of them took a particular pleasure in doing so. Justice Jackson had beckoned his law clerks to join him in his chambers after he returned from the steel seizure conference. As soon as the clerks took their seats, Jackson announced, "Well boys, the president got licked."[15]

One of those law clerks, William Rehnquist, later wrote that the case's questions of constitutional law were "more or less up for grabs [and] the whole trend of the Court's decisions in the preceding fifteen years leaned toward the government." Examining the question of why six justices voted against the administration in the steel seizure case, Rehnquist concluded, "I think that this is one of those celebrated constitutional cases where what might be called the tide of public opinion suddenly began to run against the government, for a number of reasons, and that this tide of public opinion had a considerable influence on the Court."[16]

Truman almost certainly would have agreed. The president was taken aback by the media's negative coverage of the steel seizure. He could recall "few instances in history where the press was more sensational or partisan than in its handling of the steel seizure." That the justices would be influenced by public perception seemed unfortunately inevitable amid such reporting. "News stories and editorials decrying the seizure and inflaming public opinion," Truman remembered, "were prejudging and deciding the case at the very time the Court itself was hearing arguments for both sides." In addition to the news coverage, the steel companies had spent heavily on advertising throughout the case's shotgun-run through the federal judiciary, buying full-page newspaper advertisements and other commercials to criticize the seizure. Truman accurately noted, "Large sums of money were spent to influence public opinion against the government."[17]

And the justices were reading the newspapers and, presumably, at least setting eyes on the steel companies' full-page ads. "This was a case," Rehnquist described, "that unfurled in the newspapers before the very eyes of the justices long before any papers were filed in the Supreme Court."[18] No one suggested that news coverage (or the advertisements) directly influenced any justice's vote. But no doubt each justice was aware of how the public perceived both the seizure and the administration's far-reaching legal arguments defending it.

President Truman's unpopularity only fueled public skepticism. Having lost the Democratic New Hampshire primary just a few months earlier to a senator who would not go on to win the nomination, and having announced thereafter that he would not seek reelection, Truman was as politically weak as he was unpopular. Had his political position been better in 1952, and had the Korean War not been so unpopular by that time, the Court might not have ruled against the administration six months into that same year. But, as Rehnquist recalled, Truman's "standing in public opinion at the time of the Steel Seizure case was at its nadir." Moreover, households across the nation were called upon to sacrifice for a war the Truman administration insisted was only a "police action." "We had a draft, we had price controls, we had rent controls, we had production controls," Rehnquist noted, "but these measures, which had been borne resolutely during the Second World War, were tolerated less resolutely and with considerably more grumbling during the Korean conflict."[19]

* * *

In the days following the Court's ruling, Truman continued to refuse to invoke the Taft-Hartley Act to end the steelworkers' strike. Unfortunately, the president's obstinance belied the very reason he gave for seizing the steel mills in the first place. The effects of a steel strike, Truman had warned before seizing the mills, "would be so immediate and damaging with respect to our efforts to support our armed forces and to protect our national security that it made this alternative [allowing a strike] unthink-able." Editors of the *Baltimore Sun* noted that Truman's refusal to end the current strike by using the Taft-Hartley Act made it clear that "the strike seems *not* to be the alternative that is unthinkable."[20]

Truman not only refused to invoke the Taft-Hartley Act but he refused to explain how he planned to end the strike. Rumors and guesses swirled in the vacuum. Senators from both parties openly predicted that he would call a special session of Congress to ask for steel seizure powers, despite the fact that four such bills had recently failed in the Senate.[21] As the strike dragged on into its seventh week, administration officials threatened to seize the steel mills again, this time by using a novel interpretation of the Selective Service Act.[22]

Nearly 2 million workers had been laid off or furloughed as a result of the steelworkers' strike. Defense Secretary Robert A. Lovett told reporters, "No enemy action, no form of bombing, could have taken out of produc-tion in one day 380 steel plants and kept them out for nearly two months." When asked if American forces might have to evacuate Korea on account of the steel shortage, Lovett answered no but added, "We may be over there fighting with bows and arrows if this thing goes on."[23]

Members of the administration continued to host negotiations be-tween the steel companies and union leaders. Finally, on July 24, 1952, the executives and union representatives reached a deal to end the nearly eight-week-long strike. Truman made the announcement at the White House, saying that he looked forward to "a speedy resumption of steel production."[24] He took no questions and details of the agreement were not made public until days later. What was clear, nearly two months after it was announced, was that the Supreme Court's decision in *Youngstown Sheet & Tube Co. v. Sawyer*, better known forever as the steel seizure case, had further weakened an already dampered president.

* * *

Justice Black realized how deeply the Court's steel seizure ruling had wounded Truman, both politically and personally. Two weeks after the decision was handed down, Black asked Douglas if he should invite the president to his home in Alexandria, Virginia, to have dinner with the justices. Douglas thought it was an excellent idea, and Truman accepted Black's invitation.

Truman joined the nine justices around Black's table at the men's only "stag dinner." As Douglas recalled, the president "was gracious though a bit testy at the beginning of the evening." As the bourbon flowed and the canapés were passed, Truman's mood lightened. He turned to his host and quipped, "Hugo, I don't much care for your law but, by golly, this bourbon is good."[25]

CHAPTER THIRTY

The Truman Court

SUPREME COURT HISTORIAN HENRY J. Abraham noted the traits all four of Truman's nominees held in common: "They had all held public office; they were his political, professional and personal friends; he understood them; he liked them; they liked him; he liked their politics."[1] Although Truman sometimes disagreed with their individual decisions, the men he nominated to the Court generally did not disappoint him. As two historians together wrote about the Court, "Truman, with few exceptions, got what he wanted from his appointees."[2]

Not only was Truman friends with the men he nominated to the Court but those men became friends with each other once on the bench. Fred Vinson, Tom Clark, Harold Burton, and Sherman Minton, joined by Stanley Reed, were the only justices who regularly had lunch together, with Vinson, Clark, and Minton dining together almost every day. The other justices ate alone in their chambers or sometimes took a tray in the public cafeteria.[3] Minton told Truman of the lunches after his presidency. "Fred, Tom and I meet before lunch each day," he wrote on June 3, 1953, "and discuss the State of the Union. Your judgment is vindicated every day in naming them to this Court. Fred is a champion in every way."[4]

* * *

Franklin Roosevelt's legendary battle with the Supreme Court obscured the fact that he, like every president before him, engaged the Court as a defensive endeavor: when litigants challenged laws or government actions, the administration defended those laws and actions in court. Roosevelt's frustration stemmed from the Court's repeatedly striking down laws on a specious theory (substantive due process) found nowhere in the Constitution. By and large, his administration was not forging ahead of Congress or the national polls, clearing legal brush to build a path toward a better America. Roosevelt stayed with Congress, going no further than its segregationist southern senators allowed in domestic policy and exercising relative restraint in foreign policy until Japan brought war to American soil.

The unfortunate exception that proves this rule was the Roosevelt administration's internment of Japanese Americans during World War II. Plaintiffs challenged Roosevelt's policy in federal court and ultimately were denied relief by the Supreme Court in *Korematsu v. United States*, one of the Court's most shameful rulings. But the majority of the Roosevelt administration's significant Supreme Court cases involved defending laws enacted by Congress and the president.

Truman turned this paradigm on its head. Like any president, he, as one historian wrote, "wanted [Supreme] Court decisions endorsing his political aims."[5] But his administration pushed ahead of Congress and even the American public in matters both foreign and domestic. When these actions were challenged in federal court, Truman welcomed the contest. The poker-playing president liked his odds.

Nearly two decades of Supreme Court jurisprudence had established the Court's deference to executive action. Combining those twenty years of common law and tradition with the fact that the four men Truman named to the Court generally shared his views on constitutional questions, it became clear why Truman felt comfortable wading into the far reaches of presidential power. He believed in a restrained judiciary that deferred to the executive and legislative branches. And he nominated four men to the Court who shared this belief.

* * *

Sixty-five legal scholars in June 1970 compared the ninety-six justices who served on the Court between 1789 and 1969. They placed Tom Clark in the middle group of fifty-five justices whom they rated "average." Vinson, Burton, and Minton were three of the eight justices they listed in the lowest category, marked "failures."[6] Any conclusions drawn by such a small group of self-selected academics should be examined with a healthy bit of skepticism, but their assessment of the four Truman nominees is consistent with those of many observers. In 1970 constitutional historian William Swindler relegated the time of Truman's appointees to the "Vinson Interlude," writing, "Truman, by his four appointments, had reduced the former rapid pace of the new constitutionalism to a walk."[7]

None of the four was regarded during his time or after his death as a great legal mind or pillar of the Court. For his part, Minton acknowledged as much when, on September 7 , 1956, he announced his retirement from the Court for health reasons: "There will be more interest in who will succeed me, than in my passing," he told reporters. "I'm an echo."[8]

The legal scholars' evaluations, which Minton seemed to anticipate, missed the point of why the justices Truman named to the Court proved so valuable to his administration. In all, Truman appointed 120 judges to federal courts but the Supreme Court provided the backstop. He was able to restrict civil liberties with the federal employee loyalty program and advance his progressive civil rights agenda because a majority of the Court believed his actions were constitutional. As a senator during the Roosevelt years, he had witnessed how a hostile Court could frustrate a presidency. As president, he was determined to avoid a similar fate.

Truman never relinquished his disappointment with the Court's ruling in the steel seizure case. He was especially frustrated that two of his nominees, Burton and Clark, voted to invalidate the seizure. Speaking at Columbia University years later, the former president said, "Packing the Supreme Court simply can't be done. . . . I've tried and it won't work." Either forgetting or disregarding that he remained close friends with Vinson, Clark, and Minton after they became justices, Truman added, "Whenever you put a man on the Supreme Court, he ceases to be your friend. I'm sure of that."[9]

Perhaps it is a president's destiny to be disappointed with the Supreme Court of his or her time. But Truman chose four of the nine justices who decided the cases during much of his administration and the other five were nominated by Roosevelt. He generally was satisfied with the Court until it ruled against him in the steel seizure case.

Years after leaving the White House and returning to Independence, Missouri, Truman maintained that the Court erred in ruling against his administration in the steel seizure case. "Whatever the six justices of the Supreme Court meant by their differing opinions about the constitutional powers of the President," he professed, "he must always act in an emergency. . . . The President, under the Constitution, must use his powers to safeguard the nation."[10] By seizing control of the steel mills, Harry S. Truman, even decades later, maintained that he was only fulfilling his duty to protect Americans. Given his own carefully chosen words; his well-known, defiant temperament; and all else we know about the man, one imagines that the thirty-third president of the United States, if somehow given a second chance, would again have seized the steel mills and taken his chances on getting a couple more votes from the Court.

NOTES

Prologue

1. William O. Douglas, *The Court Years, 1939–1975: The Autobiography of William O. Douglas* (New York: Random House, 1980), 242.

2. Del Dickson, ed., *The Supreme Court in Conference, 1940–1985: The Private Discussions behind Nearly 300 Supreme Court Decisions* (New York: Oxford University Press, 2001), 100–101.

3. Robert S. Allen and William V. Shannon, *The Truman Merry-Go-Round* (New York: Vanguard Press, 1950), 357.

4. Douglas, *The Court Years*, 245, 248.

5. Fred Rodell, *Nine Men: A Political History of the Supreme Court from 1790 to 1955* (New York: Random House, 1955), 318.

Chapter One

1. "Marking Time in Steel Crisis," *Pittsburgh Press*, April 7, 1952.

2. Asa Atwater, "Mill Towns Flash Alive at Cry 'Dismiss Pickets,'" *Pittsburgh Press*, April 9, 1952.

3. Maeva Marcus, *Truman and the Steel Seizure Case: The Limits of Presidential Power* (New York: Columbia University Press, 1977), 87.

4. Atwater, "Mill Towns Flash Alive."

5. "Defense Gets All Deliveries 'Immediately,'" *Pittsburgh Press*, April 7, 1952.

6. "Captive Mines Lay Off 9,000 in District," *Pittsburgh Press*, April 8, 1952.

7. "Men to Go On Working for Government," *Baltimore Sun*, April 9, 1952.

8. Patricia L. Bellia, "Story of the Steel Seizure Case," in *Presidential Power Stories*, ed. Christopher H. Schroeder and Curtis A. Bradley (New York: Foundation Press, 2009), 236–37.

9. "Wildcat Strikes Hit Steel Plants," *Pittsburgh Press*, April 8, 1952.

10. "Picket Signs Go Back in Storage," *Pittsburgh Press*, April 8, 1952.

11. "Sec. Sawyer Told to Take Charge of Operations," *Washington Post*, April 9, 1952.

12. Marcus, *Truman and the Steel Seizure Case*, 87.

13. "Text of Truman's Speech on Federal Seizure of Steel Industry," *New York Times*, April 9, 1952.

14. Marcus, *Truman and the Steel Seizure Case*, 32, 34.

15. "Text of Truman's Speech on Federal Seizure of Steel Industry."

16. "Text of Truman's Speech on Federal Seizure of Steel Industry."

17. Marcus, *Truman and the Steel Seizure Case*, 80.

18. Bellia, "Story of the Steel Seizure Case," 237–39.

19. Dewey L. Fleming, "Steel Strike Called Off by Murray as Truman Orders Seizure of Mills," *Baltimore Sun*, April 9, 1952.

20. "Text of Truman's Speech on Federal Seizure of Steel Industry."

21. Atwater, "Mill Towns Flash Alive."

22. "Men to Go On Working for Government."

23. Atwater, "Mill Towns Flash Alive."

24. Joseph A. Loftus, "Steel Freeze Ends; President to Rely on Pay Bargaining," *New York Times*, April 11, 1952.

25. "Impeach Truman on Mill Seizure: Bender," *Bridgeport [CT] Sunday Herald*, April 20, 1952.

26. John H. Fenton, "Taft Urges Steps to Remove Truman," *New York Times*, April 18, 1952.

27. "Lopsided," *Washington Post*, April 10, 1952.

28. Arthur Krock, "In the Nation: Issues of Law and Politics in Seizure," *New York Times*, April 11, 1952.

29. Alfred Friendly, "Union Heads and Industry Confer Here Again Today," *Washington Post*, April 10, 1952.

30. "Without Benefit of Law," *Washington Post*, April 10, 1952.

31. Dewey L. Fleming, "Steel Official Calls Truman Seizure," *Baltimore Sun*, April 10, 1952.

Chapter Two

1. "Justice Roberts," *Washington Post*, July 18, 1945.

2. Harry McAlpin, "No Loss Viewed in Roberts' Resignation," *Atlanta Daily World*, July 10, 1945.

3. *Smith v. Allwright*, 321 U.S. 649 (1944).

4. "Roberts' Bow Boon to Negro," *Chicago Defender*, July 14, 1945.

5. George Gallup, "Public Favors Bipartisan High Court Appointments," *Washington Post*, August 29, 1945.

6. "Hatch Backs Sen. Austin for Supreme Court," *Washington Post*, July 6, 1945.

7. C. Herman Pritchett, *The Roosevelt Court: A Study in Judicial Politics and Values, 1937–1947* (New York: Macmillan, 1948), 13.

8. "Presidents Sometimes Regret Justices They Appoint," *USA Today*, July 5, 2005.

9. C. P. Ives, "Four Justices Who Stand Together," *Baltimore Sun*, May 27, 1945.

10. "Justice Roberts Retires," *New York Times*, July 7, 1945.

11. Melvin I. Urofsky, *Division and Discord: The Supreme Court under Stone and Vinson, 1941–1953* (Columbia: University of South Carolina Press, 1997), 45–46.

12. Melvin I. Urofsky, *Felix Frankfurter: Judicial Restraint and Individual Liberties* (Boston: Twayne, 1991), 87.

13. Del Dickson, ed., *The Supreme Court in Conference, 1940–1985: The Private Discussions behind Nearly 300 Supreme Court Decisions* (New York: Oxford University Press, 2001), 96.

14. "Harold Hitz Burton," in *The Supreme Court Justices: A Biographical Dictionary*, ed. Melvin I. Urofsky (New York: Garland, 1994), 77.

15. Jim Kelley, "Harold Hitz Burton," in *Dictionary of Unitarian and Universalist Biography*, Unitarian Universalist History and Heritage Society, 2014, www.uudb.org.

16. "The Elections of 1940: Ohio Bets on Burton for Senate," *Life*, October 21, 1940, 98.

17. "Ohio Republicans Win Senate Seat, Reelect Bricker as Governor," *Baltimore Sun*, November 7, 1940. See also "Election Battle in Midwest Still in Nip-and-Tuck Stage," *Washington Post*, October 28, 1940.

18. "Roosevelt Victor in Ohio Election," *New York Times*, November 6, 1940.

19. "These Are Some Winners in Nip-and-Tuck," *Life*, November 18, 1940, 32.

20. "Roosevelt Victor in Ohio Election."

21. James D. Secrest, "District Didoes," *Washington Post*, February 9, 1941.

22. "Sen. Burton GOP Choice for D.C. Group," *Washington Post*, January 9, 1941.

23. "D.C. Leaders Vote to Form Civic Assembly," *Washington Post*, February 1, 1941.

24. Wilson D. Miscamble, *From Roosevelt to Truman: Potsdam, Hiroshima, and the Cold War* (New York: Cambridge University Press, 2007), 21.

25. "Notes of Society," *Washington Post*, May 22, 1941.

26. Gerald G. Gross, "Washingtonians of the Week," *Washington Post*, January 26, 1941.

27. Drew Pearson, "The Washington Merry-Go-Round," *Washington Post*, August 5, 1945.

28. "Senator Burton Called Possible Choice," *Baltimore Sun*, August 28, 1945.

29. William O. Douglas, *The Court Years, 1939–1975: The Autobiography of William O. Douglas* (New York: Random House, 1980), 248.

30. Drew Pearson, "The Washington Merry-Go-Round," *Washington Post*, September 25, 1945.

31. David Alistair Yalof, *Pursuit of Justices: Presidential Politics and the Selection of Supreme Court Nominees* (Chicago: University of Chicago Press, 1999), 25.

32. Urofsky, *Division and Discord*, 152n57.

33. Frances Howell Rudko, *Truman's Court: A Study in Judicial Restraint* (Westport, CT: Greenwood Press, 1988), 31.

34. Edward T. Folliard, "Resignation of Stimson Reluctantly Accepted," *Washington Post*, September 19, 1945.

35. Harry S. McAlpin, "Truman Names Burton Justice," *Atlanta Daily World*, September 19, 1945.

36. "President Tells News in Three Minutes," *New York Times*, September 18, 1945.

37. "New Justice," *Washington Post*, September 19, 1945.

38. Lewis Wood, "Senator Burton Is Named a Supreme Court Justice," *New York Times*, September 19, 1945.

39. Folliard, "Resignation of Stimson."

40. Merlo Pusey, "Judicial Nominations: New Trend Seen," *Washington Post*, September 25, 1945.

41. Wood, "Senator Burton Is Named a Supreme Court Justice."

42. "Hail Choice of Patterson, Burton," *Baltimore Afro-American*, September 29, 1945.

43. "Senator Burton as a Supreme Court Justice," *Baltimore Sun*, September 20, 1945.

44. Wood, "Senator Burton Is Named a Supreme Court Justice."

45. Rudko, *Truman's Court*, 28.

46. "New Justice."

47. Arthur Krock, "In the Nation: Laborings of the Federal Machinery," *New York Times*, September 20, 1945.

48. "New Justice."

49. Krock, "In the Nation."

50. "Senate Confirms Choice of Burton," *New York Times*, September 20, 1945.

51. Folliard, "Resignation of Stimson."

52. "Senate Confirms Choice of Burton."

53. "Senate OKs Burton for Supreme Court," *Washington Post*, September 20, 1945.

54. "The Day in Washington," *New York Times*, September 20, 1945.

55. Wood, "Senator Burton Is Named a Supreme Court Justice."

56. Vincent Swain, "Justice for All Is Burton's Creed," *New York Times*, September 22, 1945.

57. "Truman Breaks 155 Year-Old Tradition at Court Opening," *Atlanta Daily World*, October 2, 1945.

58. Lewis Wood, "Truman Watches Burton Take Oath," *New York Times*, October 2, 1945.

59. "Truman Visits High Tribunal," *Baltimore Sun*, October 2, 1945.

60. "Supreme Court to Seat Burton as First Task," *Washington Post*, October 1, 1945.

61. John Q. Barrett, "Mr. Cropley, First Monday and Supreme Court Stewardship (1952)," https://thejacksonlist.com/wp-content/uploads/2014/02/20121001-Jackson-List-Cropley .pdf.

62. "Truman Sees Burton Take Court Seat," *Washington Post*, October 2, 1945.

63. Rudko, *Truman's Court*, 28.

Chapter Three

1. "Clark Received Short Notice of Choice as Attorney General," *Washington Post*, May 24, 1945.

2. Alexander Smithfield, "Supreme Court OK's Talmadge," *New York Amsterdam News*, November 2, 1946.

3. "Negro Council Opposes Tom Clark Nomination," *Baltimore Sun*, May 25, 1945.

4. Venice T. Spraggs, "Negro Can Depend on Me—Clark," *Chicago Defender*, June 23, 1945.

5. Venice T. Spraggs, "Negroes Adopt 'Wait and See' Policy on Texas Attorney General Clark," *Chicago Defender*, June 2, 1945.

6. Spraggs, "Negroes Adopt 'Wait and See' Policy."

7. Alexander Wohl, *Father, Son, and Constitution: How Justice Tom Clark and Attorney General Ramsey Clark Shaped American Democracy* (Lawrence: University Press of Kansas, 2013), 8–9.

8. Wohl, *Father, Son, and Constitution*, 13.

9. Mimi Clark Gronlund, *Supreme Court Justice Tom C. Clark: A Life of Service* (Austin: University of Texas Press, 2010), 23.

10. Franklin D. Roosevelt, Executive Order 9066, "Authorizing the Secretary of War to Prescribe Military Areas," February 19, 1942.

11. *Hirabayashi v. U.S.*, 320 U.S. 81 (1943); *Korematsu v. U.S.*, 323 U.S. 214 (1944).

12. Wohl, *Father, Son, and Constitution*, 42, 48.

13. "New Cabinet Wives Aren't Career Gals," *Washington Post*, May 27, 1945.

14. Gronlund, *Supreme Court Justice Tom C. Clark*, 85.

15. "Tom Clarks, Miss Reynolds Given Parties," *Washington Post*, June 11, 1945.

16. Gronlund, *Supreme Court Justice Tom C. Clark*, 87.

17. Jerry Kluttz, "The Federal Diary: Justice Aides to Quit Despite Plea by Clark," *Washington Post*, May 31, 1945.

18. "Tom Clark Talks to Bar," *Baltimore Sun*, July 1, 1945.

Chapter Four

1. John W. Johnson, "Harlan Fiske Stone," in *The Supreme Court Justices: A Biographical Dictionary*, ed. Melvin I. Urofsky (New York: Garland, 1994), 425.

2. Michael R. Belknap, *The Vinson Court: Justices, Rulings, and Legacy* (Santa Barbara, CA: ABC-CLIO, 2004), 221.

3. "Stone Is Nominated for Supreme Court as M'Kenna Resigns," *New York Times*, January 6, 1925.

4. Eric Schepard, "Why Harlan Fiske Stone (Also) Matters," *Howard Law Journal* 56, no. 1 (Fall 2012): 98.

5. Schepard, "Why Harlan Fiske Stone (Also) Matters," 100.

6. "The Day in Washington," *Baltimore Sun*, January 6, 1925.

7. "Stone Is Nominated for Supreme Court as M'Kenna Resigns."

8. Belknap, *The Vinson Court*, 221.

9. Johnson, "Harlan Fiske Stone," 426.

10. "Stone a Supporter of New Deal Laws," *New York Times*, June 13, 1941.

11. J. Fred Essary, "3 Selected for Place on Highest Bench," *New York Times*, June 13, 1941.

12. "'Not Sure I'm Lucky,' Says Justice Stone," *Baltimore Sun*, June 13, 1941.

13. William V. Nessly, "Chief Justice Hughes Retires July 1; Jackson Most Likely Successor," *Washington Post*, June 3, 1941.

14. Essary, "3 Selected for Place on Highest Bench."

15. "'Not Sure I'm Lucky,'" *New York Times*, June 12, 1941.

16. Melvin I. Urofsky, *Felix Frankfurter: Judicial Restraint and Individual Liberties* (Boston: Twayne, 1991), 88–89.

17. Alpheus Thomas Mason, *The Supreme Court from Taft to Burger* (Baton Rouge: Louisiana State University Press, 1991), 60.

18. Del Dickson, ed., *The Supreme Court in Conference, 1940–1985: The Private Discussions behind Nearly 300 Supreme Court Decisions* (New York: Oxford University Press, 2001), 77.

19. Dickson, *The Supreme Court in Conference*, 77.

20. James F. Simon, *The Antagonists: Hugo Black, Felix Frankfurter and Civil Liberties in Modern America* (New York: Simon and Schuster, 1989), 101–2.

21. Simon, *The Antagonists*, 104.

22. "Black Embarrasses Colleagues in Supreme Court, Writer Says," *Washington Post*, May 11, 1938.

23. Simon, *The Antagonists*, 104–5.

24. Dickson, *The Supreme Court in Conference*.

25. Drew Pearson, "The Washington Merry-Go-Round," *Washington Post*, May 18, 1945.

26. "Counsel on Atrocities," *Washington Post*, May 4, 1945.

27. "Justice Jackson as Prosecutor in the Cases against War Criminals," *Baltimore Sun*, May 4, 1945.

28. William O. Douglas, *The Court Years, 1939–1975: The Autobiography of William O. Douglas* (New York: Random House, 1980), 28.

29. Frank R. Kent, "The Great Game of Politics: On Drafting Judges," *Baltimore Sun*, June 1, 1945.

30. Douglas, *The Court Years*, 28.

31. Simon, *The Antagonists*, 158.

32. Pearson, "The Washington Merry-Go-Round."

33. Dickson, *The Supreme Court in Conference*, 97.

34. Simon, *The Antagonists*, 159–60.

35. Dewey L. Fleming, "Death of Truman Is a Fact, Truman Declares," *Baltimore Sun*, May 3, 1945.

36. "Biased Attorney Named to Pick War Criminals," *Baltimore Afro-American*, June 2, 1945.

37. "Jackson Goes to London," *New York Times*, May 23, 1945.

38. Simon, *The Antagonists*, 161.

39. Moritz Fuchs, "Robert H. Jackson at the Nuremberg Trials, 1945–1946 as Remembered by His Personal Bodyguard," *Albany Law Review* 68, no. 1 (2004): 13–16.

40. Mimi Clark Gronlund, *Supreme Court Justice Tom C. Clark: A Life of Service* (Austin: University of Texas Press, 2010), 91.

41. Scott W. Johnson and John H. Hinderaker, "Guidelines for Cross-Examination: Lessons from the Cross-Examination of Hermann Goering," *Bench and Bar of Minnesota* 59, no. 9 (October 2002).

42. Simon, *The Antagonists*, 164–65.

43. Urofsky, *Felix Frankfurter*, 88.

Chapter Five

1. "Vinson Rise Rapid; Experience Broad," *New York Times*, June 7, 1946.

2. James A. Anderson, III, *The Judge: Fred Vinson, Legislator, Executive, Jurist* (Louisville, KY: Sulgrave Press, 1999), 12; "Vinson Rise Rapid; Experience Broad."

3. Wesley McCune, *The Nine Young Men* (New York: Harper and Brothers, 1947), 261.

4. Anderson, *The Judge*, 29.

5. James E. St. Clair and Linda Gugin, *Chief Justice Fred M. Vinson of Kentucky: A Political Biography* (Lexington: University Press of Kentucky), 103.

6. St. Clair and Gugin, *Chief Justice Fred M. Vinson*, 126.

7. "Vinson Rise Rapid; Experience Broad."

8. "Vinson to Become Head of Treasury after Big 3 Parley," *New York Times*, July 7, 1945.

9. *Public Papers of the Presidents of the United States, Harry S. Truman, April 12 to December 31, 1945* (Washington, DC: U.S. Government Printing Office, 1961), 67.

10. Drew Pearson, "The Washington Merry-Go-Round," *Washington Post*, July 11, 1945.

11. "Morgenthau Denies Ouster," *Baltimore Sun*, July 26, 1945.

12. Richard Hedlund, "Harry S. Truman and Frederick M. Vinson: A Personal Relationship," *Filson History Quarterly* 75, no. 3 (Summer 2001): 335.

13. "Unanimous Vote Confirms Vinson," *Baltimore Sun*, July 18, 1945.

14. "Oath Taken by Vinson; Cabinet Pondering Rises," *Baltimore Sun*, July 24, 1945.

15. Pearson, "The Washington Merry-Go-Round."

16. "Vinson to Become Head of Treasury."

17. Hedlund, "Harry S. Truman and Frederick M. Vinson," 336.

18. "Unanimous Vote Confirms Vinson."

19. "Vinson Rise Rapid; Experience Broad."

20. Mark Sullivan, "Vinson's Tax Plan: Double Objective," *Washington Post*, October 5, 1945.

21. Ernest Lindley, "Truman's Cabinet: Policy Changes Not Anticipated," *Washington Post*, July 9, 1945.

22. C. P. Trussell, "Five Billion Tax Reduction, Exempting 12,000,000, Urged on Congress by Vinson," *New York Times*, October 2, 1945.

23. Robert C. Albright, "Vinson Plan Would Free 12 Million of Income Tax," *Washington Post*, October 2, 1945.

NOTES TO CHAPTER SIX

24. St. Clair and Gugin, *Chief Justice Fred M. Vinson*, 150.

25. Samuel A. Tower, "Compromise Bill on Jobs Is Evolved," *New York Times*, February 3, 1946.

Chapter Six

1. "'Not Sure I'm Lucky,' Says Justice Stone," *New York Times*, June 12, 1941.

2. Del Dickson, ed., *The Supreme Court in Conference, 1940–1985: The Private Discussions behind Nearly 300 Supreme Court Decisions* (New York: Oxford University Press, 2001), 3.

3. During a recent private tour of the Supreme Court building, the author was informed that the conference room was "off-limits."

4. Dickson, *The Supreme Court in Conference*, 91.

5. Lewis Wood, "Dissents in High Court Reflect Basic Division," *New York Times*, February 25, 1945.

6. Dickson, *The Supreme Court in Conference*, 96.

7. John W. Johnson, "Harlan Fiske Stone," in *The Supreme Court Justices: A Biographical Dictionary*, ed. Melvin I. Urofsky (New York: Garland, 1994), 433.

8. C. Herman Pritchett, *The Roosevelt Court: A Study in Judicial Politics and Values* (New York: Macmillan, 1948), 25.

9. Melvin I. Urofsky, *Division and Discord: The Supreme Court under Stone and Vinson, 1941–1953* (Columbia: University of South Carolina Press, 1997), 42.

10. Pritchett, *The Roosevelt Court*, 25.

11. Lewis Wood, "Supreme Court Split Is Aired in Dissents," *New York Times*, February 13, 1944.

12. "Our New Court," *Washington Post*, June 13, 1941.

13. Pritchett, *The Roosevelt Court*, 23.

14. "Denies Court of One Mind," *New York Times*, June 20, 1942.

15. Jay Walz, "New Citizen Freed of Oath to Fight," *New York Times*, April 23, 1946.

16. *Girouard v. the United States*, 328 U.S. 61 (1946).

17. "Chief Justice Harlan Stone of Supreme Court Is Dead," *New York Times*, April 23, 1946.

18. "Chief Justice Stone Dies; Stricken in Court," *Baltimore Sun*, April 23, 1946.

19. "Chief Justice Harlan Stone of Supreme Court Is Dead."

20. "Nation Mourns Death of Chief Justice Stone," *Atlanta Daily World*, April 24, 1946.

21. "Tributes by Colleagues," *New York Times*, April 23, 1946.

22. "Truman Mourns Death of Stone," *New York Times*, April 23, 1946.

23. "Chief Justice Harlan Stone of Supreme Court Is Dead."

24. "Truman Mourns Death of Stone."

25. "Tributes by Colleagues."

26. Wesley McCune, *The Nine Young Men* (New York: Harper and Brothers, 1947), 265.

27. Dickson, *The Supreme Court in Conference*, 91.

28. Melvin I. Urofsky, *Felix Frankfurter: Judicial Restraint and Individual Liberties* (Boston: Twayne, 1991), 88.

29. Edward T. Folliard, "Chief Justice to Be Chosen from Court Membership," *Washington Post*, April 29, 1946.

30. Edward T. Folliard, "Truman Asks Hughes' Aid in Naming Justice," *Washington Post*, April 30, 1946.

31. Folliard, "Chief Justice to Be Chosen from Court Membership."

32. "Truman Gets View of Hughes on Court," *New York Times*, April 30, 1946.

33. "Truman Gets View of Hughes on Court."

34. Ernest Lindley, "Chief Justiceship," *Washington Post*, April 26, 1946.

35. Joseph Short, "Stone's Post Likely to Go to Jackson," *Baltimore Sun*, April 29, 1946.

36. Merlo Pusey, "What Kind of Court?" *Washington Post*, April 30, 1946.

37. Marquis Childs, "Washington Calling: Jackson Logical Successor," *Washington Post*, April 25, 1946.

38. Folliard, "Truman Asks Hughes' Aid."

39. Pritchett, *The Roosevelt Court*, 26.

40. James E. St. Clair and Linda Gugin, *Chief Justice Fred M. Vinson of Kentucky: A Political Biography* (Lexington: University Press of Kentucky, 2002), 161.

41. Folliard, "Truman Asks Hughes' Aid"; "Hughes Talks with Truman," *Baltimore Sun*, April 30, 1946.

Chapter Seven

1. Richard Hedlund, "Harry S. Truman and Frederick M. Vinson: A Personal Relationship," *Filson History Quarterly* 75, no. 3 (Summer 2001): 345.

2. James E. St. Clair and Linda Gugin, *Chief Justice Fred M. Vinson of Kentucky: A Political Biography* (Lexington: University Press of Kentucky, 2002), 162.

3. Michael R. Gardner, *Harry Truman and Civil Rights: Moral Courage and Political Risks* (Carbondale: Southern Illinois University Press, 2002), 169.

4. "Naming of Vinson Backed in Senate," *New York Times*, June 7, 1946.

5. "Vinson to Become Head of Treasury after Big 3 Parley," *New York Times*, July 7, 1945.

6. Edward T. Folliard, "Truman's Choices Meet Approval, Sent to Senate for Confirmation," *Washington Post*, June 7, 1946.

7. William O. Douglas, *The Court Years, 1939–1975: The Autobiography of William O. Douglas* (New York: Random House, 1980), 225.

8. Adam Aft, "Fred Vinson and the National Pastime," in *The Green Bag Almanac and Reader*, ed. Ross E. Davies (Washington, DC: Green Bag Press, 2010), 217.

9. James A. Anderson, III, *The Judge: Fred Vinson, Legislator, Executive, Jurist* (Louisville, KY: Sulgrave Press, 1999), 9.

10. St. Clair and Gugin, *Chief Justice Fred M. Vinson*, 126.

11. Hedlund, "Harry S. Truman and Frederick M. Vinson," 345.

12. Hedlund, "Harry S. Truman and Frederick M. Vinson," 336.

13. St. Clair and Gugin, *Chief Justice Fred M. Vinson*, 93.

14. Anderson, *The Judge*, 22.

15. St. Clair and Gugin, *Chief Justice Fred M. Vinson*, 66.

16. "Naming of Vinson Backed in Senate."

17. Frances Howell Rudko, *Truman's Court: A Study in Judicial Restraint* (Westport, CT: Greenwood Press, 1988), 34.

18. "Vinson Places Freedom High in Life Credo," *Washington Post*, June 8, 1946.

19. Rudko, *Truman's Court*, 34.

Chapter Eight

1. Joseph Alsop and Steward Alsop, "Public Never Told Jackson Was Choice for Chief Justice," *Washington Post*, May 19, 1946.

2. "Supreme Court Term Likely to Be Extended," *Washington Post*, May 27, 1946.

3. C. Herman Pritchett, *The Roosevelt Court: A Study in Judicial Politics and Values, 1937–1947* (New York: Macmillan, 1948), 29.

4. *Jewell Ridge Coal Corporation v. Local No. 6167, United Mine Workers of America*, 325 U.S. 161 (1945).

5. Fred Rodell, *Nine Men: A Political History of the Supreme Court from 1790 to 1955* (New York: Random House, 1955), 298.

6. "Quarrel on the High Bench," *New York Times*, June 12, 1946.

7. Joseph H. Short, "Jewell Ridge Coal Case," *Baltimore Sun*, June 12, 1946; *Jewell Ridge Coal Corporation v. Local No. 6167, United Mine Workers of America*, 325 U.S. 161 (1945).

8. Tony Freyer, "Jackson-Black Feud," in *The Oxford Guide to the Supreme Court*, ed. Kermit L. Hall (New York: Oxford University Press, 2005), 514.

9. Pritchett, *The Roosevelt Court*, 27.

10. "Quarrel on the High Bench."

11. Pritchett, *The Roosevelt Court*, 27.

12. *Jewell Ridge Coal Corporation v. Local No. 6167, United Mine Workers of America*, 325 U.S. 897, 898 (1945).

13. Pritchett, *The Roosevelt Court*, 26–27.

14. "Jackson Attacks Black for Judging Ex-Partner's Case," *New York Times*, June 11, 1946.

15. "Text of Jackson's Statement Attacking Black," *New York Times*, June 11, 1946.

16. Arthur Krock, "In the Nation: The Question of a Judge's Good Behavior," *New York Times*, June 14, 1946.

17. Pritchett, *The Roosevelt Court*, 28.

18. C. P. Ives, "Disintegration of a Court," *Baltimore Sun*, June 12, 1946.

19. James F. Simon, *The Antagonists: Hugo Black, Felix Frankfurter, and Civil Liberties in Modern America* (New York: Simon and Schuster, 1989), 168.

20. Lewis Wood, "Split of Jackson and Black Long Widening at the Capital," *New York Times*, June 11, 1946.

21. "Jackson Attacks Black."

22. "Quarrel on the High Bench."

23. Simon, *The Antagonists*, 169.

24. "Jackson Attacks Black."

25. Pritchett, *The Roosevelt Court*, 28.

26. Simon, *The Antagonists*, 169.

27. William Domnarski, *The Great Justices, 1941–54: Black, Douglas, Frankfurter, and Jackson in Chambers* (Ann Arbor: University of Michigan Press, 2006), 47.

28. William O. Douglas, *The Court Years, 1939–1975: The Autobiography of William O. Douglas* (New York: Random House, 1980), 31.

29. "House May Take Up Jackson's Charges," *New York Times*, June 11, 1946.

30. "Racial Neutrality Urged in Supreme Court Fight," *Baltimore Afro-American*, June 29, 1946.

31. James E. St. Clair and Linda Gugin, *Chief Justice Fred M. Vinson of Kentucky: A Policial Biography* (Lexington: University Press of Kentucky, 2002), 165–66.

32. Richard Kirkendall, "Fred M. Vinson," in *The Justices of the United States Supreme Court, 1789–1969: Their Lives and Major Opinions*, ed. Leon Friedman and Fred L. Israel (New York: Chelsea House, 1969), 4:2641.

33. Marquis Childs, "Washington Calling: Vinson's Job," *Washington Post*, June 8, 1946.

34. Freyer, "Jackson-Black Feud," 514.

Chapter Nine

1. Felix Belair, Jr., "Vinson in Unusual Ceremony Takes Oath as Chief Justice," *New York Times*, June 25, 1946.

2. Frances Howell Rudko, *Truman's Court: A Study in Judicial Restraint* (Westport, CT: Greenwood Press, 1988), 28.

3. Edward T. Folliard, "Vinson Takes Oath as Thirteenth Chief Justice," *Washington Post*, June 25, 1946.

4. Belair, "Vinson in Unusual Ceremony."

5. Folliard, "Vinson Takes Oath."

6. Folliard, "Vinson Takes Oath."

7. Folliard, "Vinson Takes Oath."

8. "Vinson Sworn as Thirteenth Chief Justice," *Baltimore Sun*, June 25, 1946.

9. Belair, "Vinson in Unusual Ceremony."

10. Folliard, "Vinson Takes Oath."

11. Belair, "Vinson in Unusual Ceremony."

12. Wesley McCune, *The Nine Young Men* (New York: Harper and Brothers, 1947), 268.

13. "Chief Justice Vinson Takes His Seat Today," *New York Times*, October 7, 1946.

14. Lewis Wood, "High Court Reopening in Tense Atmosphere," *New York Times*, October 6, 1946.

15. "Chief Justice Vinson Takes His Seat Today."

16. Wood, "High Court Reopening."

17. John Q. Barrett, "Farewell to the Chief Justice (1953)," Robert H. Jackson Center, www.roberthjackson.org.

18. Wood, "High Court Reopening."

19. Lewis Wood, "New Chief Justice Ends First Session," *New York Times*, October 8, 1946.

20. Dillard Stokes, "Tranquility Reigns as Vinson Opens Supreme Court Session," *Washington Post*, October 8, 1946.

21. William O. Douglas, *The Court Years, 1939–1975: The Autobiography of William O. Douglas* (New York: Random House, 1980), 225–26.

22. Julian Borger, "US Guard Tells How Nazi Girlfriend Duped Him into Helping Goering Evade Hangman," *The Guardian* (London), February 8, 2005.

23. "Nazi Myth Broken, Jackson Declares," *New York Times*, October 17, 1946.

Chapter Ten

1. George Gallup, "Democrat Strength Ebbs to Lowest Point in 16 Years," *Washington Post*, October 16, 1946.

2. Gallup, "Democrat Strength Ebbs."

3. V. O. Key, Jr., "If the Election Follows the Pattern," *New York Times*, October 20, 1946.

4. Merlo Pusey, "Midterm Elections: Should They Be Eliminated?" *Washington Post*, November 5, 1946.

5. Joseph Alsop and Stewart Alsop, "Matter of Fact: The War Chest," *Washington Post*, October 14, 1946.

6. "Rayburn Backs Truman," *New York Times*, October 13, 1946.

7. "Gov. Edge Assails Truman as Leader," *New York Times*, October 30, 1946.

8. Alsop and Alsop, "Matter of Fact: The War Chest."

9. William E. Leuchtenburg, "New Faces of 1946," *Smithsonian Magazine*, November 2006, https://www.smithsonianmag.com/history/new-faces-of-1946-135190660/.

10. Leuchtenburg, "New Faces of 1946."

11. Lawrence E. Davies, "Oregon Republicans Hold Lead; Truman's Policies under Fire," *New York Times*, October 19, 1946.

12. Leuchtenburg, "New Faces of 1946."

13. "Truman Ponders: Meat the Big Issue before Election Day," *New York Times*, October 13, 1946.

14. Leuchtenburg, "New Faces of 1946."

15. "Truman Ponders."

16. Robert J. Donovan, *Conflict and Crisis: The Presidency of Harry S. Truman, 1945–1948* (Columbia: University of Missouri Press, 1996), 235.

17. Bess Furman, "President Expected to Act on Meat, Easing Some Restrictions Tomorrow; Feeders Likely to Ship Cattle Soon," *New York Times*, October 12, 1946.

18. "Taft Hits Truman as Tardy on Meat," *New York Times*, October 17, 1946.

19. William Knighton, Jr., "Truman Ends All Meat Price Controls; Will Speed Removal of Wage Curbs," *Baltimore Sun*, October 15, 1946.

20. "News of Food: Housewives Must Again Go to Market with Full Purses for Purchasing Staples," *New York Times*, October 18, 1946.

21. Walter White, "People, Politics and Places: Merry Go Round," *Chicago Defender*, October 26, 1946.

22. Leuchtenburg, "New Faces of 1946."

23. William S. White, "Truman Reserves Opinion on Vote," *New York Times*, October 25, 1946.

24. David McCullough, *Truman* (New York: Simon and Schuster, 1992), 522.

25. Joseph R. Short, "President Talks on War Horrors," *Baltimore Sun*, November 3, 1946.

26. "President Still Silent on Eve of Elections," *Washington Post*, November 5, 1946.

27. "The House Goes Republican," *New York Times*, November 6, 1946.

28. "Bilbo Admits He's Klansman, Always Will Be," *Chicago Tribune*, August 10, 1946.

29. Charley Cherokee, "To Err Is Human," *Chicago Defender*, October 26, 1946.

30. Leuchtenburg, "New Faces of 1946."

31. "Opinion: We've Had More Than Enough," *Baltimore Afro-American*, November 2, 1946.

32. "President Still Silent on Eve of Elections."

33. McCullough, *Truman*, 523.

34. Leuchtenburg, "New Faces of 1946."

35. "Truman Returns, Silent on Defeat," *New York Times*, November 7, 1946.

36. Robert Shogan, *Harry Truman and the Struggle for Racial Justice* (Lawrence: University Press of Kansas, 2013), 91.

37. "Fulbright, Chicago Sun Suggest Truman Resign," *Baltimore Sun*, November 7, 1946.

38. "Fulbright Invites Truman to Resign," *New York Times*, November 7, 1946.

39. "Fulbright, Chicago Sun Suggest Truman Resign."

40. "Fulbright Invites Truman to Resign."

41. Leuchtenburg, "New Faces of 1946."

Chapter Eleven

1. "Papers Halted in Cleveland," *Baltimore Sun*, January 5, 1946.
2. "City Workers Quit Jobs in Stockton," *New York Times*, January 4, 1946.
3. Lawrence Resner, "Stamford Tied Up 3 Hours in Demonstration by Labor," *New York Times*, January 4, 1946.
4. "Capital Phone Operators Strike," *Baltimore Sun*, January 5, 1946.
5. "Negotiations Broken Off in Truck Drivers' Strike," *Baltimore Sun*, January 5, 1946.
6. Cabell B. H. Phillips, *The Truman Presidency: The History of a Triumphant Succession* (New York: Macmillan, 1966), 113.
7. Max Hall, "1946's Labor Warfare Historic," *Washington Post*, December 22, 1946.
8. "Picket-Line Scuffle," *Baltimore Sun*, January 5, 1946.
9. Phillips, *The Truman Presidency*, 113.
10. Walter W. Ruch, "Detroit Riot Squads Avert Fight by Pickets, Workers," *New York Times*, January 4, 1946.
11. Phillips, *The Truman Presidency*, 113.
12. *U.S. v. United Mine Workers of America*, 330 U.S. 258, 262n1 (1947).
13. Arthur F. McClure, *The Truman Administration and the Problems of Postwar Labor, 1945–1948* (Cranbury, NJ: Associated University Presses, 1969), 141.
14. Harry S. Truman, *Memoirs*, vol. 1, *Year of Decisions* (Garden City, NY: Doubleday, 1955), 495–96.
15. McClure, *The Truman Administration*, 42.
16. McClure, *The Truman Administration*, 13.
17. Phillips, *The Truman Presidency*, 119.
18. Truman, *Memoirs*, 502.
19. Joseph H. Short, "Soft Coal Strike Settled after 45 Days," *Baltimore Sun*, May 30, 1946.
20. "Truman Satirical on Policy Critics," *Baltimore Sun*, May 30, 1946.
21. "Mine Strike's Cost in Coal and Money," *Baltimore Sun*, May 30, 1946.
22. Walter Lippmann, "Today and Tomorrow: The Contracts of John L. Lewis," *Washington Post*, November 19, 1946.
23. McClure, *The Truman Administration*, 148.
24. "U.S. Breaking of Coal Pact Charged; Strike Could Start Nov. 20," *Baltimore Sun*, October 22, 1946.
25. William S. White, "Lewis Hints of Strike Nov. 1 if Krug Does Not Open Pact," *New York Times*, October 23, 1946.
26. Leo Wolman, "Beam in Labor's Eye," *Washington Post*, December 22, 1946.
27. Edward T. Folliard, "Truman Begins Week's Rest in Key West Sun," *Washington Post*, November 18, 1946.
28. Phillips, *The Truman Presidency*, 122.
29. Dillard Stokes, "UMW Gives No Sign of Yielding to Government," *Washington Post*, November 19, 1946.
30. Louis Stark, "Contract Upheld," *New York Times*, November 19, 1946.
31. Stokes, "UMW Gives No Sign of Yielding."
32. Joseph H. Short, "Truman Orders Aides to 'Fight It Out' with Lewis," *Baltimore Sun*, November 18, 1946.
33. Edward T. Folliard, "Truman Steers All-Out Fight against Lewis," *Washington Post*, November 19, 1946.
34. Folliard, "Truman Begins Week's Rest."

Chapter Twelve

1. A. H. Raskin, "Miners Ready to Back Union, Right or Wrong," *New York Times*, November 24, 1946.

2. "Miners Await Move by Lewis," *Baltimore Sun*, December 5, 1946.

3. "Off the Deep End," *Washington Post*, November 17, 1946.

4. Raskin, "Miners Ready to Back Union."

5. "Miners Await Move."

6. Raskin, "Miners Ready to Back Union."

7. A. H. Raskin, "Miners See 'Trouble' If Lewis Is Jailed," *New York Times*, December 4, 1946.

8. Louis Stark, "Defense Is Enraged," *New York Times*, December 5, 1946.

9. Gerald Griffin, "Lewis Fined $10,000 and UMW $3,500,000," *Baltimore Sun*, December 5, 1946.

10. "Steel Industry Hardest Hit By Strike, with 70,000 Out," *New York Times*, December 7, 1946.

11. "Truman versus Lewis," *Harvard Crimson* (Cambridge, MA), November 19, 1946.

12. Joseph A. Loftus, "Capital Surprised," *New York Times*, December 8, 1946.

13. Cabell B. H. Phillips, *The Truman Presidency: The History of a Triumphant Succession* (New York: Macmillan, 1966), 125.

14. A. H. Raskin, "Rush to the Pits Due," *New York Times*, December 8, 1946.

15. Raskin, "Miners Ready to Back Union."

16. Walter H. Waggoner, "Rules End Quickly," *New York Times*, December 8, 1946.

17. Raskin, "Miners See 'Trouble.'"

18. Phillips, *The Truman Presidency*, 125.

19. Dillard Stokes, "Supreme Court Hears Debate in Coal Case," *New York Times*, January 15, 1947.

20. James E. St. Clair and Linda Gugin, *Chief Justice Fred M. Vinson of Kentucky: A Political Biography* (Lexington: University Press of Kentucky), 203.

21. St. Clair and Gugin, *Chief Justice Fred M. Vinson*, 203–4.

22. William O. Douglas, *The Court Years, 1939–1975: The Autobiography of William O. Douglas* (New York: Random House, 1980), 139.

23. Douglas, *The Court Years*, 139.

24. *United States v. United Mine Workers of America*, 330 U.S. 258 (1947).

25. Lewis Wood, "UMW Fined $700,000," *New York Times*, March 7, 1947.

26. "Court Breaks 14-Year Custom with Ruling on a Thursday," *Baltimore Sun*, March 7, 1947.

27. "Court Breaks 14-Year Custom."

28. *United States v. United Mine Workers of America*, 330 U.S. 258, 263 (1947).

29. "Court Breaks 14-Year Custom."

30. Douglas, *The Court Years*, 139.

31. "Capitol Hails Lewis Ruling," *Baltimore Sun*, March 7, 1947.

32. Douglas, *The Court Years*, 139.

33. "High Court Backs Lewis Fine," *New York Times*, March 7, 1947.

34. "Miners 'Surprised, Shocked' at Ruling," *New York Times*, March 7, 1947.

35. "President Gratified by Court's Ruling," *New York Times*, March 7, 1947.

36. "High Court Backs Lewis Fine."

37. Harvey Gresham Hudspeth, "The Best Laid Plans: Fred M. Vinson and the Decline and Fall of the Roosevelt Court, 1946–1949," *Essays in Economic and Business History* 19, no. 1 (2001): 125.

Chapter Thirteen

1. George Gallup, "Democrat Strength Ebbs to Lowest Point in 16 Years," *Washington Post,* October 16, 1946.

2. "GOP Ruins OPA: Blames Truman," *Chicago Defender,* October 26, 1946.

3. Joseph Alsop and Stewart Alsop, "Matter of Fact: Two Years of Mess," *Washington Post,* November 6, 1946.

4. William E. Leuchtenburg, "New Faces of 1946," *Smithsonian Magazine,* November 2006, https://www.smithsonianmag.com/history/new-faces-of-1946-135190660/.

5. David McCullough, *Truman* (New York: Simon and Schuster, 1992), 552.

6. Executive Order 9835, March 21, 1947, https://www.trumanlibrary.gov/library/execu tive-orders/9835/executive-order-9835.

7. Jerry Kluttz, "Civil Service Loyalty Test Plan Going to Truman Today," *Washington Post,* February 20, 1947.

8. C. Herman Pritchett, *Civil Liberties and the Vinson Court* (Chicago: University of Chicago Press, 1954), 266.

9. Harry S. Truman, *Memoirs,* vol. 2, *Years of Trial and Hope, 1946–1952* (Garden City, NY: Doubleday, 1956), 280.

10. Melvin I. Urofsky, *Division and Discord: The Supreme Court under Stone and Vinson, 1941–1953* (Columbia: University of South Carolina Press, 1997), 159.

11. Mimi Clark Gronlund, *Supreme Court Justice Tom C. Clark: A Life of Service* (Austin: University of Texas Press, 2010), 116.

12. Jerry Kluttz, "Federal Diary: Federal Loyalty Program of Truman Is Fairest of Lot," *Washington Post,* October 7, 1948.

13. Robert W. Ruth, "Loyalty Program Welcomed by AFL," *Baltimore Sun,* September 16, 1947.

14. "Officials Give Assurances on Loyalty Probe," *Baltimore Sun,* September 6, 1947.

15. "The News of the Week in Review," *New York Times,* March 23, 1947.

16. Gronlund, *Supreme Court Justice Tom C. Clark,* 119.

17. "President's Order on Loyalty Hailed," *New York Times,* March 23, 1947.

18. "President's Order on Loyalty Hailed."

19. "Congressmen Praise Purge," *Baltimore Sun,* March 23, 1947.

20. "President's Order on Loyalty Hailed."

21. "Congressmen Praise Purge."

22. William S. White, "House, 319–61, Votes for Tests of Loyalty for Federal Jobs," *New York Times,* July 16, 1947.

23. "Checks Federal Workers," *New York Times,* September 12, 1948.

24. Anthony Leviero, "883 Federal Employees Resign Jobs Rather Than Face Loyalty Trials," *New York Times,* September 23, 1948.

25. "Truman Plans to Ask [for] Purge Funds Soon," *Washington Post,* March 30, 1947.

26. Gronlund, *Supreme Court Justice Tom C. Clark,* 119, 118.

27. Tom C. Clark, "Civil Rights," Speech before the Chicago Bar Association, Chicago, Illinois, June 21, 1946.

Chapter Fourteen

1. James E. St. Clair and Linda Gugin, *Chief Justice Fred M. Vinson of Kentucky: A Political Biography* (Lexington: University Press of Kentucky, 2002), 192.

2. Harry S. Truman, *Memoirs,* vol. 2, *Years of Trial and Hope, 1946–1952* (Garden City, NY: Doubleday, 1956), 489.

3. Richard Kirkendall, "Fred M. Vinson," in *The Justices of the United States Supreme Court, 1789–1969: Their Lives and Major Opinions,* ed. Leon Friedman and Fred L. Israel (New York: Chelsea House, 1969), 4:2648.

4. Felix Belair, Jr., "Mr. Truman's Friend—And His Nominee?" *New York Times,* December 16, 1951.

5. St. Clair and Gugin, *Chief Justice Fred M. Vinson,* 191.

6. Jeff Jacoby, "Supreme Court Justices Shouldn't Attend State of the Union," *Boston Globe,* January 11, 2015.

7. James McManus, "Bluffing at the Highest Levels," *Wall Street Journal,* November 7, 2009.

8. Raymond H. Geselbracht, "Harry Truman, Poker Player," *Prologue* 35, no. 1 (Spring 2003), https://www.archives.gov/publications/prologue/2003/spring/truman-poker.html.

9. Michael R. Gardner, *Harry Truman and Civil Rights: Moral Courage and Political Risks* (Carbondale: Southern Illinois University Press, 2002), 164.

10. James McManus, "Presidential Poker," *American History,* April 2010, https://www.historynet.com/presidential-poker.htm.

11. McManus "Bluffing at the Highest Levels."

12. Geselbracht, "Harry Truman, Poker Player."

13. Geselbracht, "Harry Truman, Poker Player."

14. Harry S. Truman Library and Museum, "'The Buck Stops Here!' Desk Sign," www.trumanlibrary.org/buckstop.htm.

15. Gardner, *Harry Truman and Civil Rights,* 167.

16. Robert Shogan, *Harry Truman and the Struggle for Racial Justice* (Lawrence: University Press of Kansas, 2013), 98.

17. Shogan, *Harry Truman and the Struggle for Racial Justice,* 100.

18. Rawn James, Jr., *The Double V: How Wars, Protest, and Harry Truman Desegregated America's Military* (New York: Bloomsbury Press, 2013), 217.

19. "Address before the National Association for the Advancement of Colored People," June 29, 1947, Public Papers of Harry S. Truman, 1945–53, https://www.trumanlibrary.gov/library/public-papers/130/address-national-association-advancement-colored-people.

20. Shogan, *Harry Truman and the Struggle for Racial Justice,* 101.

21. "Address before the National Association for the Advancement of Colored People," June 29, 1947.

Chapter Fifteen

1. Barton J. Bernstein, "The Ambiguous Legacy: The Truman Administration and Civil Rights," in *Politics and Policies of the Truman Administration,* ed. Barton J. Bernstein (Chicago: Quadrangle Books, 1970), 277.

2. Committee members were Sadie T. Alexander, James B. Carey, John S. Dickey, Morris L. Ernst, Roland B. Gittelsohn, Frank P. Graham, Francis J. Haas, Charles Luckman, Francis P. Matthews, Franklin D. Roosevelt, Jr., Henry Knox Sherrill, Boris Shishkin, Dorothy Tilly, Channing Tobias, and Charles E. Wilson.

3. Rawn James, Jr., *The Double V: How Wars, Protest, and Harry Truman Desegregated America's Military* (New York: Bloomsbury Press, 2013), 217.

4. James, *The Double V,* 218.

5. Michael R. Gardner, *Harry Truman and Civil Rights: Moral Courage and Political Risks* (Carbondale: Southern Illinois University Press), 44.

6. Gardner, *Harry Truman and Civil Rights,* 51.

7. *To Secure These Rights: The Report of the President's Committee on Civil Rights*, 3–9, Harry S. Truman Presidential Library, Independence, MO.

8. *To Secure These Rights*, 151–73.

9. Gardner, *Harry Truman and Civil Rights*, 61, 62.

10. Gardner, *Harry Truman and Civil Rights*, 63.

11. Lynda G. Dodd, "Presidential Leadership and Civil Rights Lawyering in the Era before *Brown*," *Indiana Law Journal* 85, no. 4 (Fall 2010): 1638.

12. *To Secure These Rights*, 68.

13. *Buchanan v. Warley*, 245 U.S. 600 (1917).

14. Leland B. Ware, "Invisible Walls: An Examination of the Legal Strategy in the Restrictive Covenant Cases," *Washington University Law Quarterly* 67, no. 3 (1989): 752.

15. *Kraemer v. Shelley*, 198 S. W. 2d 679 (Mo. 1946).

16. Robert Shogan, *Harry Truman and the Struggle for Racial Justice* (Lawrence: University Press of Kansas, 2013), 167.

17. Ware, "Invisible Walls," 759.

18. Rawn James, Jr., *Root and Branch: Charles Hamilton Houston, Thurgood Marshall, and the Struggle to End Segregation* (New York: Bloomsbury Press, 2010), 201.

19. James, *Root and Branch*, 202.

20. Del Dickson, ed., *The Supreme Court in Conference, 1940–1985: The Private Discussions behind Nearly 300 Supreme Court Decisions* (New York: Oxford University Press, 2001), 635–36.

21. *Sipuel v. Board of Regents of the University of Oklahoma*, 332 U.S. 631, 632–33 (1948), citing *Missouri ex rel. Gaines v. Canada*, 305 U.S. 337 (1938).

22. James, *Root and Branch*, 192.

23. Gardner, *Harry Truman and Civil Rights*, 175.

24. James, *Root and Branch*, 192.

25. James, *Root and Branch*, 192.

26. Ware, "Invisible Walls," 766.

27. James, *Root and Branch*, 194.

28. Ware, "Invisible Walls," 767.

29. Ware, "Invisible Walls," 767.

30. James, *Root and Branch*, 194.

31. Frances Howell Rudko, *Truman's Court: A Study in Judicial Restraint* (Westport, CT: Greenwood Press, 1988), 72–73.

32. James, *Root and Branch*, 196.

33. *Shelley v. Kraemer*, 334 U.S. 1 (1948).

34. James, *Root and Branch*, 197.

35. Gardner, *Harry Truman and Civil Rights*, 177.

Chapter Sixteen

1. David Pietrusza, *1948: Harry Truman's Improbable Victory and the Year That Transformed America* (New York: Union Square Press, 2011), 205.

2. Pietrusza, *1948*, 205.

3. J. R. Wiggins, "Truman on 1st Appears Sure as Eisenhower Reiterates 'No,'" *Washington Post*, July 10, 1948.

4. Wiggins, "Truman on 1st Appears Sure."

5. Arthur Krock, "Truman Gives Notice He's in Fight to Finish," *New York Times*, June 13, 1948.

6. Harry S. Truman, *Memoirs*, vol. 2, *Years of Trial and Hope, 1946–1952* (Garden City, NY: Doubleday, 1956), 223.

7. Pietrusza, *1948*, 209.

8. David J. Garrow, "The Tragedy of William O. Douglas," *The Nation*, March 27, 2003, https://www.thenation.com/article/archive/tragedy-william-o-douglas/.

9. Bruce Allen Murphy, *Wild Bill: The Legend and Life of William O. Douglas, America's Most Controversial Supreme Court Justice* (New York: Random House, 2003), 351.

10. Murphy, *Wild Bill*, 215.

11. Murphy, *Wild Bill*, 218.

12. Clark Clifford, *Counsel to the President: A Memoir* (New York: Random House, 1990), 216.

13. William O. Douglas, *The Court Years , 1939–1975: The Autobiography of William O. Douglas* (New York: Random House, 1980), 288–89.

14. Pietrusza, *1948*, 209.

15. Douglas, *The Court Years*, 289.

16. Murphy, *Wild Bill*, 259.

17. Pietrusza, *1948*, 228.

18. Murphy, *Wild Bill*, 261.

19. Douglas, *The Court Years*, 289.

20. Truman, *Memoirs*, 190.

21. Douglas, *The Court Years*, 290.

22. Murphy, *Wild Bill*, 265.

23. C. Herman Pritchett, *Civil Liberties and the Vinson Court* (Chicago: University of Chicago Press, 1954), 18.

24. Robert H. Ferrell, ed., *Off the Record: The Private Papers of Harry S. Truman* (New York: Harper and Row, 1980), 141–42.

25. Murphy, *Wild Bill*, 266–67.

26. Clifford, *Counsel to the President*, 216.

Chapter Seventeen

1. Harry S. Truman, *Memoirs*, vol. 2, *Years of Trial and Hope, 1946–1952* (Garden City, NY: Doubleday, 1956), 212, 215.

2. Truman, *Memoirs*, 212–13.

3. Truman, *Memoirs*, 215.

4. Ken Hechler, *Working with Truman: A Personal Memoir of the White House Years* (New York: G. P. Putnam's Sons, 1982), 98.

5. Clark Clifford, *Counsel to the President: A Memoir* (New York: Random House, 1990), 232–33.

6. Truman, *Memoirs*, 213.

7. Truman, *Memoirs*, 216.

8. Truman, *Memoirs*, 214.

9. Truman, *Memoirs*, 213–14.

10. "President to Greet Marshall at Airport," *New York Times*, October 9, 1948.

11. Associated Press photograph, *Washington Post*, October 10, 1948.

12. "Truman Abandons Mission of Vinson," *New York Times*, October 10, 1948.

13. James Reston, "Truman Blocked in Move to Send Vinson to Stalin," *New York Times*, October 9, 1948.

14. "Vinson Trip Abandoned by Truman," *Washington Post*, October 10, 1948.

15. "Statements on Mission," *New York Times*, October 10, 1948.

16. Arthur Krock, "Truman's Plan for Vinson Causes Anxiety in Capital," *New York Times*, October 10, 1948.

17. Bertram D. Hulen, "Situation Cleared," *New York Times*, October 10, 1948.

18. Gerald Griffin, "British Link Vinson Move to Campaign," *Baltimore Sun*, October 12, 1948.

19. "Soviet Reacts on Vinson," *New York Times*, October 11, 1948.

20. "Soviet Reacts on Vinson."

21. Lerdin Kuhn, Jr., "Marshall Persuades Truman to Drop Vinson Peace Trip; Deplores Talk of Policy Rift," *Washington Post*, October 10, 1948.

22. Krock, "Truman's Plan for Vinson."

23. Clifford, *Counsel to the President*, 232–34.

24. "Dulles Was Not Informed of Truman's Vinson Plan," *New York Times*, October 10, 1948.

25. "Thurmond's View Caustic," *New York Times*, October 11, 1948.

26. "Dewey Aides Split on 'Vinson Affair,'" *New York Times*, October 12, 1948.

27. Hechler, *Working with Truman*, 99.

28. "Dewey Aides Split."

29. Edward T. Folliard, "Dewey Hits 'Clumsiness' of Truman," *Washington Post*, October 13, 1948.

30. Thomas O'Neill, "Dewey to Aid GOP Nominees," *Baltimore Sun*, October 10, 1948.

31. Philip White, *Whistle Stop: How 31,000 Miles of Train Travel, 352 Speeches, and a Little Midwest Gumption Saved the Presidency of Harry Truman* (Lebanon, NH: ForeEdge, 2014), 148.

32. "Truman Outpaced in Campaign, State Department's 'Voice' Says," *New York Times*, October 11, 1948.

33. "Truman Outpaced in Campaign."

34. Folliard, "Dewey Hits 'Clumsiness.'"

35. White, *Whistle Stop*, 149–50.

36. Harry S. Truman, "Address in Harlem, New York, upon Receiving the Franklin Roosevelt Award," October 29, 1948, Harry S. Truman Presidential Library, Independence, MO, https://www.trumanlibrary.gov/library/public-papers/265/address-harlem-new-york-upon-receiving-franklin-roosevelt-award.

37. White, *Whistle Stop*, 140.

38. White, *Whistle Stop*, 171.

39. White, *Whistle Stop*, 234–35.

40. Clifford, *Counsel to the President*, 232–34.

41. James E. St. Clair and Linda Gugin, *Chief Justice Fred M. Vinson of Kentucky: A Political Biography* (Lexington: University Press of Kentucky, 2002), 193–94.

Chapter Eighteen

1. "Justice Murphy Lauded by Truman and Vinson," *Atlanta Daily World*, July 20, 1949.

2. "Justice Murphy Dies at 59 in Detroit of Heart Attack," *New York Times*, July 20, 1949.

3. John P. Frank, "Frank Murphy," in *The Justices of the United States Supreme Court, 1789–1969: Their Lives and Major Opinions*, ed. Leon Friedman and Fred L. Israel (New York: Chelsea House, 1969), 4:2499.

4. "Frank Murphy," *Washington Post*, July 20, 1949.

5. Howard M. Schott, "Frank Murphy," Letters to the Editor, *Washington Post*, July 23, 1949.

6. *Korematsu v. United States*, 323 U.S. 214, 233 (1944), J. Murphy, dissenting.

7. Lawrence S. Wrightsman, *The Psychology of the Supreme Court* (New York: Oxford University Press, 2006), 188.

8. "Justice Murphy," *Atlanta Daily World*, July 20, 1949.

9. Wrightsman, *The Psychology of the Supreme Court*, 187.

10. "President Sends Tribute to Family," *New York Times*, July 20, 1949.

11. Tom C. Clark, oral history interview, February 8, 1973, 206, 207, Harry S. Truman Presidential Library, Independence, MO.

12. Alexander Wohl, *Father, Son, and Constitution: How Justice Tom Clark and Attorney General Ramsey Clark Shaped American Democracy* (Lawrence: University Press of Kansas, 2013), 129.

13. Clark, oral history interview, 207.

14. David Alistair Yalof, *Pursuit of Justices: Presidential Politics and the Selection of Supreme Court Nominees* (Chicago: University of Chicago Press, 1999), 36.

15. James E. St. Clair and Linda Gugin, *Chief Justice Fred M. Vinson of Kentucky: A Political Biography* (Lexington: University Press of Kentucky, 2002), 169.

16. William Domnarski, *The Great Justices, 1941–54: Black, Douglas, Frankfurter, and Jackson in Chambers* (Ann Arbor: University of Michigan Press, 2006), 58.

17. St. Clair and Gugin, *Chief Justice Fred M. Vinson*, 177.

18. St. Clair and Gugin, *Chief Justice Fred M. Vinson*, 173.

19. William O. Douglas, *The Court Years, 1939–1975: The Autobiography of William O. Douglas* (New York: Random House, 1980), 248.

20. St. Clair and Gugin, *Chief Justice Fred M. Vinson*, 174.

21. Harvey Gresham Hudspeth, "The Best Laid Plans: Fred M. Vinson and the Decline and Fall of the Roosevelt Court, 1946–1949," *Essays in Economic and Business History* 19, no. 1 (2001): 129.

22. St. Clair and Gugin, *Chief Justice Fred M. Vinson*, 179.

23. Domnarski, *The Great Justices*, 66.

24. Douglas, *The Court Years*, 248.

25. St. Clair and Gugin, *Chief Justice Fred M. Vinson*, 180.

26. St. Clair and Gugin, *Chief Justice Fred M. Vinson*, 180.

27. St. Clair and Gugin, *Chief Justice Fred M. Vinson*, 175.

28. James A. Thomson, "Frederick Moore Vinson," in *The Supreme Court Justices: A Biographical Dictionary*, ed. Melvin I. Urofsky (New York: Garland, 1994), 492.

29. John P. Frank, "Fred Vinson and the Chief Justiceship," *University of Chicago Law Review* 21 (1954): 242.

30. "Praise, Blast Tom Clark," *New York Amsterdam News*, August 13, 1949.

31. "Ickes and Rogge Assail Tom Clark," *Baltimore Sun*, August 11, 1949.

32. Alice E. Dunnigan, "Leftists Strike at Tom Clark," *Atlanta Daily World*, August 16, 1949.

33. "Praise, Blast Tom Clark."

34. "Tom Clark Gets NAACP Backing," *Baltimore Afro-American*, August 20, 1949.

35. "Local Dems 'Steamed Up' over 'Judgeship Plum,'" *New York Amsterdam News*, August 18, 1949.

36. "Tom Clark Gets NAACP Backing."

37. Yalof, *Pursuit of Justices*, 34.

38. Richard Kirkendall, "Tom C. Clark," in Friedman and Israel, eds., *Justices of the United States Supreme Court*, 4:2667. See also Frances Howell Rudko, *Truman's Court: A Study in Judicial Restraint* (Westport, CT: Greenwood Press, 1988), 29.

39. Yalof, *Pursuit of Justices*, 36.

40. "Ickes and Rogge Assail Tom Clark."

41. Mary Spargo, "Senate Confirms Tom Clark and McGrath in New Posts," *Washington Post*, August 19, 1949.

42. Lewis Wood, "Clark Is Approved by Senate Body, 9–2," *New York Times*, August 13, 1949.

43. Spargo, "Senate Confirms Tom Clark and McGrath."

44. "Truman Sees Clark Sworn in by Vinson at the White House," *New York Times*, August 25, 1949.

45. "Clark Will Be Sworn in Today," *New York Times*, August 24, 1949.

46. "The New Associate Justice," *Washington Post*, August 25, 1949, photograph and caption.

47. Marie McNair, "Society Sees Tom Clark Take Oath," *Washington Post*, August 25, 1949.

48. "Clark Sworn in as Justice," *Baltimore Sun*, August 25, 1949.

49. "Truman Sees Clark Sworn In."

50. "Clark Sworn in as Justice."

51. Rudko, *Truman's Court*, 29.

Chapter Nineteen

1. "Rutledge Died of Overwork," *Baltimore Sun*, September 12, 1949.

2. "Justice Wiley Rutledge Dies of Brain Hemorrhage at 55," *New York Times*, September 11, 1949.

3. Fred L. Israel, "Wiley Rutledge," in *The Justices of the United States Supreme Court, 1789–1969: Their Lives and Major Opinions*, ed. Leon Friedman and Fred L. Israel (New York: Chelsea House, 1969), 4:2598.

4. "Rutledge Died of Overwork."

5. Israel, "Wiley Rutledge," 4:2598.

6. "Rutledge Died of Overwork."

7. "Vinson Praises Career," *New York Times*, September 12, 1949.

8. "Colleagues Praise Rutledge for Work," *New York Times*, September 11, 1949.

9. Israel, "Wiley Rutledge," 4:2598.

10. David Alistair Yalof, *Pursuit of Justices: Presidential Politics and the Selection of Supreme Court Nominees* (Chicago: University of Chicago Press, 1999), 37.

11. "Rutledge Died of Overwork."

12. Lewis Wood, "Liberals to Press for Court Vacancy," *New York Times*, September 11, 1949.

13. Joseph H. Short, "Judge Minton Named to Supreme Court, Former Indiana Senator Who Backed 'Court-Packing' Bill to Succeed Justice Rutledge," *Baltimore Sun*, September 16, 1949.

14. William Franklin Radcliff, *Sherman Minton: Indiana's Supreme Court Justice* (Indianapolis: Guild Press of Indiana, 1996), 129–30.

15. "Minton Reported Choice for the Supreme Court," *Baltimore Sun*, September 15, 1949.

16. Lewis Wood, "Minton Named to the Supreme Court; Was a New Dealer in Senate," *New York Times*, September 16, 1949.

17. Edward T. Folliard, "He Favored Packing It—Minton Nominated for Supreme Court," *Washington Post*, September 16, 1949.

18. "Truman Nominates Judge Sherman Minton to U.S. Supreme Court," *Atlanta Daily World*, September 16, 1949.

19. "GOP Weighs Fight to Oppose Minton," *New York Times*, September 18, 1949.

20. "Judge Minton Appointed to Supreme Court," *Baltimore Sun*, September 16, 1949.

21. "Truman Nominates Judge Sherman Minton."

22. Wood, "Minton Named to the Supreme Court."

23. Folliard, "He Favored Packing It."

24. Folliard, "He Favored Packing It."

25. "Truman Nominates Judge Sherman Minton."

26. Folliard, "He Favored Packing It."

27. Short, "Judge Minton Named to Supreme Court."

28. "The Minton Appointment," *New York Times*, September 16, 1949.

29. "GOP Unsure on Minton," *Baltimore Sun*, September 18, 1949.

30. "Senate Group Sets Thursday for Hearing on Judge Minton," *Washington Post*, September 21, 1949.

31. "Minton Hearings to Be Sept. 27," *New York Times*, September 21, 1949.

32. "Minton Hearings to Be Sept. 27."

33. "Text of Minton Letter to Senate Group," *New York Times*, October 4, 1949.

34. Lewis Wood, "Senate Unit Backs Minton for Court," *New York Times*, October 4, 1949.

35. Radcliff, *Sherman Minton*, 134.

36. "Minton and Truman Watch That Homer," *New York Times*, October 6, 1949.

37. Chalmers M. Roberts, "Minton Takes High Court Seat, About 400 See Oath Ceremony," *Washington Post*, October 13, 1949.

38. "Minton Sworn in as Supreme Court Justice," *New York Times*, October 13, 1949.

Chapter Twenty

1. John P. Frank, "The United States Supreme Court: 1949–1950," *University of Chicago Law Review* 18, no. 1 (Autumn 1950): 1.

2. James E. St. Clair and Linda Gugin, *Chief Justice Fred M. Vinson of Kentucky: A Political Biography* (Lexington: University Press of Kentucky, 2002), 237.

3. James A. Gorfinkel and Julian W. Mack, II, "*Dennis v. United States* and the Clear and Present Danger Rule," *California Law Review* 39, no. 4 (December 1951): 1.

4. *People v. Feiner*, 300 N.Y. 391, 395 (N.Y. 1950).

5. *People v. Feiner*, 300 N.Y. 391, 396 (N.Y. 1950).

6. *People v. Feiner*, 300 N.Y. 391, 396–97 (N.Y. 1950).

7. *People v. Feiner*, 300 N.Y. 391, 398 (N.Y. 1950).

8. *Feiner v. New York*, 340 U.S. 315, 320, 321 (1951).

9. *Feiner v. New York*, 340 U.S. 315, 323, 328 (1951).

10. *Feiner v. New York*, 340 U.S. 315, 323, 331 (1951).

11. Douglas Martin, "Irving Feiner, 84, Central Figure in Constitutional Free-Speech Case, Is Dead," *New York Times*, February 2, 2009.

12. Melvin I. Urofsky, *Division and Discord: The Supreme Court under Stone and Vinson, 1941–1953* (Columbia: University of South Carolina Press, 1997), 158.

13. Linda C. Gugin and James E. St. Clair, *Sherman Minton: New Deal Senator, Cold War Justice* (Indianapolis: Indiana Historical Society, 1997), 217.

14. Urofsky, *Division and Discord*, 161.

15. Frank, "The United States Supreme Court," 4.

16. *American Communications Association v. Douds*, 339 U.S. 382, 386 (1950).

17. *American Communications Association v. Douds*, 339 U.S. 382, 389 (1950).

18. *American Communications Association v. Douds*, 339 U.S. 382, 390, 393 (1950).

19. *American Communications Association v. Douds*, 339 U.S. 382, 390, 393 (1950).

20. *American Communications Association v. Douds*, 339 U.S. 382, 407 (1950).

21. *American Communications Association v. Douds*, 339 U.S. 382, 407, 415, 397, 396 (1950).

22. *American Communications Association v. Douds*, 339 U.S. 382, 407, 415, 397, 396 (1950).

23. *American Communications Association v. Douds*, 339 U.S. 382, 417, 421–22 (1950).

24. *American Communications Association v. Douds*, 339 U.S. 382, 422, 423 (1950).

25. *American Communications Association v. Douds*, 339 U.S. 382, 446 (1950).

26. Frank, "The United States Supreme Court," 3.

27. St. Clair and Gugin, *Chief Justice Fred M. Vinson*, 236.

28. Fred Rodell, *Nine Men: A Political History of the Supreme Court from 1790 to 1955* (New York: Vintage Books/Caravelle, 1955), 307.

29. *United States v. Rabinowitz*, 339 U.S. 56, 59 (1950).

30. *United States v. Rabinowitz*, 339 U.S. 56, 63 (1950).

31. *United States v. Rabinowitz*, 339 U.S. 56, 59, 60 (1950).

32. *United States v. Rabinowitz*, 339 U.S. 56, 61–64 (1950).

33. *United States v. Rabinowitz*, 339 U.S. 56, 72 (1950).

34. "Case Analysis: *Dennis v. United States*," Columbia University Freedom of Global Expression, https://globalfreedomofexpression.columbia.edu/cases/dennis-v-united-states.

35. C. Herman Pritchett, *Civil Liberties and the Vinson Court* (Chicago: University of Chicago Press, 1954), 71–72.

36. "Harold Medina, U.S. Judge, Dies at 102," *New York Times*, March 16, 1990.

37. "Harold Medina, U.S. Judge."

38. "Harold Medina, U.S. Judge."

39. Pritchett, *Civil Liberties and the Vinson Court*, 72.

40. *Schenck v. United States*, 249 U.S. 47, 52 (1919).

41. Del Dickson, ed., *The Supreme Court in Conference, 1940–1985: The Private Discussions behind Nearly 300 Supreme Court Decisions* (New York: Oxford University Press, 2001), 278–79.

42. "Straight-Jacketing Free Speech," *The Nation*, June 14, 1951.

43. Michal R. Belknap, "Why *Dennis*?" *Marquette Law Review* 96 (2013): 1021.

44. Pritchett, *Civil Liberties and the Vinson Court*, 73.

45. Terry Eastland, ed., *Freedom of Expression in the Supreme Court: The Defining Cases* (Lanham, MD: Rowman and Littlefield, 2000), 112.

46. Dickson, *The Supreme Court in Conference*, 278–79.

47. Belknap, "Why *Dennis*?" 1018.

48. "Freedom with Security," *Washington Post*, June 6, 1951.

49. Ralph Blumenthal, "When Suspicion of Teachers Ran Unchecked," *New York Times*, June 15, 2009.

50. Dennis Hevesi, "Irving Adler, Teacher Fired in Red Scare, Dies at 99," *New York Times*, September 27, 2012.

51. Hevesi, "Irving Adler."

52. *Adler v. Board of Education of the City of New York*, 342 U.S. 485, 493 (1952).

53. *Keyishian v. Board of Regents*, 385 U.S. 598 (1967).

Chapter Twenty-One

1. Robert Shogan, *Harry Truman and the Struggle for Racial Justice* (Lawrence: University Press of Kansas, 2013), 172.

2. Michael R. Gardner, *Harry Truman and Civil Rights: Moral Courage and Political Risks* (Carbondale: Southern Illinois University Press, 2002), 165.

3. Gardner, *Harry Truman and Civil Rights*, 177.

4. Rawn James, Jr., *Root and Branch: Charles Hamilton Houston, Thurgood Marshall, and the Struggle to End Segregation* (New York: Bloomsbury Press, 2010), 211.

5. Richard Kluger, *Simple Justice: The History of Brown v. Board of Education and Black America's Struggle for Equality* (New York: Vintage Books, 1977), 268.

6. Kluger, *Simple Justice*, 268.

7. James, *Root and Branch*, 211–12.

8. Chalmers M. Roberts, "Minton Takes High Court Seat, about 400 See Oath Ceremony," *Washington Post*, October 13, 1949.

9. James, *Root and Branch*, 204–5.

10. James, *Root and Branch*, 207.

11. James, *Root and Branch*, 207.

12. James, *Root and Branch*, 206–8.

13. Kluger, *Simple Justice*, 276.

14. "N.C. to Close Schools If Sweatt Wins Case," *Baltimore Afro-American*, March 25, 1950.

15. "Vets File Briefs in Sweatt, McLaurin Cases," *Atlanta Daily World*, February 5, 1950.

16. "188 Law Professors Back Sweatt's Plea," *Baltimore Afro-American*, January 28, 1950.

17. James, *Root and Branch*, 208.

Chapter Twenty-Two

1. Richard Kluger, *Simple Justice : The History of Brown v. Board of Education and Black America's Struggle for Equality* (New York: Vintage Books, 1977), 271.

2. Louis Lautier, "Justice Department Urges: End 'Separate but Equal' Doctrine," *Atlanta Daily World*, February 12, 1950.

3. Lautier, "Justice Department Urges."

4. Alexander Wohl, *Father, Son, and Constitution: How Justice Tom Clark and Attorney General Ramsey Clark Shaped American Democracy* (Lawrence: University Press of Kansas, 2013), 143.

5. Mark V. Tushnet, *Making Civil Rights Law : Thurgood Marshall and the Supreme Court, 1936–1961* (New York: Oxford University Press, 1994), 144.

6. Wohl, *Father, Son, and Constitution*, 143.

7. Tushnet, *Making Civil Rights Law*, 144.

8. "Sweatt to Attend School in the North If He Loses Case," *Atlanta Daily World*, April 14, 1950.

9. "Heman Sweatt Meets the Press as Supreme Court Sweats Out His Case," *Chicago Defender*, April 22, 1950.

10. John P. Frank, "The United States Supreme Court: 1949–1950," *University of Chicago Law Review* 18, no. 1 (Autumn 1950): 34.

11. William E. Leuchtenburg, *The White House Looks South: Franklin D. Roosevelt, Harry S. Truman, Lyndon B. Johnson* (Baton Rouge: Louisiana State University Press, 2005), 169.

12. Tushnet, *Making Civil Rights Law*, 139.

13. Tushnet, *Making Civil Rights Law*, 141.

14. Tushnet, *Making Civil Rights Law*, 141.

15. Tushnet, *Making Civil Rights Law*, 141.

16. Tushnet, *Making Civil Rights Law*, 141.

17. Del Dickson, ed., *The Supreme Court in Conference, 1940–1985: The Private Discussions behind Nearly 300 Supreme Court Decisions* (New York: Oxford University Press, 2001), 638.

18. Dickson, *The Supreme Court in Conference*, 638–39.

19. Dickson, *The Supreme Court in Conference*, 640.

20. Dickson, *The Supreme Court in Conference*, 639.

21. Dickson, *The Supreme Court in Conference*, 642.

22. Dickson, *The Supreme Court in Conference*, 642.

23. Dickson, *The Supreme Court in Conference*, 643.

24. Dickson, *The Supreme Court in Conference*, 644.

25. Dickson, *The Supreme Court in Conference*, 644.

26. Kluger, *Simple Justice*, 280.

27. Kluger, *Simple Justice*, 281.

28. *Henderson v. United States*, 339 U.S. 816 (1950).

29. Kluger, *Simple Justice*, 282.

30. Rawn James, Jr., *Root and Branch : Charles Hamilton Houston, Thurgood Marshall, and the Struggle to End Segregation* (New York: Bloomsbury Press, 2010), 214.

31. "Texas Girds for Sweatt Victory," *Chicago Defender*, August 26, 1950.

32. "U.S. Court Bans Segregation in Diners and Higher Education," *Atlanta Daily World*, June 6, 1950.

33. "U.S. Court Bans Segregation."

34. "Report for Class, Dean Tells Sweatt," *Baltimore Afro-American*, August 12, 1950.

35. "U.S. Court Bans Segregation."

36. Harry S Truman, "Commencement Address at Howard University," June 13, 1952, Harry S. Truman Presidential Library, Independence, MO, https://www.trumanlibrary.gov /library/public-papers/169/commencement-address-howard-university.

Chapter Twenty-Three

1. Mark V. Tushnet, *The NAACP's Legal Strategy against Segregated Education, 1925–1950* (Chapel Hill: University of North Carolina Press, 1987), 135.

2. Mark V. Tushnet, *Making Civil Rights Law: Thurgood Marshall and the Supreme Court, 1936–1961* (New York: Oxford University Press, 1994), 147.

3. Richard Kluger, *Simple Justice : The History of Brown v. Board of Education and Black America's Struggle for Equality* (New York: Vintage Books, 1977), 294.

4. Tushnet, *Making Civil Rights Law*, 147.

5. James T. Patterson, *Brown v. Board of Education: A Civil Rights Milestone and Its Troubled Legacy* (New York: Oxford University Press, 2001), 19.

6. John P. Frank, "The United States Supreme Court: 1949–1950," *University of Chicago Law Review* 18, no. 1 (Autumn 1950): 36.

7. Kamina A. Pinder and Evan R. Hanson, "360 Degrees of Segregation: A Historical Perspective of Segregation-Era School Equalization Programs in the Southern United States," *Amsterdam Law Forum* 2, no. 3 (2010): 57–58.

8. Tushnet, *Making Civil Rights Law*, 141.

9. Alexander Wohl, *Father, Son, and Constitution: How Justice Tom Clark and Attorney General Ramsey Clark Shaped American Democracy* (Lawrence: University Press of Kansas, 2013), 143.

10. Tushnet, *Making Civil Rights Law*, 165–66.

11. Kluger, *Simple Justice*, 539.

12. Del Dickson, ed., *The Supreme Court in Conference, 1940–1985: The Private Discussions behind Nearly 300 Supreme Court Decisions* (New York: Oxford University Press, 2001), 646.

13. Dickson, *The Supreme Court in Conference*, 646–47.

14. Dickson, *The Supreme Court in Conference*, 648.

15. Dickson, *The Supreme Court in Conference*, 649.

16. Dickson, *The Supreme Court in Conference*, 649.

17. Dickson, *The Supreme Court in Conference*, 653.

18. Dickson, *The Supreme Court in Conference*, 653.

19. Kluger, *Simple Justice*, 613–14.

20. Dickson, *The Supreme Court in Conference*, 653; Kluger, *Simple Justice*, 615.

Chapter Twenty-Four

1. Executive Order 10340, Harry S. Truman Presidential Library, Independence, MO, https://www.trumanlibrary.gov/library/executive-orders/10340/executive-order-10340.

2. "Men to Go On Working for Government," *Baltimore Sun*, April 9, 1952.

3. "Men to Go On Working."

4. Joseph A. Loftus, "Steel Freeze Ends; President to Rely on Pay Bargaining," *New York Times*, April 11, 1952.

5. Joseph A. Loftus, "Sawyer, Taking Over Steel, Plans No Pay Changes Now," *New York Times*, April 9, 1952.

6. Loftus, "Steel Freeze Ends."

7. Loftus, "Sawyer, Taking Over Steel."

8. Maeva Marcus, *Truman and the Steel Seizure Case: The Limits of Presidential Power* (New York: Columbia University Press, 1977), 102.

9. Dewey L. Fleming, "Steel Official Calls Truman Seizure 'Corrupt Political Deal' to Repay CIO," *Baltimore Sun*, April 10, 1952.

10. "Special Message to the Congress Reporting on the Situation in the Steel Industry," April 9, 1952, Public Papers of Harry S. Truman, 1945–53, https://www.trumanlibrary.gov/library/public-papers/83/special-message-congress-reporting-situation-steel-industry.

11. "Steel-Makers Lose First Battle in Fight against Order from White House," *Zanesville [OH] Times-Recorder*, April 10, 1952.

12. Steel-Makers Lose First Battle in Fight against Order from White House."

13. Arthur F. McClure, *The Truman Administration and the Problems of Postwar Labor, 1945–1948* (Cranbury, NJ: Associated University Presses, 1969), 213.

14. "Truman Seizure of Steel Lashed as Corrupt Deal," *Daily Oklahoman* (Oklahoma City), April 10, 1952.

15. "Scott Views Steel Move as Politics," *Baltimore Sun*, May 2, 1952.

16. Neal Devins and Louis Fisher, "The Steel Seizure Case: One of a Kind?" *Constitutional Commentary* 19 (2002): 68.

17. Marcus, *Truman and the Steel Seizure Case*, 89.

18. "Murray Charges Steel Attempts to Create Strike," *Boston Evening Globe*, April 17, 1952.

19. Marcus, *Truman and the Steel Seizure Case*, 91–92.

20. "Senate to Probe Steel Mill Seizure to Determine Legality of Truman Act," *Sarasota [FL] Herald-Tribune*, April 21, 1952.

21. John Harris, "Taft Talks Impeachment," *Boston Evening Globe*, April 17, 1952.

22. "Impeachment Remark 'Ridiculous'—Kefauver," *Boston Evening Globe*, April 17, 1952.

23. Marcus, *Truman and the Steel Seizure Case*, 96.

24. Devins and Fisher, "The Steel Seizure Case," 67.

25. "GOP Leaders Awaiting Court Decision on Steel," *Post-Standard* (Syracuse, NY), April 29, 1952.

26. Marcus, *Truman and the Steel Seizure Case*, 109–10.

27. Andrew Glass, "Truman Declines to Seek Another Term," *Politico*, March 29, 2019, https://www.politico.com/story/2019/03/29/truman-declines-to-seek-another-term-march-29-1952-1238358.

28. Linda C. Gugin and James E. St. Clair, *Sherman Minton: New Deal Senator, Cold War Justice* (Indianapolis: Indiana Historical Society, 1997), 220.

Chapter Twenty-Five

1. "David A. Pine, of U.S. Court Dies," *New York Times*, June 12, 1970.

2. "Judge Pine, 60, Little Known Outside Capital League Circles," *Baltimore Sun*, April 30, 1952.

3. Meava Marcus, *Truman and the Steel Seizure Case : The Limits of Presidential Power* (New York: Columbia University Press, 1977), 114–15.

4. Marcus, *Truman and the Steel Seizure Case*, 117.

5. Marcus, *Truman and the Steel Seizure Case*, 117.

6. *Youngstown Sheet & Tube Co. v. Sawyer*, 103 F. Supp. 569, 573 (D.D.C. 1952).

7. Marcus, *Truman and the Steel Seizure Case*, 117.

8. Marcus, *Truman and the Steel Seizure Case*, 117.

9. Neal Devins and Louis Fisher, "The Steel Seizure Case: One of a Kind?" *Constitutional Commentary* 19 (2002): 68–69.

10. Marcus, *Truman and the Steel Seizure Case*, 121.

11. William H. Rehnquist, *The Supreme Court* (New York: Random House, 1987), 160.

12. Marcus, *Truman and the Steel Seizure Case*, 125.

13. Rehnquist, *The Supreme Court*, 162.

14. Del Dickson, ed., *The Supreme Court in Conference, 1940–1985: The Private Discussions behind Nearly 300 Supreme Court Decisions* (New York: Oxford University Press, 2001), 171.

15. "GOP Delays Action on Steel Seizure," *Washington Post*, April 29, 1952.

16. Alfred Friendly, "Murray Declares Judge's Decision Leaves Strike as Only Alternative," *Washington Post*, April 30, 1952.

17. "GOP Delays Action."

18. *Youngstown Sheet & Tube Co. v. Sawyer*, 103 F. Supp. 569, 573 (D.D.C. 1952).

19. *Youngstown Sheet & Tube Co. v. Sawyer*, 103 F. Supp. 569, 573, 576 (D.D.C. 1952).

20. "Murray Holds Out for 26-Cent Boost," *Baltimore Sun*, April 30, 1952.

21. Marcus, *Truman and the Steel Seizure Case*, 134.

22. "Murray Holds Out."

23. Friendly, "Murray Declares Judge's Decision."

24. Friendly, "Murray Declares Judge's Decision."

25. Friendly, "Murray Declares Judge's Decision."

26. William Knighton, Jr., "Legislators Laud Court's Decision," *Baltimore Sun*, April 30, 1952.

27. Marcus, *Truman and the Steel Seizure Case*, 131–32.

28. "Press Views on Steel Ruling," *Baltimore Sun*, May 1, 1952.

29. "U.S. Judge Refuses to Block Seizure," *Daily Oklahoman* (Oklahoma City), April 10, 1952.

30. Marcus, *Truman and the Steel Seizure Case*, 133.

31. Rehnquist, *The Supreme Court*, 163.

32. Marcus, *Truman and the Steel Seizure Case*, 134.

33. William Knighton, Jr., "Moves Divided in Congress over Steel Case," *Baltimore Sun*, May 1, 1952.

34. "Murray Holds Out."

35. Marcus, *Truman and the Steel Seizure Case*, 135.

Chapter Twenty-Six

1. Alfred Friendly, "Decision Follows Truman Threat of Pay Increase by Government," *Washington Post*, May 4, 1952.

2. Friendly, "Decision Follows Truman Threat."

3. Meava Marcus, *Truman and the Steel Seizure Case: The Limits of Presidential Power* (New York: Columbia University Press, 1977), 147.

4. Joseph A. Loftus, "High Court Bars Steel Pay Raise after Truman Says He Plans It," *New York Times*, May 4, 1952.

5. Del Dickson, ed., *The Supreme Court in Conference, 1940–1985: The Private Discussions behind Nearly 300 Supreme Court Decisions* (New York: Oxford University Press, 2001), 168–70.

6. Dickson, *The Supreme Court in Conference*, 170–71.

7. Marcus, *Truman and the Steel Seizure Case*, 320nn72, 73.

8. Friendly, "Decision Follows Truman Threat."

9. Robert F. Whitney, "High Court Hears Argument on Steel Seizure Today," *New York Times*, May 12, 1952.

10. "Courtroom Acoustics," *Washington Post*, May 14, 1952.

11. A. H. Raskin, "Steel Union Hurls New Strike Threat," *New York Times*, May 14, 1952.

12. Philip Potter, "Supreme Court Fires Question Barrage at Perlman, Seldom Interrupts Davis," *Baltimore Sun*, May 13, 1952.

13. William H. Rehnquist, *The Supreme Court* (New York: Random House, 1987), 185.

14. Potter, "Supreme Court Fires Question Barrage."

15. Chalmers M. Roberts, "Right to Grab Steel Mills Is Argued in High Court," *Washington Post*, May 13, 1952.

16. "Two Points of View: Excerpts," *Baltimore Sun*, May 13, 1952.

17. Potter, "Supreme Court Fires Question Barrage."

18. Potter, "Supreme Court Fires Question Barrage."

19. Potter, "Supreme Court Fires Question Barrage."

20. Potter, "Supreme Court Fires Question Barrage."

21. Potter, "Supreme Court Fires Question Barrage."

22. Marcus, *Truman and the Steel Seizure Case*, 329n75.

23. Philip Potter, "Attorneys Finish Oral Arguments; Some Delay Expected on Ruling," *Baltimore Sun*, May 14, 1952.

24. Potter, "Attorneys Finish Oral Arguments."

25. Potter, "Attorneys Finish Oral Arguments."

26. "Is It War?" *Washington Post*, May 15, 1952.

27. Potter, "Attorneys Finish Oral Arguments."

28. Joseph A. Loftus, "High Court Is Told 'War' Justifies Seizure of Steel," *New York Times*, May 14, 1952.

29. Loftus, "High Court Is Told 'War.'"

30. Marcus, *Truman and the Steel Seizure Case*, 173–74.

31. Loftus, "High Court Is Told 'War.'"

32. Loftus, "High Court Is Told 'War.'"

33. Loftus, "High Court Is Told 'War.'"

Chapter Twenty-Seven

1. "Decision on Steel Today Is Possible," *Baltimore Sun*, May 19, 1952.

2. Drew Pearson, "Washington Merry Go-Round: 8 Justices Have Upheld Seizure," *Washington Post*, May 19, 1952.

3. "President's Power Facing Curb," *New York Times*, May 20, 1952.

4. Meava Marcus, *Truman and the Steel Seizure Case: The Limits of Presidential Power* (New York: Columbia University Press, 1977), 195.

5. "President's Power Facing Curb."

6. William H. Rehnquist, *The Supreme Court* (New York: Vintage Books, 2002), 186.

7. Del Dickson, ed., *The Supreme Court in Conference, 1940–1985: The Private Discussions behind Nearly 300 Supreme Court Decisions* (New York: Oxford University Press, 2001), 172–73.

8. Dickson, *The Supreme Court in Conference*, 173.

9. "Truman Declines to Talk on U.S. 'at War' Question," *New York Times*, May 16, 1952.

10. Dickson, *The Supreme Court in Conference*, 174.

11. Dickson, *The Supreme Court in Conference*, 174.

12. Dickson, *The Supreme Court in Conference*, 174–75.

13. Dickson, *The Supreme Court in Conference*, 175–76.

14. Dickson, *The Supreme Court in Conference*, 176–77.

15. Dickson, *The Supreme Court in Conference*, 177.

16. Dickson, *The Supreme Court in Conference*, 178–79.

17. Dickson, *The Supreme Court in Conference*, 179.

18. Dickson, *The Supreme Court in Conference*, 180.

19. Dickson, *The Supreme Court in Conference*, 180.

20. "Strike Food Plane Riddled," *New York Times*, June 12, 1937.

21. Dickson, *The Supreme Court in Conference*, 180.

22. Dickson, *The Supreme Court in Conference*, 180–81.

23. Dickson, *The Supreme Court in Conference*, 181.

24. Ralph E. Edwards, "Letters to the Editor: Steel Seizure and Movie Pickets," *Baltimore Sun*, May 24, 1952.

25. Marcus, *Truman and the Steel Seizure Case*, 179.

26. George Gallup, "Voters Familiar with Issue Disapprove Steel Plant Seizure," *Washington Post*, May 28, 1952.

27. A. H. Raskins, "Union Is Disillusioned by U.S. Role in Steel," *New York Times*, May 18, 1952.

Chapter Twenty-Eight

1. Maeva Marcus, *Truman and the Steel Seizure Case: The Limits of Presidential Power* (New York: Columbia University Press, 1977), 220.

2. Linda C. Gugin and James E. St. Clair, *Sherman Minton: New Deal Senator, Cold War Justice* (Indianapolis: Indiana Historical Society, 1997), 218.

3. *Youngtown Sheet & Tube Co. v. Sawyer*, 343 U.S. 579, 584 (1952).

4. *Youngtown Sheet & Tube Co. v. Sawyer*, 343 U.S. 585, 587 (1952).

5. *Youngtown Sheet & Tube Co. v. Sawyer*, 343 U.S. 587, 588 (1952).

6. *Youngtown Sheet & Tube Co. v. Sawyer*, 343 U.S. 588–89 (1952).

7. *Youngtown Sheet & Tube Co. v. Sawyer*, 343 U.S. 660 (1952).

8. *Youngtown Sheet & Tube Co. v. Sawyer*, 343 U.S. 663–66 (1952).

9. Gugin and St. Clair, *Sherman Minton*, 219.

10. Gugin and St. Clair, *Sherman Minton*, 213.

11. *Youngtown Sheet & Tube Co. v. Sawyer*, 343 U.S. 634–35 (1952).

12. *Youngtown Sheet & Tube Co. v. Sawyer*, 343 U.S. 635 (1952).

13. *Youngtown Sheet & Tube Co. v. Sawyer*, 343 U.S. 637 (1952).

14. *Youngtown Sheet & Tube Co. v. Sawyer*, 343 U.S. 637–38, 640 (1952).

15. Chalmers M. Roberts, "Vinson, Minton, Reed Dissent as Black Delivers Majority Opinion," *Washington Post*, June 3, 1952.

16. Joseph A. Loftus, "Black Gives Ruling," *New York Times*, June 3, 1952.

17. Roberts, "Vinson, Minton, Reed Dissent."

18. Harry S. Truman, *Memoirs*, vol. 2, *Years of Trial and Hope, 1946–1952* (Garden City, NY: Doubleday, 1956), 476.

19. Truman, *Memoirs*, 476.

Chapter Twenty-Nine

1. "U.S. Supreme Court Rules against Seizure," *Atlanta Daily World*, June 3, 1952.

2. Anthony Leviero, "Next Move in Crisis Is Called Truman's," *New York Times*, June 3, 1952.

3. Chalmers M. Roberts, "Highest Court Rules Steel Seizure Illegal," *Washington Post*, June 3, 1952.

4. "U.S. Supreme Court Rules against Steel Seizure."

5. Joseph A. Loftus, "Black Gives Ruling," *New York Times*, June 3, 1952.

6. Maeva Marcus, *Truman and the Steel Seizure Case: The Limits of Presidential Power* (New York: Columbia University Press, 1977), 214.

7. Leviero, "Next Move in Crisis."

8. "Stocks Flip-Flop on News of Steel," *New York Times*, June 3, 1952.

9. C. P. Trussell, "Congress Hails End of Steel Seizure," *New York Times*, June 3, 1952.

10. Trussell, "Congress Hails End."

11. Walter Lippmann, "Today and Tomorrow: The Court and the Steel Case," *Washington Post*, June 5, 1952.

12. Harry S. Truman, *Memoirs*, vol. 2, *Years of Trial and Hope, 1946–1952* (Garden City, NY: Doubleday, 1956), 476.

13. Marcus, *Truman and the Steel Seizure Case*, 214.

14. Frances Howell Rudko, *Truman's Court: A Study in Judicial Restraint* (Westport, CT: Greenwood Press, 1988), 32.

15. William H. Rehnquist, *The Supreme Court* (New York: Random House, 1987), 186.

16. Rehnquist, *The Supreme Court*, 189.

17. Truman, *Memoirs*, 475.

18. Rehnquist, *The Supreme Court*, 189.

19. Rehnquist, *The Supreme Court*, 190–91.

20. "Mr. Truman Shifts His Steel Unthinkables," *Baltimore Sun*, June 5, 1952.

21. "Truman Declines to State Next Move in Steel Strike," *Atlanta Daily World*, June 13, 1952.

22. "Truman May Seize Mills Again, Officials Say," *Atlanta Daily World*, July 19, 1952.

23. "Steel Peace Move Taken by Truman," *Baltimore Sun*, July 24, 1952.

24. Robert W. Ruth, "Steel Strike Settled," *Baltimore Sun*, July 25, 1952.

25. William O. Douglas, *Go East, Young Man: The Early Years, the Autobiography of William O. Douglas* (New York: Random House, 1974), 450.

Chapter Thirty

1. Henry J. Abraham, *Justices and Presidents: A Political History of Appointments to the Supreme Court*, 2nd ed. (New York: Oxford University Press, 1985), 238.

2. Linda C. Gugin and James E. St. Clair, *Sherman Minton: New Deal Senator, Cold War Justice* (Indianapolis: Indiana Historical Society, 1997), 222.

3. Gugin and St. Clair, *Sherman Minton*, 228.

4. William Franklin Radcliff, *Sherman Minton: Indiana's Supreme Court Justice* (Indianapolis: Guild Press of Indiana, 1996), 139.

5. Frances Howell Rudko, *Truman's Court: A Study in Judicial Restraint* (Westport, CT: Greenwood Press, 1988), 37.

6. Rudko, *Truman's Court*, 33.

7. Rudko, *Truman's Court*, 36.

8. Gugin and St. Clair, *Sherman Minton*, 282.

9. Rudko, *Truman's Court*, 32.

10. Harry S. Truman, *Memoirs*, vol. 2, *Years of Trial and Hope, 1946–1952* (Garden City, NY: Doubleday, 1956), 478.

INDEX

Note: numbers preceded by "P" refer to plate images, with plate number.

education, 31; and Burton, swearing-in
of, 21; and conflicts of interest, 66; and
Coolidge, friendship with, 31–32; death of,
34, 56–57; Douglas as former student of,
32; funeral of, 58; on Jackson as Nuremberg
prosecutor, 38–39; and *Jewell Ridge Coal*
case, 66; on judicial restraint, 31; as law
professor, 32; and New Deal, support
for, 31, 33, 35; and Nuremberg trials,
opposition to, 39; as respected jurist, 31
Stone, as associate justice, 31; break from
conservative majority, 33; criticism
of Black, 35–37, 39; dislike of Court
leadership, 51; evaluation of, 57; as first
to have Senate confirmation hearing, 33;
nomination and confirmation, 32
Stone, as chief justice: and Court animosities,
13–14, 31, 35, 53–54, 55, 57; and Court
debate, encouragement of, 51–52, 53–54;
and Court's strong disagreement on basic
legal issues, 71; dissenting opinions under,
increase in number and vitriol, 51–52,
54; evaluation of, 57–58; and *Girouard
v. United States* (1946), 56; and judicial
restraint, 56; and Murphy's case load,
148; nomination, 34; replacement for,
58–60; and slowing of decision process,
53; speculation on successor, 58–59, 65;
swearing-in ceremony, 73; time served as,
34
Stone, replacement for, 58–59; choice of
Vinson for, 60, 61; consultations on, 59–60;
Jackson's furious response at being passed
over, 65–66, 67–68; reactions to Jackson's
furious response, 68–70; speculation on,
58–59, 65
substantive due process jurisprudence: end of,
55; Roosevelt's frustration with, 255
subversive speech: First Amendment and,
165–68, 171, 174–77; Smith Act and, 174,
176
Sullivan, John L., P7
Supreme Court: Court inherited by Truman,
37; and geographical representation, 33;
"massing" of justices in, 34–35; political
balance, public opinion favoring, 12; as
political body, postwar recognition of, 12;
Truman's willingness to challenge, 256. *See*

also Justices of Supreme Court; Truman
Court
Supreme Court building, construction of, 51
Supreme Court conferences, 52–54; rancor of,
under Stone, 53–54; special room for, 52;
typical conduct of, 52–53
Sweatt, Heman Marion: Court-ordered
acceptance at University of Texas Law
School, 196, 197; harassment at University
of Texas Law School, 199; on plans after
Sweatt, 191
Sweatt v. Painter (1950): and African
American admissions to graduate schools,
197–98; American Veterans' Committee
amicus brief in, 186–87; *amicus* brief from
law professors, 186–87; announcement
of ruling, 196; Court conference on,
192–94; Court's refusal to affirm *Plessy*
in, 199; facts of case, 184–86; granting
of *certiorari* to, 187; importance of, 186;
importance of unanimous Court opinion
on, 195; Justice Department *amicus* brief
on, 189–90; Justices's review of ruling, to
reach unanimity, 195–96; little practical
impact of, 199; media attention to, 189; oral
arguments, 191–92; and *Plessy v. Ferguson*,
190, 192, 194–96; reactions to ruling,
196–98, 199–200; and separate but equal
doctrine, challenge to, 185; states aligned
with Texas in, 186; as unanimous ruling,
196; Vinson's writing of opinion, 195

Taft, Robert: on Burton's nomination, 18,
20; on Clark's nomination, 155, 156; and
miners' strike of 1946, 91; and Supreme
Court conferences, 53; and Truman's
seizure of steel mills, 7, 211, 221
Taft, William Howard: advocacy for Supreme
Court as coequal branch of government,
51; efficient management of Court, 51;
on massing the court, 34; and right-wing
Court majority, 33; and Supreme Court
building, 51
Taft-Hartley Act: denial of benefits to unions
with Communist Party leadership, 168–69;
Truman's disregard of, in seizure of steel
mills, 207–8, 221, 226–27, 229, 230, 232,
234, 238, 239, 243, 251–52